Discover the Magic of Colour

To Dearest Mo

The best friend ever

lots of love & light
always

Lilian x

1994.

Discover the Magic of Colour

LILIAN VERNER BONDS MIACT, Dip.

An OPTIMA book

First published by Optima in 1993

Copyright © Lilian Verner Bonds 1993

The right of the author has been asserted.

ISBN 0 356 21031 6

Typeset in Sabon by Solidus (Bristol) Limited
Printed and bound in Great Britain by
Clays Ltd, St. Ives plc

Optima
A Division of
Little, Brown and Company (UK) Limited
165 Great Dover Street
London SE1 4YA

**Nothing in this book is to be construed as taking
the place of appropriate medical advice,
diagnosis or treatment.**

While the case histories described in this book are based on real people
and their experiences, the author has created pseudonyms, altered
identifying characteristics to preserve the privacy and anonymity of the
individuals and their families. The author is grateful to the clients who
allowed their stories to be shared.

Dedicated to my daughter, Louise Jane Verner

The joy and light of my life

Contents

THE COLOUR CATALOGUE
The psychology and language of colour

To Dr Ronald L. Bonewitz

The man who said I could write this book when I said I couldn't.

Acknowledgements

I am especially grateful to Joseph Corvo for his continuous insight and support.

I also want to express gratitude to my literary agent, Darley Anderson, for his guidance and encouragement; to my editor, Jayne Booth, for her extreme patience; and to my publisher, Hilary Foakes.

I also want to express my gratitude to the following people for being significant in my life:

John Grassom. Francis Gladys Ham. William Ham. Gladys Meyer. Violet Grassom. Rosina Meyer. Miss Marsh. Mrs Gibbs. Mrs Flaxman. Rita Smith. Maude Wells. Aida Foster. Merle Lee. Pam Nicolson. Peter Sasdy. Daphne Shadwell. Bebe Lyon. Ben Lyon. Tony Hancock. Charlie Chaplin. James Verner. Peter Penrose. Beryle Penrose. Mo Townsend. Barry Townsend. Sally Kemp. Mr Raffhead. Jean Wallis. John Wallis. Michael Meeks. Hamed Mused. Carol Whimster. Lilian Gattrel. Elaine Howard. John Howard. Sir Lew Grade. Oscar Beuselinck. Monty Norman. Val Guest. Robert Patterson. Geoffrey Baynard Bonds. Alan Draper. Geoffrey Robinson. Sandra Raebin. Harry Kaufman. John Mason. Patricia Meadows. Harvey Meadows. Joyce Poole. Bill Poole. Ken Mongston. Charles Bell. Claire Sauters. Margo Baynard. Yvonne Fisher. Sonia Luper. Horace Luper. Elaine Jouhl. Ajit Jouhl. Barbara Seghal. Hiro Seghal. Valerie Cox. Ron Cox. Russell Harris. Kitty Hagenback. Keith Hagenback. Shanie Moss. Irene Dupaere. Vicky Wall. Margaret Cockbain. Mike Booth. Michael Deffries. Pamela Deffries. Joanne Haig. Pamela Allsop. Barbara Scott. Sophia Stainton. James Postlewaithe. Tom Fallowell. Celia Fallowell. Wendy Fallowell. Hugh Wates. Graham Brown. Babette Hayes. Monique Allen. Lilla Beck. Dr Victor Bloom. Inga Laird. Michael Laird. Olive Dewhurst Maddox. Geraldine Saabor. John Esam. Andrew Carrington. David Lawson. Jim Frecklington O.A.M. Mavis Keating. Hazel Hill. Margaret Simon. Harry Simon. Sabine McNeil Kurjo . . . and others . . .

Foreword

I have always known about my psychic gifts. Through a traumatic childhood during the London Blitz, and then as a successful actress, the gift was always there.

Later, I learnt to harness the power and channel it into colour therapy. Colour is an integral part of the make-up of human beings; it is a psychic sense.

Colour therapy is individual. The art of the colour therapist is first to assess by the use of colour, to use colour in an intuitive way, and then to find the unique treatment for the person. Colour sets you free.

If you do not know why something keeps happening in your life, why you are having the same illness, why you feel the same negative reactions to someone or something, why you are stuck in a useless pattern of behaviour, then colour therapy will help. Colour can reveal the significance of our actions that cannot otherwise be observed.

Colour therapy is enabling. It will allow the individual to discover new things about themselves, about others, and about the world in general. It will enable you to use colour in your everyday life. Simple techniques that help you to make your own assessment – mentally, emotionally, physically and spiritually. Discover the magic of colour ...

Lilian Verner Bonds

Making room for a gift

'I give you one month to clear out your spare room and I will send you your first client.'

'Pardon,' I said.

'I give you one month to the day to be ready to receive your first client.'

Peter, I thought, has gone mad.

It was mid-1984, and I was having my tarot cards read by Peter Penrose, a specialist in this field. I had known for at least two years that my acting career was, if not completely over, at least no longer to be of any great importance in my life. But I still had no idea what, if anything, was supposed to replace it. I had visited Peter often before and, over the years, he and his wife, Beryl, had become my friends. Once a year I would visit and have my cards read. On this occasion I could not believe what I was hearing.

'Set up as what?' I asked.

'To do what you have always done,' came his reply. 'Read palms psychically.'

On my return home I thought about this, and then pushed it to the back of my mind. One week later Peter rang. 'Have you got that room ready yet?'

'No.'

'You'd better. I'll call again,' he said – and he did.

After the second call, I found myself suggesting to Valerie Cox, my home help, that we take the spare bed out and see what the room looked like. We did.

Decorating followed, a friend lent me a table, I borrowed a magnifying glass and a lamp, and began to get the shakes. Dear God, what *was* I doing?

Two days before the deadline, Peter was on the line again: 'I'm sending you Beryl. She'll be with you tomorrow. Good luck.'

I was going to need the luck – Beryl was no mean psychic herself, and a very good critic. Two days later, Beryl arrived. I was very nervous; I had no idea what I was going to do. We started the reading . . .

After a few minutes something happened, something that has happened all through my life – I slip into a feeling, a kind of space in which I am 'tuned in'. In this 'place', my identity vanishes and I am in a kind of no-man's land. There are no rules or regulations and the truth can come through unhindered by my personality's beliefs and shortcomings. I am totally available. This happened now and I was away. I could see what Beryl's life had been, where she was now, and where she was going to be in the future. The shaking had gone. It was never to come back.

I was forty-four years old and had finally accepted my inheritance, my 'gift'.

THE GIFT YOU GET WHETHER YOUR FAMILY LIKES IT OR NOT

I am seven years old and walking along the road with my mother. She is carrying a small table.

'Mummy,' I say pleasantly, 'when you go round the corner of the next road you are going to fall down the kerb and drop the table and a leg is going to break off.'

'Stop talking.'

We turn the corner, my mother falls off the kerb, the leg falls off the table.

'There,' she says, giving me a smack, 'you've done it again.'

And I had. I was always doing 'it' and getting smacked, because, they said, when what I said would happen *did* happen it was 'my fault'. To be psychic was to be faulty. Not that I even knew the word for it until much later, or that it was an unusual thing to be. I thought everybody could do it. What I didn't know then was that my great-grandmother, Granny Meyer, a famous clairvoyant, had had the same 'problem'. There was something suspect about her. My mother told me that she and her brother and sister had been banned from seeing Granny Meyer because her father 'did not believe in all that nonsense'. And just as they had banned it in her family, so they were now trying to suppress it in me.

There wasn't a chance they would succeed, of course: 'it' had been in the family longer than my mother, longer than anyone. It was older, much, much older and more powerful than any of us. It had been travelling, I am sure, down through the family for generations like a mysterious entity with an agenda of its own. I had inherited a gift that was stronger and more powerful than any particular time's fear and prejudice. Not so much a gift, though, if the fear it created in my mother was anything to go by – more of an affliction. In our family, it seemed, a woman was likely to get the gift whether she wanted it or not. Someone in each generation had to carry it forward.

I could try to ignore it, put it away in the attic marked 'Not Wanted On Voyage'. Sooner or later, though, it was going to have to come out – as all real talents must, if we are to be balanced and complete people.

This was a process destined to take many years and pass through several stages – theatrical as well as psychological – before it would be complete. In the meantime, I had to try and survive my childhood. From the moment of birth, I was surrounded by the noise, confusion and destruction of a world at war, and another war taking place within my own immediate family; more local perhaps, but at least as fierce as and certainly much longer than World War II – and then there was dyslexia.

WHY DYSLEXIA CONTROLLED THE CROSSROADS

'A drop of ink may make a million think.'
Lord Byron

The adversity in my childhood enabled me to develop psychically. The gift was in my family, but circumstances forced me to discover it in myself during the first years of my life. It was an anchor I found within my being that kept me from being swept away by the currents of the wild disaster going on all around me and becoming totally lost.

Many psychics seem to have required this blocking off of the outer world through pain and distress to drive them in on themselves. If things are so terrible in what is laughingly called 'reality' you have to go somewhere. You either go mad, die, or you shift. If you cannot go somewhere else in outer space, you find a way out in inner space.

Living in surroundings that cause continual fear and misery can drive a person, even a very young person, to ask: 'What is going on here, and how do I get out of it?' I must have asked this as a child because I got answers and they worked for me.

I can see now that by this process I was being taught that there were answers to what was happening to me and in the world around me, but that I had to go somewhere else to get them. I couldn't ask my father or my mother what was going on – they didn't seem to know. But if I just opened myself and asked, an understanding of what it was all about would be given to me. I called it my daydreaming.

I would be told things. Something that was going to happen would come into my mind. If I didn't examine it, it always happened. A voice told me. But it was a voice that had no sound.

If I didn't want what I heard to come true, I had a way of stopping it. The voice might tell me that I would hurt my leg before the dancing contest. To stop this happening, I would have to look very intensely at an object outside me – a flower, a teacup, the leaf on a plant. At the same time, I would focus my mind on the subject and say: 'This will not happen, this will not happen ...' If I repeated this phrase over and over again for five minutes, I could stop whatever it was from taking place. Nowadays, it's called affirmation and is taught in personal growth workshops.

It is clear to me that there was an 'it', a guardian angel, if you like, in charge of this teaching process, an intelligence. From the point of view of, say, a welfare worker, its methods could be seen as harsh, even sometimes brutal. I don't consider them so, particularly in the light of what I was led to by them.

It's not that I imagine that World War II or my parents' fear and their miserable marriage was staged for my psychic advancement. But, like any creative artist, 'it' certainly took full advantage of the opportunities they provided.

My dyslexia is another case in point. It was not enough that I couldn't read as a child (no one had heard of 'dyslexia' in the 1940s); my parents also tried to cure me of this obstinacy by a strange process. My younger sister (who could read beautifully at three years of age) would be given a storybook and my punishment for 'refusing' to read would be to sit across the room watching her reading the story to herself. That was one part of the process. The other part, the bit that gave me a practical lesson in psychic perception, was that I would sit opposite her staring at the book and thinking to myself: 'I *will* know what the story in that book is, I *will*!'

Thirty years later, I found myself sitting in a group at a personal growth seminar in which the exercise was to hold an unopened book between your hands and visualise what was in it. I took to this like a duck to water and could not understand why the others found it so frustrating.

I don't think it was an accident that the solace of books that has always been the salvation for so many lonely children was barred to me. When I came to the sign at the crossroads with 'reading' pointing one way and 'something else' the other, dyslexia stood there making sure I went the way our family 'gift' required.

Reading would only have distracted me at a time that was vital to my real education. I wasn't going to become a professor of literature, I was going to become an artist and psychic. My sister, on the other hand, went on to read many more books and become a cancer researcher.

As I look back on my school days, I can see the comic absurdity, the mad perfection of it all. I can explain it away as being nobody's fault, just the inevitable outcome of harried adults trying to do their best in collision with a child with an affliction they were not equipped to understand. The child had to come off second best.

I can also take the spiritual high ground and put it down to a necessary learning experience in the larger school of my life. My real teachers were within. Perhaps there should be another word that is the opposite of in-tuition – out-tuition, maybe. My sister was good at out-tuition, which is why she became a scientist while I became a psychic.

MEETING THE PSYCHIC CIRCLE

Another important part of my education came about many years later when I went to my first meeting of the Psychic Circle. It was a developing Circle specifically designed to bring out psychic potential.

I don't believe I met the Circle accidentally. Rather, it contacted me through a chain of circumstances, people and coincidences that ended with a friend, Joyce Poole, saying to me: 'My husband's cousin is a very famous medium and has just set up a psychic circle. It's in Camden Town, and it's run by her friend, Charles Bell. Would you like to come along?'

She explained her invitation: 'I'm only saying this to you because the medium who leads it, Clare, said to me, "You've got a blonde friend. She's supposed to join the Circle, I've just had a message. Ask her to come along."'

I was immediately both excited and apprehensive. But I went. So started a twelve-year training in my life's real work. It was obvious that I had been more or less recruited. Naturally I wondered why. Part of the answer lay in the role that the Circle would play in providing me with an understanding and supportive environment in which to develop my psychic abilities. It was a beautiful space in which to develop my own natural psychic skill. It was both a place of initiation and a very valuable training ground for me.

The first evening I attended the Circle I was very nervous. I found myself on the spot quite quickly. Within a couple of minutes, Clare brought through a message from Jack. 'Jack,' she said, 'apologises for what his son has done to you.'

Jack was my ex-husband's father. He had been killed in the Second World War at El Alamein when James was still a baby. She then said that there was another message for me. 'There's a Rose here in spirit and she is going to help you tremendously with your psychic work.' This was comforting, but also puzzling because I didn't know a Rose at the time. It wasn't until I discovered much later that my psychic Granny Meyer's first name was Rosina that this piece of information fell into place.

What the Circle did was to create a space in which you could watch, listen and learn, in which you could practise and make all the necessary mistakes. Like any other skill in life, the psychic has techniques which must be mastered if you are to become a useful member of the profession. We were shown how to become skilled at perceiving the patterns of the messages that were coming through. This ability to recognise a psychic pattern as opposed to just imagination is a skill in itself. With my background in the theatre and the training required for that I was quite at home with this approach.

Each person has to develop their own way of receiving. We are shown signs constantly – sounds, pictures, colours, feelings, shapes and symbols reach us all the time. But unless we know how to recognise and decode these, they appear to be meaningless jumble. Another way of looking at this is that just as we all have a physical body and can learn how it works by study, so we have a psychic body whose functioning can also be studied.

The essence of the thing was, of course, that we learned to open ourselves in the Circle to whoever or whatever wanted to come through – and it usually did! This we did by jumping in the deep end.

As we sat quietly in the Circle, a message would come to someone. The receiver would look at the person the message was for and say, 'I think this may be for you'. For me receiving was not a problem. It simply happened without my having to do very much at all.

One evening, I had to give a woman in the Circle a message from a friend. The sender was a woman in spirit who told me she had lost a leg in a bombing raid in the war.

The two women had been friends for years, but had parted on very bad terms. The woman's dead friend had accused her of stealing. The breach caused deep distress and they had never been able to bring themselves to communicate after the incident. Eventually, the friend who had lost a leg died.

The message that I had to give to the survivor was this: 'Your friend says she realises that she was wrong and she is really very sorry about it. She knows now that it was not you who stole the money and she's sad that she passed over before she had time to put it right.'

The woman in spirit went on to ask her friend's forgiveness. It was a very moving moment. The friend in the Circle came to me afterwards and said, 'I've been to many circles. I've waited twenty years for this. Thank you.'

So much completion goes on in the Circle. It can be very healing. People have things that worry them, that keep them stuck or blocked. Messages that come through can release a great deal. They have a marvellously therapeutic value in people's lives. It can sometimes save years in therapy! The joy of witnessing and sharing an individual's breakthrough, their release and relief from the often years of pain and confusion that they have been trapped in, is always for me a most humbling experience. I never cease to be amazed at the courage of the human race.

The Circle was not static. In the twelve years that I was

a member, it underwent many changes. It had an extraordi-
nary dynamism. One factor in this was that people came and
went. There was a fairly constant core group who were in
the Circle week after week, month after month. But around
them was a cloud of temporary members who would vary
in numbers and types by the week – birds of psychic passage
who had just alighted for the night. And each one of these
transients brought his or her own psychic connections and
energy into the Circle.

Then there was the factor of the messages that came
through. No one ever knew what these would be, or from
whom. But there were also fluctuations in the energy of the
Circle from week to week that seemed to have nothing to do
with the people present. It was like being on an ocean. Some
weeks it was very strong and calm; the next week, it would
be all over the place and have everyone agitated.

We could never say, 'Next week we'll do this'. It didn't
work like that. We were dealing with something that was
unpredictable – we knew something would happen, but not
exactly what. I noticed that there was an even longer cycle
of fluctuation – some years were better than other years. The
Circle developed all the time. Yet this development never
seemed to be heading towards a particular end or outcome.
And as it developed, so did we.

Each week, time would be given to absent healing and
special prayers for people who needed some extra help. The
person's special needs would be focused on psychically. The
format would be: 'Mrs So-and-So is going through a
difficult time and needs support and energy.' It sometimes
took the form of a prayer.

One night, Charles led us in a prayer for someone in need.
A slight sense of desolation passed across my heart as he did
and I thought, 'I'm sure that not one time in my whole life
has anybody ever thought to say a prayer for me.' It was a

brief but quite deep feeling, and then I thought, 'Oh well, it's not important. It doesn't matter.'

The Circle ended. I was just about to leave when an elderly woman came over and sat next to me. She was someone who attended the Circle about once a year. We chatted for a moment and then, just as she was about to leave, she put her hand on mine and said, 'Lilian, I always mention you every night, dear, in my prayers before I go to sleep.' You never know how speedily your prayers are going to be answered!

It is important to understand that psychic ability is a natural talent of the human body/mind, and not something mysterious and out-of-this-world. It is something that we all possess. Colour is also part and parcel of the psychic makeup of human beings. It is as inherent as our eyesight or sense of smell. Colour is a psychic sense. However, just as we are not trained to develop our psychic senses, so it is with colour – it is a talent nobody ever taught us to develop or make use of, far less trust and embrace.

I believe that we all have psychic talent to a greater or lesser degree. Almost everyone could develop this inherent ability with the right training and, most important of all, if society had the right attitude towards it. Some of us have a talent that can stretch further. We can all walk, run and dance. But not all of us can dance like Fred Astaire or Ginger Rogers!

Rainbow puddles

As a kid I was absolutely amazed when it rained and petrol
that had been spilled from the cars on the road
became the most amazing,
exquisite patches of rainbow puddles.
I would spend hours sitting on the kerb, my chin
cupped in my hands, staring into these
patches of oil or petrol that seemed to come alive when
the rain poured on them. It was a real joy.
I loved it when it rained because I knew that
the rainbow puddles would come.
I found them so . . .
It was like a deep . . .
I can even feel it now.
I used to feel such a fullness, a contentment came
into my stomach as I sat there looking at
the colours. It was beautiful.
A great well-being used to
come over me. I was happy. The colours would shimmer.
They gently touched my face
as they floated upwards like brightly coloured butterflies.
I used to point
these out to people, but nobody took
any notice of them. I used to say,

'Look at all the colours' and they used to say, 'Yes'.
and move on. They had no interest in them.
When the puddle dried they disappeared. I knew
I would have to wait until it
rained again. I couldn't even see the patches of
grease on the road. But come the rain and they
just used to appear like magic.
It wasn't like there was a patch on the road
where you thought there was going
to be a rainbow, you didn't see
anything until it rained and
then they popped up all over the place.
It was probably because the cars leaked so much
in those days of post-war Britain.

The magic of colour

Colour has been magic for me. The magic is that it sets me free. When I don't know why something keeps happening in my life – why I'm getting the same illness time after time, why I keep having the same negative reaction to someone or something, if I'm stuck in any pattern of useless behaviour – colour will tell me why it is like that for me. Then I can work out what I need to do and the colours I need to use to bring myself back into balance. I call it the Great Corrective.

PINK!

Someone asked me when I had first discovered that colour was magic. I thought about this and remembered the rainbow puddles. But finally I tracked the moment back to a pair of pink ballet shoes under a piano when I was eight, a few years after the war.

Colour always depicts the history and climate of the times. There was not much colour about when I was very young during and after the war, at least not where my family was in the East End of London. For the first eight years of my life, the world seemed to be made of dark shades of grey, black and brown. We didn't even have flowers in the garden,

14

only vegetables. (You could be fined if you grew flowers.) Even the blankets on our bed were army issue slate grey, and the rats that ran around outside the house we lived in (it had been condemned because of the bombing, but we stayed anyway) were grey. My mother would have a blue fit when she saw one – I thought that they looked quite friendly chaps.

Colours have both positive and negative meanings. Grey only becomes positive when it starts to move up into its silver tones. The negative of grey depicts criticism, fear and illness, which certainly was the feeling of that time.

There was also brown. The houses were brown, brown bricks, brown paintwork, brown walls – if they were still standing. Grey, black and brown. Even after the war, things remained drab, dark and austere for the first few years. It was as though people were not yet ready for the stimulation of real colour after all the shocks of the previous years.

One day in 1948, I persuaded my mother to take me up the road to a house where dancing classes had just started. I walked into the room and there under the piano was a pair of *pink* satin ballet shoes! I couldn't believe my eyes. I couldn't move, I was transfixed. It was love at first sight. Bliss.

I had never seen anything so beautiful in my life, and I was determined that I was going to get those pink ballet shoes on my feet if it was the last thing I did. It was as though I had never seen colour until that moment.

Other people have told me they have similar memories of the all-pervading greyness of the time. There must have been other colours around – blood red, for instance – but I don't remember them. Perhaps the dark psychological state that predominated during those years prevented us from seeing them.

When a young person chooses pink it means that she or

he is ready to develop their full potential. I certainly was, not only as a dancer but also in my relationship to colour. So, it seems, was post-war Britain. A friend and I were discussing that period and he recalled how, in 1948, suddenly everyone's house was painted pink inside and out. Wallpapers were not available at the time, nor emulsion paint, and something called distemper was all you could get to cover the walls. White or green were the first colours, and then this pink which exploded over everything as though a giant pink bomb had fallen to announce that the war really was over at last and we could now begin to develop our potential, individually and collectively.

ENCOUNTERING THE SPIRIT OF COLOUR

It is clear to me that I fell in love with colour the moment I saw the pink ballet shoes when I was eight. But it wasn't until more than thirty-five years later that I began to discover the true grandeur of colour's domain and the serious affair began. It was like coming home to a place I had always been part of but had forgotten existed.

It was about six months after I had cleared out my spare room and begun reading palms professionally. As so often happens when we have managed to stumble onto our real path in life, it began with a quiet hint from destiny, or my guardian angel, or whatever name you like to give to that which guides us on these occasions. In this case, the nudge took the form of a casual remark by an acupuncturist friend that she was going to an 'evening on colour that would be right up your street'.

Colour, I thought. What is she talking about? Of course, I went and it was like a duck finding water. I seemed to know exactly what to do.

The evening happened to be given by a leading colour therapist, Marie-Louise Lacy. In one exercise, we took a partner and each made three different coloured marks on a piece of paper. Then we had to swap papers and attempt to assess what we could of the other's life from the coloured marks. Without thinking, I wrote down what had happened to my partner in her life, where she was now, and what was coming in for her. My partner was dumbfounded by the accuracy of it all. She had just spent a large sum of money having her astrological chart cast and everything had turned up in my reading as well.

I was not as surprised as she was. Even though I had never done it before, the process was second nature to me. I didn't seem to have to learn it, the colours seemed to tell me. I knew I had encountered something of the greatest importance to me. It felt as though I had made contact with a presence, an intelligence, that spoke to me through colour. It was also strangely familiar and I knew I was meant to add it to my palmistry. I decided that I had better do some further study.

Once again somebody pointed out the next step: 'There's the high priestess of colour, Vicky Wall. Go and see her.' So I did. I studied colour with Vicky for several years. She was an inspirational teacher for me; her knowledge and experience helped me unlock my intuitive knowledge of colour. When I was at her lectures, I would be so enthused by what she was saying that I would find myself spontaneously commenting from the group. I couldn't help it. Her understanding so excited my understanding, it was as though her words set fire to the fuse of a string of crackers in me.

I will always be grateful for Vicky's grace and openness, which expressed itself in her humorous patience with my irrepressible enthusiasm. While she was lecturing one day, a long pause developed after she had made a point. I wondered what she was waiting for?

'Where's my echo?' she said.

I realised she meant me, and felt both acknowledged and accepted.

After I had been with Vicky for about a year, she and her partner Margaret Cockbain asked me to help them on their stand at the Mind, Body and Spirit Exhibition in London. When I arrived, I stood behind the stand surrounded by all Vicky's jewel-like colour bottles wondering what I was supposed to be doing. Vicky was on the stand, but had not given me any instructions. I had only been standing there a few minutes when 'something' quite firmly told me: 'Get off the stand and go down where the people are'.

I followed orders and within a minute was talking with the nearest member of the public, a middle-aged man in a suit and tie, about his ailments and needs, and how colour could help. I pointed to the array of colour bottles on the stand and asked him to tell me the ones he felt drawn to. Other people began listening, and asking what their colours said about them. Within minutes it had developed into a large crowd.

I looked over at Vicky – she was beaming. I heard her say to Margaret: 'The Red Ray is here. She's out there doing it.'

The Red Ray is the ray of the pioneer. Someone coming under this influence has the particular energy and abilities required to take new information (which may be old knowledge in new bottles) out into the market place. They are not afraid to tread new ground, even though they know this may sometimes draw ridicule upon them. Vicky saw that this was my role. It still is. My great wish is to make the healing powers, spiritual beauty and mysteries of colour accessible to everyone.

Vicky passed on in January 1991. I feel that I was very privileged to have known her, and been guided by her, when she was at the peak of her career.

It was at the same Mind, Body and Spirit Exhibition that an American psychologist Dr Ron (Ra) Bonewitz, introduced himself to me. Two months later, he invited me to speak on the psychology of colour at one of his fascinating crystallography seminars. This was held at the famous colour healing school founded by Lily Cornford: the Maitreya School of Healing.

There is a saying that when the pupil is ready the teacher appears, and appear he had! Dr Bonewitz was already established in his field and was able to direct me towards avenues that as yet I had not considered. My circle of exposure had widened yet again. Ron's seminar was my first experience teaching colour to a group. The workshop members were very enthusiastic about what they were hearing. As for me, it was confirmation of what I already knew: that lectures and workshops were to be a large part of my red ray role of bringing the magic of colour to a wider audience.

After my initiation into the world of workshops, we embarked upon tours in the UK, and abroad. The workshops we did together were based on colour and crystals. They proved to be very powerful. It was wonderful exposure and experience as well as fun. Finally, I attended a series of personal growth workshops and entered into counsellor training not only to advance my own personal growth but also to compile techniques that could be incorporated into my own courses. My own workshops were to be based on colour, personal development and palmistry.

Palmistry is a very ancient art. The hands are the mirror of your soul and the nails are the window into you. The Romans would look at them to assess people mentally, emotionally and physically. In fact, the only positive thing I can say about Hitler is that he taught me palmistry! Being in the bomb shelter was the first recollection I have of using the hand to get information and communicate without words. I remember the noise of the bombing as being so great you couldn't hear what anyone said. I used to hold on to people's hands to find out what I needed to know without asking them. This way, I knew who they were and what they wanted to say.

It was quite natural to me – I thought everybody did it. As with being 'psychic', it was years later that I found that the name for what I was doing was 'palmistry'. Except that by then, as my friend Peter was to point out to me, I had put the two together and got 'psychic palmistry'. Even in the street, I would look up at the hand of whoever it was who was holding on to mine. The hand *was* the person for me; it was the only reliable way of communication I had with people.

I remember there was a little boy I used to play with and I liked him very much. My father came in one day and told us that he had got caught in a bombing raid and been blown to bits. It upset my father very much because he had given him a penny for sweeties about five minutes before and all they found afterwards was the little hand clutching the penny. The terror that stayed with me for years was in the picture of the little hand, the hand that was my connection to everybody, being all that was found.

No description could exaggerate the torture of childhood at this time. No one seemed to speak to us children. And when they, the adults, spoke to each other about the war, about the bombing, the deaths and devastation, it was always in hushed tones. It seemed that they believed that, by speaking in low voices, we children wouldn't know what was happening – as though we couldn't see the carnage and destruction going on day and night all around us.

I don't know where they thought we were. Obviously, not

in the same world as them. But we were, you know ...
Unfortunately, this adult denial of the shock that we children
were in was a sure way of making us candidates later on for
what modern psychiatry calls post-traumatic stress disorder.
In other words, total nervous wrecks!

By 1986, the promise of colour that I had been aware of
since childhood had flowered and become an integral part of
my work. I had always been psychic and a palmist: now
colour had arrived. Not only did it bring a great expansion
of my understanding, it also provided an almost miracu-
lously powerful instrument of focus for my psychic eye.

I know that colour and I work together in a unique way
and that I am under colour's spell. As in all love affairs, it
is difficult, often impossible, for me to explain exactly what
happens between us. However, I am still under the influence
of the red ray and in the next few pages of this book I want
to attempt to give at least an impression of how I work with
colour. And perhaps more importantly, how colour works
with me – and the people who come to see me in my
consultation room.

When I was teaching at the Aromatherapy School in
North London, the school's director, Christian Le Xingrean,
said he would like to recommend me to people. He asked me
to submit 'a format' for my sessions, including a list of the
questions I would ask a client.

I told him I didn't work from a list. He looked baffled:
surely I must have a format that I asked clients when they
came for their first session? I had to tell him that I didn't ask
them anything very much, apart from to sit down. In fact,
I don't want to know anything about a client at all. In their
first session (which may be all that's necessary), I just want
him or her to sit down, allow me to look at their hands and
then choose some colours from the bottles on my colour

table. From this simple process I can do my readings.

There are actually two types of readings that I give. One reading consists of assessing with the palms first. The hands give a wealth of information about a person. I follow this with a colour relate reading where I ask the person to choose from a selection of coloured bottles. The colours they choose will give an overall understanding beginning with the karma colour which shows what the person brought in with them at birth, progressing to what was happening for them as a child and then up to the present day. The reading will then continue to give an indication of what will be coming in the future. Both the palm and colour readings are complete in themselves but they do confirm each other. The second reading I give is a card reading that incorporates the colours and palms. I didn't intend to work with cards when I started my practice. But, as has so often been the case in my life, something else decided I should add cards to my repertory. While walking around an exhibition soon after I had started up my private practice, I came across a pack of cards. They were from France and had hand palms printed on them. Each card had different colours, which also appealed to me. I bought them without knowing what I was going to do with them, put them away in a drawer and forgot about them. Two years later I was drawn to buy a book on cards and promptly put that on a shelf and forgot about it, also. All through this time I was continuing with my colour work.

One evening I absent-mindedly pulled the card book from the shelf. It fell open at a page depicting a card-spread in the shape of a circle. I didn't read what it meant, but I instantly knew what I had to do with the palms and colour pack languishing in the drawer. I spent the rest of the night setting out and arranging my pack in a wheel shape and working out what each place setting represented. I realised that this would be a very concentrated reading which would focus on and predict for one year ahead only. The card reading looks back over the last six months to give me an idea of what has been happening, and then continues to give detailed month-by-month information on what will be coming for the person in the following year. It also reveals the hindrances that may be ahead and the help that will be given to the person.

Each place setting has four cards to be read. Together, they make a very powerful and effective tool. What is so helpful about this reading is the first card of the setting. It is called the Enquirer and it indicates what the whole reading will be about. A person may have come to learn about one particular aspect of their life, be it health, work, love or relationships; but the Enquirer will tell what the next year's focus will be irrespective of their idea of what is important. Although I am not a classic Tarot card reader, it seems so right and natural for me to have developed this one-year divination. The use of prediction is that it gives an indication of possibilities. A map for the future. Both of the readings can give valuable information as to the kind of therapy, counselling or healing that may be needed. There is no point, as far as I can see, of having the means to see past, present and future happenings if you cannot assist the client with changing their lives if they wish to do so.

I often do not remember what has been said after a reading. It's nice to get calls confirming that the reading was of help. Once I've said what has been said to me I pass it on to where it's meant for and I don't retain it as it isn't mine. I've often been asked how I know what to say. If I was to go before a group of scientists, how would they measure it? All I could say would be that I 'mind' and listen. I pause and go into a space and see what comes through. It's not a personal line to God as some people explain it. I know it's not something just outside of me. I listen to within which somehow seems to go without. If I try to get a message the very trying blocks it. I put my personal desires and thinking to one side and become available. I can then receive 'pure understanding' which I pass on. I interpret precisely what comes through. If I leave anything out because I think it won't mean anything to them, then I later find it was most relevant.

If I try to give a message in my own words which I feel they will understand, it's no good – it's lost. I must only decode what comes through. Once they receive it they can share it or discuss it if they want, it's up to them. There is a difference between getting a message for them and a message about them. The first is purely for them but the latter is a guide to help me be of help to them. If something comes through as a warning I will not be negative about the message. I will look for a positive solution.

A woman came seeking guidance concerning the next year's events. The first card, the Enquirer, had indicated that this was a very important year for her career. As I read further, I began to see why: it seemed she was going to go into research of some kind. This didn't surprise me as she looked like the type of person who would be drawn to research. But what did take me aback was when TV flashed into my mind: she would be on television. No, I thought, she won't be on TV, she doesn't look as though she would be in front of cameras.

At the last card – which is called the culmination place – TV came up again. I have to give it, I thought.

'Well, Paula, although it may seem a bit far-fetched, I'm getting that you are going to be involved with TV. In fact, right now I'm getting that you're going to be a researcher first and then a TV newscaster within a few years.'

'Oh, good,' she said, 'you've just seen my uncle, he's

one of Australia's leading newscasters. I've been asked by the TV company to go into their research section for a year with a view to becoming a newscaster myself. Now I know I'm on the right track. Thank you.'

To me this is just another example of the truth that the psychic world never lies. You just have to give exactly what you receive and not try to judge whether it is 'reasonable' or not.

The intelligence of colour

'All forms of matter are light waves in motion.'
Albert Einstein

THE PURE LIGHT

Sometimes during a reading a client says to me, 'How do you know this?'

I used to wonder myself. How on earth *do* I know things about the people I see? I wanted some complicated explanation. But since I have accepted the magic of colour, I have been able to accept the simplicity of the answer: I know because the colours tell me.

Each colour can have many meanings. The crunch in being a colour therapist comes in knowing how the colour relates to your client – to know which aspect of that colour belongs to them. For me it is a matter of listening. I don't know what the story is going to be this time. The colour tells me. What I have to do is empty myself of myself so that I can first hear, and then translate, its message. To quote from D.H. Lawrence's poem 'Not I, Not I, but the wind which blows through me!' For me, the wind is colour.

Colour is a language, yet it transcends the language

barrier. Like music, it is a universal language. I simply know what it means. I listen to what the colour is saying and try to translate it into English. It can be difficult – sometimes I have to struggle to find the words I need to convey exactly what it is saying. And sometimes there aren't any.

Someone asked me what, or who, is speaking to us in this colour language. I have thought about this often and will try to give an answer. Colour comes out of pure light. The clear light that holds all colour is the clear brilliance. It is the cosmic law, or, if you prefer, the Universal Intelligence. Light is a higher order of intelligence. So colour transcends the solid form. It is a glimpse into the infinite. It can be seen as the way Light talks to us. When the sun's and stars' light reaches the earth, the colours of the spectrum break out of its brilliance. It's like birth – I wonder sometimes whether it is not painful for a colour to be born out of the light.

Physical science also tells us that all light is visible radiant energy that travels through space in wave form at a speed of 186,000 miles per second. The light vibrates at different wavelengths and frequencies. Red has the longest wavelength and violet the shortest. The speed at which it travels has a great effect upon anything that receives it. We react to colour automatically. Colour is a gift of evolution. It influences our thoughts, our social behaviour, our health, our relationships; in fact we cannot live without the light which contains all colour. If you put a plant in a cupboard and shut out the light, it withers and dies. Colour can be measured. All organs and parts of our bodies when they are healthy hold to a particular set of harmonious vibrations. It has been proved that it is part and parcel of the psychic and physical make-up of human beings. We are given this proof that light is not only without shining on us, but that it is also a part of us within, in our dreams. When you go to sleep at night, you have your eyes shut in a dark room and yet you see your dreams. Have you ever considered where the light comes from to illuminate your dreams? It must surely come from within. The light was and is always with you – your dreams are proof of that. If we dream in black and white it is of the past and a colourful dream is of the future. A nightmare represents a 'backslip'. Even if the nightmare is in colour, its origins come from the past.

Another simple form of light is a candle. A candle represents the light in the darkness. It also represents the uncertainty of life as it is easily extinguishable. As dreams show the light within, candles represent the light without – our essential self. People who have had near-death experiences often remark on the light that leads the way. No wonder light has been considered divine – the divine light from where all colour comes from that leads the world.

We cannot close ourselves off to this Intelligence. If we could, we would wither and die because it invisibly sustains us through every moment. We can only forget that this is our relationship to it. We can blinker ourselves to its clear truth with the limitations of our intellect and become simultaneously clever and ignorant. Or we can blind ourselves to the magnificence of the Intelligence that is light with the 'sense's shadow show' that is the material world.

Our knowledge of colour has never been truly lost. How could it ever be, as long as the sun continues to shine upon the earth and paints its lessons on all things? It can be ignored but not lost. In every age, those willing to learn its language will be given the gift of the healing wisdom it contains, and directly experience the deep benevolence that the Intelligence which speaks through colour has towards us in our struggle with life.

THE AGES OF COLOUR

This is being called the colour age. People are beginning to give recognition to its vital influence. History shows that colour has always thrilled and fascinated human beings since the beginning of time. Even though we have modern technology, the world is turning with renewed interest to the study of light – reviewing and understanding ancient healing methods as well as examining modern scientific data.

Each day we wake up to a world pulsating – sounds, sights and vibrations of all descriptions. Each day is new and different from the one before, changing constantly. But the one thing that never changes is the fact that colour is an integral part of this world. When we start to explore the world of colour, we realise there is more to colour than meets the eye. We experience a multitude of responses to colour all the time on a conscious and unconscious level. Colour is our universe. It affects everything that we touch, eat, drink, use and are surrounded by. Colour helps us delve into our history. Through colour we can move from the bloom we are in the present to the roots beneath the earth of the past.

If we look back in time we can actually trace our evolution by looking at the colours that depicted that time. For instance, Stone Age people, 50,000 years ago, decorated their caves in Altimira in Spain with drawings of bears, bulls and other animals of that time. Prehistoric art in Africa, Europe and other parts of the world were concerned with physical survival. The colours used by the artists were very primitive. The dark reds show the physical hardship and brutality of that time – the hunting of flesh to survive. The ochres and dark oranges and blacks show the restrictions of the time. The brown earth indicates the great potential yet untapped. These magnetic colours represent a way of life and an environment that was concerned with the physical.

Humanity has moved up the colour spectrum as the ages have passed. I believe that when humans started to domesticate animals and keep them captive for food in an enclosure rather than hunting for them, they were starting to work from the intellect and not from the brawn.

In Roman times thousands of snails had to be crushed to produce enough dye for the Emperor's purple robes. Purple the leader, the ruler taking his own power. In fact, all through history the pecking order in society could be seen by the colour of the clothes you wore. The poor were not allowed to wear colour. In Renaissance times, artists loved to use crushed crystals to make murals, crushed crystals having been used for their colour content for medicines centuries back. In Puritan times the predominant colour was grey. Grey slows things down and deprives. Grey is not into sexuality, and nor were the Puritans! Post-war Britain was a grey time, a time of austerity and criticism. My father, like all men of that time, would not have been seen dead without his grey suit. But grey is like a coat of armour – you can't move in it – which is exactly how the nation felt at that time. When times are prosperous and people are gay and feel like rejoicing, out come the bright colours. This has been shown throughout history as humans have discovered the magic of colour.

We now come to mankind in modern times – the Aquarian Age. The colour of today is blue. We are in the space age. The pace has quickened and we are moving faster. It is the age of the scientist, but science is combined with the higher spiritual self. In this new age, we are seeking the truth. The one reason that may prevent mankind from being in the blue of truth is fear. Fear makes us walk backwards; it makes us contract. Fear will turn us away from the truth. Blue will not only help us to keep to the truth, it is also the great healer; the carer that combats pain, brutality and cruelty.

COLOURS IN THE ENVIRONMENT

Colours surround us all the time, in homes, offices, factories, schools, shopping centres, public buildings and so on. The colours in our environment can have a great effect on us. For instance, in the workplace it was found that by painting stairways red, this will stop people idling for a chat. The red vibrations keep them moving. In the USA, managers were faced with the problem of their male employees spending too much time in the loo, so they decided to paint the walls in the gents a sizzling electric green, and no one hangs around in there now. In a lipstick factory it was discovered that the women working there were being over-exposed to red. Absenteeism was high because of headaches and migraine. But when the walls were painted green, it counter-acted the effect of the red and the headaches disappeared.

An overload of white can also cause problems. For instance too much white in hospitals should be avoided as this will give a sterile feeling causing frustration. Pastels would be better. And if you are visiting someone in hospital, give a thought to the flowers you take them. Don't take red flowers which say 'get up and go' particularly if they've just had an operation. Lavender is a good colour to help eliminate anaesthetics or for anyone who is ill or convalesc-ing.

Airports have neutral colours with bold red signs for directions. It's best not to use yellow in an aeroplane as this will cause nausea, but used in classrooms yellow would focus the concentration and stimulate the intellect. Primrose can be used for children at exam time – it helps their confidence and focuses the mind. (It also helps with elimination – if they feel constipated because they are sitting down and not getting enough exercise!)

The best colours in assembly halls or conference centres are the sombre dignified colours such as dark blue and indigo which encourage structure and planning. In cafés, reds and oranges are the best colours to ensure that customers don't linger too long over a cup of coffee. These colours make you eat more quickly so it will certainly help speed up the turnover. A survey was conducted on colouring prison cells pink to quieten the inmates. I saw this on television and I thought 'They won't be quiet for long, there's too much red in it,' when the prison orderly said, 'But after an hour they were fighting again!' They needed more white in the pink to keep them contented. Football crowds flooded with yellow were found to get very disruptive and hostile and angry. Pale blue would have been better. Autistic children who have a problem with communication have been found to respond well to peach and social orange. Even looking at the colour of flags of different countries can be most illuminating about the character of the people. In law courts the surroundings are usually mature brown wood which gives a feeling of solidity. The judge is often red robed and surrounded by red carpet. He is going to put into action what happens in a case. The jury have blue carpet, blue being the colour of thinking and contemplation.

Surgeons wear dark green gowns in the operating theatre. Dark green has been proven to help staunch the flow of blood. First aid kits are usually dark green too.

Decor in the home is of a profound significance. The colour schemes we use can alter the amount and type of light our skin tissues and internal organs receive. Light is known to be the next most important influence affecting our bodily functions after food. Upstairs in the bedrooms, keep to the cool electrical colours like blues and lavenders for rest and relaxation. Touches of pale pinks and peaches can be brought in for warmth. In work rooms like the kitchen, choose the action colours from the magnetic range – reds, oranges or yellow. Green will go with anything, but don't use it in rooms where you spend a lot of time, such as the sitting room, as it brings on a static heaviness. The baby's room should never be painted white. The baby will be more content and not so frustrated if you use pastels.

It always amazes me when I visit other people's houses and I see hot magnetic colours like orange in the bedroom and the cool electrical colours like blue in the kitchen. So a wake-up colour is in the bedroom where they should be relaxing and sleeping and the go-to-sleep colour is in the kitchen where they should be chopping and peeling!

A RED STORY ... THE WALLPAPER

I had a workman doing some painting for me in my home and I noticed he was very tired. He told me, 'I can't understand it, but just lately I have felt exhausted.' I asked him what colour he had used to decorate his bedroom.

'Well, I've just redone it and the wall by the side of my bed is a lovely bright red,' he said.

'You won't get a good night's sleep with that,' I said.

'Oh no. It's lovely wallpaper, all flocked and velvety. It cost me a bomb. I'm not going to change it.'

I saw him in the street a year later and asked him how he was. 'Well,' he said, 'I had to change that red wall, you know. I didn't get a wink of sleep with that red. I've got a lovely cream wallpaper up now and I sleep like a baby. Beautiful.'

The sense of colour

Colour is a vibration, it shimmers. Each colour of the spectrum vibrates at a slightly different rate to the one either side of it, and we can appreciate the beauty of each. But there is more than beauty in a colour for me.

There is also information about myself and others. Some of the many meanings and connections associated with the different colours can be found in the Colour Catalogue on pages 194–346.

If I am in a room that is blue and I feel a certain kind of sensation in my body, I know that there is some information for me in that colour. It is as though the blue is trying to contact me. It is not always the same feeling. It can be physical or it can be emotional. Sometimes it will be a slight tightening or slight fluttering in my solar plexus, as of fear or warning; another time it will be a feeling of opening, of lightening. But whatever form it takes, it always involves one or more of my senses.

When I feel this signal, I simply give myself over to the colour. I know that if I allow myself to be immersed in the blue, I will understand what it is I need – or what it is I don't need. If I am willing to listen, the colour will tell me.

We all have colours radiating out of us all the time. The colours sometimes come out in little puffs. Sometimes, I can look intently at a person and their physical body dissolves and leaves just an outline where they were into which I can see. Then I see a multitude of colour rays coming out from all parts of their body. Their outer flesh goes, and I can see the patches of different colours that are their organs. There is, in fact, a level at which the person is a colour body, like Joseph's coat of many colours.

This inner colour body gives us information about ourselves and others. If an organ is poorly, then it will not send out a strong, bright coloured light. The colour will be dim and weak. Sometimes the organ will appear to be dark, indicating that it is not as healthy as it could be.

I was at a seminar. The room was full of people, but my eyes were drawn to a young man sitting some distance away. He seemed very animated and very happy, but I could see little puffs of colour, little lilac puffballs, coming from his body. I quite often see this with people, little puffs of colour that are shaped like a ball. They always come from around the head and pop out upwards. In this young man's case, they were a pale lilac. I knew I had to say something to him, so I went over and sat next to him.

We started talking and after a minute or two I suggested to Brian that I thought it would be a good idea for him to look to his immune system at this time because it needed some strengthening. Tears came into his eyes and he told me that he had been diagnosed as HIV positive a week before the seminar.

The young man at the seminar didn't have to tell me that he didn't feel well. In his case, it was the colour coming from his body that told me what was wrong. But there are other ways. In a private reading, for instance, I would have asked him to select some colours from my colour table.

When I ask a person to choose colours, they are drawn to the colours which connect with their own inner colour vibrations. The colours they choose intuitively, and the sequence they choose them in, give me information about their physical, emotional and mental states. This can be information about their present state, but it can also be about their birth, first months, childhood, adolescence – any time, even pre-birth and pre-conception.

This is another aspect of colour's magic: it opens up a door into a person's history like Aladdin's 'Open Sesame' at the cave entrance. And not only the past, the colour body sometimes seems to know the future, also.

A woman came to see me. She chose some colours and I had to tell her that she would have two children before eighteen months were up. She was not particularly pleased by this information and told me that she did not want any more children.

I told her that she had just chosen the colour of birthing, and that I saw two children – although I found myself telling her that she would only have one. She said that she couldn't see how she was going to have even one because she had no intention of having any. I was a bit puzzled myself. Two children in eighteen months?

Four years later I met her at a cocktail party. She came over to me, smiling, and pointed to the three-year-old boy holding her hand.

'You were right,' she said. 'I did get pregnant. I had twins but I lost one, and here is my son.' The little boy looked at me and I felt I knew him well. He had, after all, let us know he was coming!

Her conscious self had been convinced of one thing, but

her colour body had known better. Something – maybe someone – else in her was already well started on the course she was sure was not for her.

FOLLOWING COLOUR INTO THE BODY ... AND BEYOND

Colour goes beyond the surface. We can see with our eyes, but colour sees deeper, and further.

Colour sees right through us. It doesn't stop at the surface of the body. Nor at the surface of time and space, either. At every moment, colour is streaming effortlessly through our bodies like light through a window. Colour can reveal the significance of our actions that could not otherwise be observed.

When I am using colour to see with, I see as though I *am* the colour. I become the colour that comes up for the person. Then I can see through into the body: I see with the eyes of colour. Another way of putting this is that the energy of colour is like an X-ray that allows me to penetrate through the surface of the physical body to the organs and parts within.

It is not just the body, as it is in the present moment, that I see. Colour seems to open up a person's body to me from the time it was conceived. The body on the chair in front of me is open; but so also is that body which stretches away from this present moment back to its conception and forward into the future. I call this the 'time body'.

If someone chooses a dark green I become that dark green myself, and then I can go into their situation on the wave or vibration of the colour.

In the physical body, the dark green may lead back to

inflammation of the joints, for instance – rheumatism. Rheuma is the Greek for flow – the flow of subtle energy through the body. The energy travels in waves through our tissue fluids. Dark green represents resentment. In relation to rheumatism, it indicates a child who was manoeuvred in a direction that was not in harmony with his or her abilities and talents. The child was misdirected, its aspiration smothered by a wet flannel. The resulting pattern of behaviour can be summed up in one word: reluctance – and so can rheumatism.

Rheumatism with its stiffness, its inflammation and swelling, is a *physical* form of the *emotional* response of resistance. The child could not resist successfully, but what it did do was stiffen like a dog being pulled against its will. When muscles stiffen, the flow of rheuma is impeded, even cut off.

If this pattern of muscular resistance continues all our life, our body chemistry changes, and if we continue to live with this chemical make-up, rheumatism/arthritis eventually become the physical symptoms. The pushing around does not necessarily cease just because we grow larger and become adults.

When the rheuma flow is held up long enough, the machinery of the body suffers – particularly the muscles, ligaments and joints. The outcome is the familiar symptom picture of rheumatism – the degeneration of muscles and joints, and the resulting inflammations and swellings.

It is important to understand that when we are being pushed around as a child we react *emotionally* as well as physically. Not to be treated as who and what we really are by our parents is emotionally painful. To be treated as a future accountant when what you really are is a future dancer is traumatic in its denial and suppression of your real vocation. The emotional pain can be so great, in fact, that we can only deal with it by going numb. I have often experienced this emotional numbness with rheumatic sufferers. It is as though the unfelt and long-stored emotional pain has come out as physical pain and degeneration. Thus, rheumatism has a strong emotional component. This is the resentment of dark green. In the person's time body, it may be something that happened when they were five, or the same thing happening many times. The green will take me to the area of their body that is being affected by the resentment, and also back in time to the origin of their pattern of resentment.

The same colour does not always lead to the same place. Another person may choose dark green and we will end up somewhere quite different in their body or their life. Heart conditions, jealousy, envy and greed are all negative aspects of the dark green. It's only when I go with the colour the person has chosen that I discover what it relates to for them personally.

A colour can pinpoint an event. But it can also point to a general predisposition within the person. One of the negative aspects of indigo, for instance, is connected with addiction and obsession. So someone choosing indigo could signal a tendency towards physical addiction. It could also express itself as extreme devotion. Perhaps the person has become emotionally obsessed with someone or some cause. Or obsessed by certain ideas which they cannot let go. In the realm of past lives, indigo might lead back to a lifetime of devotion and austerity as a monk in a monastery or maybe show a lack of structure in previous lives. The particular events for two people who choose indigo are likely to be quite different, but they will usually relate to the general themes of the colour.

Colour also speeds up the therapy process. Working with colour saves a great deal of talking – something which is sometimes the cause of suspicion and misunderstanding in our word-centred society.

Using colours that a client has intuitively chosen means that I don't have to ask the person what their mummy did, what their daddy did, and everybody else did. It shortens therapy time immensely because, on the first reading, I will be able to tell exactly what has been happening, where we are going and what may be needed. We don't have to spend a long time finding out what the person's issues are.

There is often some confusion about 'therapy'. The general idea is that you only need therapy if you are psychologically ill in some way – if you have a psychological condition that more or less incapacitates you in the way cancer or the flu does physically. For some, this is true enough and many people do come to me with specific complaints – physical and psychological. However, when we go to a therapist we are also asking for support or assistance. We may not be aware that this puts us in a state of humility – which allows us to be teachable. When we are teachable, we are ready to learn and grow. Ralph Waldo Emmerson said 'What lies behind us and what lies before us does not compare with what lies within us.'

Many people come, both for private consultations and to my public seminars, who do not need 'therapy' in the normal sense. Their aim is wider: they are seeking enlightenment – to 'know themselves'. My function as a therapist is to be a catalyst (a catalyst is an agent that effects change without becoming involved itself), that is to be available for people while they enlighten themselves.

The colours of self-knowing

'He who knows others is clever,
but he who knows himself is enlightened.
He who overcomes others is strong,
But he who overcomes himself is mightier still.'
Lao Tsu

Colour is a whole new dimension of self-discovery. With colour you can totally dissemble yourself, then re-assemble yourself with something new. Colour is a non-invasive means of discovering yourself. Getting to know yourself is an essential part of life. Some would say the most essential. Looking at it from a purely practical level, we are likely to function better when we know what we are and how we work. Or don't work. As the American author Norman Mailer puts it quite bluntly, 'There was that law of life so cruel and so just which demanded that one must grow or pay more for remaining the same.'

People have always known this truth. The great philosopher, Socrates, devoted much of his life to reminding his fellow citizens of it in Athens over 2,000 years ago. We may be more advanced technologically than the ancient Greeks, but we have not escaped from the necessity to 'Know Thyself'.

To further this process of self-knowing by any one of the many forms of counselling that depend upon talking, upon words, is of some help. The trouble is that we will usually answer the questions from the conscious mind only.

My experience is that we need to go further, deeper, than that. We have to go into our subconscious or emotional self to be able to get to the real truth. Only then does this work of knowing ourselves begin to bring about permanent changes, enabling us to free our present actions and relationships from the old hurts and fears of childhood.

We are all made up of light and darkness. One way into the hidden side of ourselves is to explore darkness and silence. And the black.

Black has a special magic in this journey to our shadow self. Black is known as the non-colour. With black there is no crutch – it is the colour that makes you stand on your own.

If we dare to embrace black, it becomes the liberator.

AN EXPERIENCE OF BLACK

'He who walks in the sun casts shadows.'

A new client began the first session with these words: 'I don't think you're going to be able to do anything for me, because deep down inside I know I am a really bad person.'

This woman was speaking of something real: deep within herself there was, in fact, a dark side. Each of us has a dark side – mainly, we know nothing about this shadow self because nobody has ever taught us about it. But if we are willing and can find a way to come face-to-face with this feared or despised part of ourselves, we release ourselves from its destructive power. We make a friend of the enemy.

Black is the other side of our coin. It is as essential to our wholeness as night is to day. When we are able to embrace our shadow side and bring it into our picture of ourselves, we bestow upon ourselves the treasure of unity.

I experienced this transformation of the black myself when training as a counsellor.

Several weeks into the course we were split up into small groups of ten. These were T-Groups – unstructured training groups. We were given no direction as to what we were to do next. But we were told a teacher would join us for the process. We sat in our group and stared at each other in silence for a minute or two ... Suddenly, the door opened and a man we had not seen before walked in, came up to our group and sat down. Our teacher.

We waited – he said nothing ...

We went on waiting – he went on saying nothing ...

The tension became unbearable. People began asking him what he wanted them to do. He asked them what they wanted to do.

More silence, greater tension ...

I realised I was in a group process that revolved around the technique of silence. It was a most nerve-wracking experience. The only thing you can do is to go with whatever comes up – and it usually does!

We did this for two hours every day. As the weeks went by, I became the scapegoat of the group – apparently one person in each group always does. I was accused by one of the participants, who was the headmistress of a girl's school, of being a liar, a cheat, sinful, etc. No one defended me. I was shocked and mortified by this attack. Even though one part of me knew it was a training device, I was still shattered.

I cried all evening and into most of the night. The only comfort I could think of was that if it got too bad I could take a bottle of pills! I felt like I was an astronaut in space who had just had his lifeline cut and was adrift on a spinning journey into oblivion. As a therapist, you have to be careful that you do not remove a person's habitual support system either too soon or too abruptly. Otherwise that person can be left floundering around in space. This is what happened to me.

Death seemed to be my only solution. I was being drawn into the negative of black. What was going through my mind in the night was: how could a terrible person such as myself survive? I was deep in the pit.

At four o'clock in the morning, I went beyond being afraid. I had reached the bottom. A strange sense of detachment set in. I could look at this terrible person the group saw me as being. It was as though I could look into the dark side of my soul and the more I looked the more I saw.

The black wall I had been up against seemed to lift like the lid of a chest. Inside was full of light and colour. Through the colour I understood what was happening. Yes, I was a liar, a cheat, a murderer and so was everyone else! In fact we all have these within us, but usually we never look at them, or even know that they are there. As a little girl I was trained to be good, sweet, kind and perfect in every way. Anything else that I was, such as bad, selfish, angry or unhappy, was pushed far away into the shadows. It was not nice little 'Lilian'.

Not until I could look at the natural human, undesirable negative side of myself which had been exiled to darkness and integrate it within myself could I be released from its perpetual threat. As the French philosopher, Pascal, said: 'He who would be an angel must become a beast.'

When I was able to embrace and love that 'delinquent' part of my child-self as much as the 'good' part, I was free from its grip and in a state of grace. But it isn't easy. These old memories and connections are hidden from us for a good reason. There is often much pain clinging to them. In a very real way, the child we once were still exists within us and is still suffering.

An old Chinese sage is reported to have said to his students: 'I can turn back one corner for you. The rest you will have to do for yourselves.' Like Socrates, he, too, was speaking of the work that in our time has come to be called 'personal growth': the work of coming to know who you are, how you got to be that way, and what you can do about it. Dogged persistence is sometimes required to remain on our path of self-discovery. But colour can help enormously.

And if, as weeks go round, in the dark of the moon
my spirit darkens and goes out, and soft strange gloom
pervades my movements and my thoughts and words
then I shall know I am walking still
with God, we are closer together now the moon's
in shadow.
Shadows, D.H. Lawrence

THE JOURNEY TO OUR TRUE SELF

Colour, my clients' and my own experiences have taught me, can be as magical as any sage in our journey along the path to our true self. So many clues to our current difficulties and dilemmas lie in our earliest days. And sometimes even earlier.

We are all born in truth. As babies, every single one of us knows only the real self which is creative and divine. The truth is the real self. The untrue self, like negativity, will have to be learned. All children react spontaneously from the truth. But if someone says to them, 'Don't do that', the child will think, 'Oh dear, I'd better obey. If I don't I might not be liked' and the subconscious belief would be: if I'm not liked, I could be abandoned, and then I would die. Because of this threat to the child's basic survival, they will respond by ignoring their spontaneous truthfulness and work from the adapted self – the fake self – because they are rewarded for this. According to how far a child has to go along with this will affect how they function. Eventually they may operate only from the adapted self. The child's identity becomes 'I adapt' and later they may have an identity crisis 'Who am I?' This does not mean adults must not give guidance to a child. All children need appropriate direction that their parents' experience can give them. What they don't need is indoctrination.

Truth allows us to be authentic which enables us to be author of our own experience. It gives us the authority to direct our own lives. Truthfulness is spontaneous. It happens on the moment and is never the same twice. That's why it can be so fearful. You can't measure the truth, and modern man is so keen to measure everything to feel secure that an imbalance occurs which actually interrupts the flow of truth. A very simple way to break this pattern is to take a long deep breath, filling the lungs to capacity. A breath taken this way short-circuits the rational mind and frees us to flow again. The false self knows and remembers by habit – by addiction. The real self is not addicted. It always does things for the first time. The false self always tries to hang on to form or matter because of its compulsion to seek security no matter what, which brings about a descent of spirit. Its idea of emotion is negative emotion – which includes all the fears, greed, envy and jealousies. Every negative emotion is learned. It is not natural to us, it comes from the fear of survival – the fear that the universe won't look after us. Because of this lack of trust we will have to learn to manipulate our environment to be safe.

Emotions are the only reliable truth. An emotion is a chemical event that is experienced in the body. The emotion is always the first thing we have. After the emotion comes the feeling, so when I say I feel this or that, it means already an emotion has happened in my body and right now I can express the feeling I have from it. After this I will interpret the feeling I got from the emotion and then I will act on the interpretation or not. How we interpret it will be according to how we experienced our environment as a child. When we are afraid of emotion we are afraid of the truth.

Emotions do not have to run away with you. They enhance your communications and relationships. They give another dimension; help you to have a richer existence. So the false self is adapted behaviour. It's the behaviour I learned would be *all right*. It learns an habitual response; it's not creative, it becomes ritualistic, compulsive, obsessive.

All addictions are another way of obliterating the pain of not being allowed to be who we are. Adaptations in early childhood are responsible for much suffering and unhappiness in adulthood. We never fully lose our inner knowing of truth, but we may have become so conditioned that we find these negative patterns of behaviour extremely difficult to break, so difficult that we may be pushed to the extreme act of ending it all. To get back to who we really are can have extreme consequences. I believe that when a person commits suicide, it is a last vain attempt to get back or forward to a moment of truth. It may be the only way a person can connect with the identity of the true self. After all, the moment of death is a fundamental truth – unfortunately it will interrupt the span of natural life.

Since being is related to feeling, it is also related to those spontaneous and involuntary movements and gestures that constitute the true self-expression. In our spontaneous movements and utterances, we experience directly the life force within us. We will always subconsciously strive to get back to a state of truth. Truth will always dissolve the fake self. It is the real, divine self incarnated in the body as 'me'. It is a state of grace.

LEAVING HOME TO FIND OUR INNER CHILD

Colour is a non-invasive means of discovering your true self. Colour is the yellow brick road into the realm of childhood past – and, many times, even further back. It can open the door to your childhood that has been kept closed to the conscious mind all these years since.

Colour has the ability, if you learn its language, to tell you how it really was for you at any time in your past. Only the road isn't brick. And it's not even always yellow ... Sometimes it's pale green.

Adele came to me in a state that she called 'a mid-life crisis'. She told me she had a 'good' life. She had a grown-up family, a pleasant home, and still got on well with her husband. They travelled, played golf and went out together; she had many friends, but ... And she chose pale green from my selection of colours.

'Sometimes, I don't know who I am any more. I don't know what I want. I don't know if there even is a real me who wants anything. I say I like something, but is that what I really like, or am I only saying that because somebody else said that I liked it? I feel so depressed for no reason. It's as though I'm living someone else's life and

I want to run away and find my own.'

Adele didn't really have to tell me, the green had already spoken. Pale green opens up that period of our childhood when we were, or should have been, learning what was good and what was not good by experience. These are the years between three and five when we should be developing a will of our own. It is our bud time. At this experimental stage, a child picks up something. What does this taste like? What does it feel like? Do I like it? Yes, I do like it, it's good. No, it's bad, it's not for me. Throw it away! By being allowed to do this, we gain confidence in our own judgement.

If one, or both, of the parents are over-protective during this time, or if they try to tell the child what he or she likes – which usually means what they would like it to like – the child is robbed of its own experience. The sense of self – what *I* like, what *I* want – is damaged. The child's experience of his or her own will is weakened, confused by being over-ridden by the much stronger will of the parent.

Like Adele, a person suffering from the incomplete development of their will at this pale green stage may find it difficult to make decisions in adult life, to know who they are and what they want. After all, to have self-confidence, you must first of all have a self to be confident in! This explains that well-known stage that many adolescents go through in which they take on other people's or the media's opinions and attitudes with alarming fervour. The leader-of-the-gang syndrome wherein the don't-knows follow the one who seems to know.

Someone in such a state of self-confusion may reach a point where they feel that they are not much more than an echo of somebody else's will. By mid-life the feeling that something is wrong with them becomes overwhelming. They are in great despair about themselves. In this state of mind, a person who has been 'happily married' for twenty years can – to the bewilderment of their spouse, friends and neighbours – suddenly disappear from the family home for 'no reason at all'. The reason is not in the family home, but in the past.

Far from being a tragedy, it is a wonderful moment. The person has at last been driven to go out (which, in fact, means that they are going in) and look for their real self. With some luck – and guidance from a skilled therapist or personal growth counsellor – this means to, first, find the inner child they lost contact with long ago, and then to give it the kind of love and understanding he or she still needs.

It isn't necessary for a person to leave their bricks-and-mortar home literally. 'Home' in this context can be as much a state of mind as a place.

How colour can heal your inner child

'The snow goose need not bathe to make itself white.
Neither need you do anything but be yourself.'
Lao-Tse

A young child is pure essence. When we do not get the kind of loving attention we expect and need as a child, its absence hurts us. This is to say nothing of the effect that the presence of the negative attention of angry words, indifference and beatings has. The child is perfect – nothing changes that. It is only the stuff others put into the child, or what the child takes on, that leads us falsely to identify that child differently or as something less.

At first we have no defence against this hurt, but we soon begin to create one. We put a shell around our essential self. But things often turn into their opposites in psychological matters. Which is why, in our adult self, this childhood shell becomes a hollow, unreal self inside of which our child essence is no longer defended but imprisoned.

The major work of what is known as self-growth is to dissolve this castle that has become a prison and release its small prisoner. Quite often, it begins to crumble from the

passage of time without any conscious work by the person
concerned – or even any understanding of what is going on.

'PEOPLE LEAVE ME'

A person's inner child may be buried very deeply,
unmourned and apparently long forgotten. But, if you know
what to look for, you will find the abandoned child still
manages to make its presence felt, and its old unmet needs
interfere in many subtle ways with your adult life.

Late one afternoon a client I had seen once before arrived.
She was a woman in her mid-forties. It was obvious that
Maria had been crying; in fact, she still was. She told me
that she had just seen her niece off at the airport.
Embarrassed and puzzled, she went on: 'I don't know
why, but whenever I see anybody off at an airport or a
train station, I just cannot stop crying. I can be perfectly
happy, and suddenly a terrifying sorrow comes up in me
and I cry like a child.'

The truth was that it was a child who was crying. There
is a technique I use to take a person back to the child they
once were. It involves bathing them in coloured light and
wrapping them in coloured silk. The colour depends upon
the person and what stage of their childhood I feel we
need to contact. For Maria, it was the first years of her
life.

Maria had been born in Germany in 1937. She was
Jewish and her mother had had to keep leaving her with
non-Jewish families for her own safety. Eventually, she
had been put in a Catholic home to conceal her. But it
wasn't this denial of her origins that had caused her such
grief, it was having to say goodbye to her mother so many

times. Furthermore, in growing up, she had herself left her own little child, the child she had been, behind.

The experience of Maria's earliest years, of her child, had been: 'People leave me'. Now, over forty years later, someone leaving for a holiday was enough to open up a tiny channel in the grown woman through which the continuing anguish of her old child could well up again.

Sometimes, childhood experiences are so painful that we have to abandon the child in order to continue to grow. We disconnect from it. Maria had had to do this.

Each stage of our life has a certain time allotted to it. Every child is born needing the environment and parental attention within which the stages of its development may unfold in their correct sequence. If the events of a particular stage are so painful that we cannot discharge the feelings they cause and integrate them before time pushes us on to the next stage, they remain within us, incomplete and seeking completion every day of the rest of our lives. Our emotional growth is held up at that point. What we resist persists.

What Maria had to do was to recover her long-lost hurt child and help her complete the process of grief. Even as adults we are only rarely able to complete the grief process on our own: young children never can.

To help Maria recover from this, I flooded her with a deep rose light. Rose is the colour of comfort, of security, contentment and affection, all states that she did not experience as a child. I also had her use a process by which she could hold her inner child and let her know that she was never going to be left again. It was very moving, and I asked her to repeat it every day for a month – or until her little child believed it. This process is given on pages 170–71.

The child within us is a very real person, and we should

treat it as such. In training, I experienced this with a therapist I was working with who taught me this in one short sentence.

I had had a dream in which my little child appeared crying inconsolably and looking so uncared for and dirty. It was very hard for my mother to keep us clean in wartime, even though she was almost paranoid about cleanliness. There was no such thing as hot running water. We were lucky to get water to drink, let alone to have a bath – which in our house was probably full of bricks from the bomb-damaged walls, anyway.

'How can I possibly cuddle and love my little child when it's so dirty and it smells?' I asked my therapist.

She turned round to me and said, 'Well, give it a wash.'

I hadn't thought of that. I'd forgotten that *I* could now parent my inner child the way it had never been parented.

The idea that the child we once were may still be trying to complete its growth may seem strange at first glance. However, many people have discovered, with the aid of the many kinds of therapies and personal growth techniques we have developed, that it is true.

We can be fully grown physically but still have not completed the stages of emotional and mental growth that were required to become adults in all these parts of ourselves.

We hold our own child, the child we once were, within us in our abdomen until the day we die. Our child contains many children within it. Each phase of our childhood will be a different child. Our reaction to life as an adult will be at least partly determined by that little child. It holds the keys to the patterns of our relationships with each other and with the world.

If our child was unloved or abused in any way, that inner child will, even though we are now an adult, seek fulfilment of its unsatisfied needs from our present partner. This will be true of not just our love partners but also of our business, work and social partners. Unfortunately, it is not possible or appropriate for our partners to fill this old gap. Only we can.

Now, as an adult, we can be the parent, or parents, our child never had and give it what it never got and still seeks: the kind of parenting that will allow it to grow through each stage of its development correctly.

Accepting our child just as it is, and then giving it the parenting it needs, allows us to complete our growth. We cease being a victim to it. We do need to parent ourselves appropriately, of course. So often as adults we parent our own little child the way we were parented – and sometimes our own children, which then continues the problem into the next generation.

However, this coin has another side too: we must release our parents from us, from our old resentments and accusations, in order to become good parents ourselves. We have to sever the cord.

This is not so easy. Many people have claims upon their parents that they are unwilling to surrender. The difficulty is that we are often completely unaware that we have such claims. Some people want to stay a dependent child for instance. It is as though the person decided: 'It's better to have a connection through dependency than no connection at all.'

In a very real way, the child we once were and the parents we once had are still back twenty, thirty, forty years ago, still caught in whatever painful events they had to live through together at the time. And tremors from those events and that relationship reach us every day, no matter what the distance is in time.

Clients often make a statement along the lines of: 'Well, my childhood was difficult and there's nothing I can do about it.' They are quite often drawn to dark blue which, in its negative form, is saying 'I am the victim of my childhood'.

It may be true that we cannot change what happened to us: what was done was done and cannot be undone. There is no point in blaming our parents either. They were parenting the only way they knew how. But, though we may not be able to change the circumstances or the event itself, we certainly can discharge the emotional energy still held in the memory of the event. It is this undischarged energy – the grief, desolation, anger, fear or helpless resentment – that keeps seeping through or boiling up into our lives and bedevilling all our relationships, health and happiness.

Until the charge is released, the event is energetically incomplete for us; it is, in effect, still happening. Once this energy is gone, the event becomes history. What happened in the past loses its power to cripple our present. We will be able to remember the event, but there will be no pain in it for us.

Colour is one way to let light into these incomplete times of childhood. It can also be the way they can be completed, the balance restored and the person allowed to have the exhilarating experience of finding themselves free to live their lives in a present no longer haunted by the past.

WHEN BEING YOURSELF MEANS GIVING BACK WHAT WAS NEVER YOURS

The child we once were still lives in us. But so, also, does its mother. And what happened between them twenty, thirty, forty years ago is still happening. My experience has been that using colour means it is not always necessary to relive all the pain of a traumatic birth or a grievous childhood.

The healing colour vibration will penetrate space and time. If that sounds like magic, it is probably because it is.

One day when I was in my thirties, I woke up feeling terribly agitated. The feeling stayed with me all morning. It was an intense edginess, as though I was about to go on stage and it was most uncomfortable. About midday, I suddenly recognised where I had felt it before: I used to get it as a little child.

The thought came to me: sit down and ask: 'Does this state belong to my little child?' I sat down, closed my eyes and I quickly went back through the years. I asked her 'Did you ever feel the way I feel now?' The answer was 'Yes', it had also been her experience. Gradually I realised it was how I used to feel every day of my life as a child. I had got it from my mother. Nowadays, it would probably be called an anxiety neurosis.

Between the stress and uncertainty of war and all that she had to contend with from my father, my mother lived every day in a state of total anxiety. A young child has no choice but to learn from its mother and father, so from mine I could not but learn anxiety. What about didn't matter: I existed, therefore I was anxious.

This was a revelation to me. Not that my mother had been anxious – that I knew. What I had not known was that this feeling was her anxiety, not mine: it was something I had taken on long ago, I had learned it from her.

Having realised this, I could let my inner child know that being in a state of anxiety was not necessary to her survival; it was simply something she had learned from her mother. I also realised that this alone would not be enough. I had to get the energy of the anxiety out of my system in some way. I remembered a process I had intuitively discovered years before when I was having trouble getting my ex-husband out of my system after our divorce.

I sat in front of the mirror and opened my mouth and imagined a root that went right down my throat, right down my gullet, way, way down deep ... I could see all its little tendrils spread throughout my body. This was where the attachment lay, the root of the anxiety neurosis. I visualised the colour of the root. It was a pale primrose yellow – yellow often indicates mother issues.

I opened my mouth wide, and with both of my hands, pulled the root up and up ... and out of my mouth. Then I put it in the palm of my right hand where it now looked very deflated and crumpled, lifted my hand up in the air and offered it back to my mother – it was her attachment, it wasn't mine.

I thanked her very much for it, but told her that I didn't need it now and, as it didn't belong to me, I was giving it back to her. I did this by visualising my mother. She had already passed on, but death is no barrier to the effectiveness of such a process. Then, with my left hand, I reached up. I didn't quite know why I was doing this, but I felt a need for healing as there was a sore emptiness where the root had come out.

I had an image of an emerald green pot of balm being placed in my left hand. Emerald is connected to heart, pain and relationships. There was no colour in the balm itself; it was from the Brilliance (see pages 200–207), from the clear light that all colours are held within. I scooped out the balm with my right hand and spread it all over my heart area and solar plexus, the areas from whence the roots had been wrenched. I felt it melt away into my body like a translucent dew. Then I gave the pot back.

* * *

Mothers have the greatest responsibility for moulding the human race. History and scriptures have always pointed this out, but we rarely bother to learn from them. A newborn child gets the influence of the woman who launches him or her. The mental state of the child is open and clear. It receives impressions and suggestions very easily. Its life will be formed by these primary impressions. The mother's role is not limited to feeding; with love she also imparts positive and constructive impressions. These are the key to the child's success in later life.

The colours in the womb

Sometimes we can't find the place that the colours refer to between now and birth. In this case, I gently regress the person back to the womb and ask them to tell me the colours they see there.

We are swamped with colour the moment we are born, but we also see colours in the womb. Very few people can remember what happened in the womb simply by thinking about it. But nevertheless it has been recorded.

Problems in the womb will affect our stability and clarity in later life – 99 per cent of human happiness is determined in the womb. Our mother's state of mind and emotions, her relationship with our father, her physical state (i.e. diet), can affect us intensely. So, as with early childhood, it is often necessary to recover these events.

The colours that the person reports seeing in the womb speak of what was happening to him or her in that first environment of our stay on Earth. They are usually very accurate. Many clients have asked their mothers whether what we seemed to have uncovered was, in fact, happening at the time, and found that it was true. The foetus evidently knows exactly what is going on around it, outside the womb as well as within.

These memories seem to be colour-coded for later recall.

Or perhaps our memory is colour?

Mother was our whole world in the womb. Many people report not wanting to leave at the time – others, it seems, couldn't wait to get out. Mother was our entire universe as we floated like tiny astronauts in the life-support suit she provided. This was the time when mother and child were truly one. Separation when it came was – or should have been – an inevitable and natural event so that life could begin its next stage. However, occasionally mother and child will conspire to keep the bond intact long after physical birth has occurred.

THE MAN WHO WAS FIFTY-NINE YEARS IN THE WOMB

James was fifty-nine, and was the headmaster of a school. For many years, he had been concerned with the running of the school but he had decided to go back into the classroom to teach and to be where the action was. It wasn't hard to see the symbolic significance of the move in general terms. But he didn't seem able to tell me much about his life and I couldn't see how exactly it related to his problem with his mother. He was very softly spoken and hesitant. And, I felt, he was extremely angry.

James was looking after his elderly mother. He was an only child and still lived with her. He had never been married and didn't even seem to have a girlfriend. He knew that he wanted to leave his mother but he also knew that he couldn't. He had tried before and hadn't been able to make it stick.

'I left home once for a few weeks,' he said, 'and I felt so guilty and full of shame that I had done this to my mother.'

It wasn't necessary to be psychic to see that he was caught in some desperate trap. As to why, he had few clues to offer. I felt that whatever it was that was holding him had begun earlier than his childhood. On his third visit, I regressed him back to the womb and asked him what he saw, particularly what colours.

All he saw in the womb was red. A vivid, bright red. For me, it was a bright red key. One aspect of red is deep shame and guilt.

'Does your mother tell you how she sacrificed herself and gave up her life for you? How you nearly killed her at birth?' I asked James (physical sacrifice is connected with red). She had. Often. Every day. For years.

'Whatever I do is never enough for her,' he said. No matter what he did for her, his mother never once said, 'Well done'. He had spent years trying to please her, his whole life, in fact, but it was never enough. James' mother needed to keep her control over him. If she had ever said she was completely pleased with him, she would have given up her hold on him and he would have been released and free to go. It was significant that James had been born very late. Perhaps he already had an idea of what he was in for and decided to delay coming out as long as possible.

Our internal mother now is how we feel about ourselves. In effect, his mother had kept James in the womb by never relinquishing the grip of guilt and shame she had established in the first months of his life. With these reins, she could control him. From the moment of conceiving him, James was going to remain hers forever.

Father was hardly spoken of. When he was it was only to mention that he, too, was 'devoted to mother'.

Some part of James was extremely enraged about being on his mother's hook, but this rage had never been able to break through. If it had, it would have changed the situation in favour of James' life, no matter what the cost to his mother.

James was one of the sweetest men I have ever met. When he gave up his very good job as principal of the school he became a teacher of little children. I believe that he wanted to try and get back to the little child who had been stolen.

James' mother imprisoned – or more accurately, had been driven to imprison – her son because she only felt safe being a mother – and then only when the child was in the womb. Her career was to be an eternal mother. She had sacrificed her son's life to maintain her own. The mother's milk that James had received had been sour. Her one great fear was that James would not love her as he grew older and independent. So she must keep him a baby. The irony – as always in these cases – is that she never realised that he would have loved her, anyway!

No one does something like this deliberately. It always stems from their having been a hurt, unloved or abused child. Personal growth dogma says that each of us must take 100 per cent responsibility for anything that has happened to us, even as a tiny child. However, I also believe that it is not helpful to try to maintain some theoretical 'fairness' which treats the child as though it were equal in responsibility to its adult parent. That is simply throwing the baby out with the parent's bathwater.

James, for instance, needed to become quite clear about his innocence. As a foetus in the womb, he was not responsible for his mother's situation. Before he could break away and live what was left of his own life, no longer have guilt and shame his mother could hook on to, he would have to come to see what had been done to him as a baby and not agree to perpetuate it any longer.

The colour psychology of this story is that of the opposite aspects of negative red dovetailing. James' mother was operating out of the dominance and control aspect. James himself was at the opposite pole of guilt and shame. Both had a fear of life. Together, they made a perfect negative red match – it takes two to tango.

Some writers have suggested that the womb is the original of the Garden of Eden. Certainly it is, or should be, a place of complete security without threat. Tranquil and peaceful, it is the receiver of new hope. But when parents quarrel, the energy of the quarrel enters the heart of the child. We cannot escape the impact of the acts of our parents, even if they took place before we were born.

The womb is our doorway into this world. Through it, we enter life and go on from there towards the equally mysterious door at the other end.

Sometimes, in order to discover why a certain pattern of behaviour is occurring in this life, we have to go back to the other lifetimes that seem to continue to exist outside of this life's two doors.

Lives before life

SOMETIMES WE MAKE PROGRESS BY GOING BACKWARDS

Colour enables us to bring past events up-to-date – it helps us to go backwards into our pasts. Men, I find, are less at ease with the womb experience than women. Men much prefer to be regressed back further into preconception. They are much keener to slip back to before their appearance in the womb than women are. I'm not sure why this is. Perhaps it is something to do with power – maybe they do not feel that they have much power in the womb. But they really like to get into past lives.

Women, on the other hand, usually have no problem with womb regressions. Perhaps it is because, as I believe, all women are magicians. It has taken me years to understand this magic and to become free enough of my personal limitations to be able to use it consciously. That she uses magic every day is a woman's dark secret. A woman's magic is that she can take energy and give it form. An ancient understanding of this was in the idea that the woman takes the light energy of the male into her dark and secret womb and there transforms it into a human being. A child is born from a woman's inner magic; the womb is just the vehicle in which the magic takes place.

PAUL'S SON

Paul was a millionaire businessman in his forties. He was very self-assured. He was 'happily divorced' and rather prided himself on his ability with women. But I also felt a deep sorrow in him.

On the face of it, Paul had everything a man needed to live a happy life. Wealth, loving women and the health to enjoy them – what was he seeking from me? He was looking for help but personal growth was not his aim.

Some people come to me looking for a deeper under-standing of themselves rather than to free themselves from a specific physical problem or psychological distress. I could see that this was not true of Paul. Underneath his success, the man was in pain and he wanted me to fix his problem for him instantly. He was used to being obeyed too.

He chose a set of colours and I discovered he had a son. Paul couldn't seem to tell me much about the boy. At first I thought that he wouldn't talk about him. Then I realised that it was not wouldn't but couldn't. His silence about his son was the result of a deep block.

I do not push or even try to encourage a person to force themselves to speak about anything. It's not necessary. Colour will take us into whatever it is, no matter how painful or how deeply buried. I got an impression, a fleeting picture, of the boy himself caught behind a block of stone, like someone trapped in a cave. While we talked about almost everything else in Paul's life but his son, I put him in the yellow light. I felt we needed to do a bit of unravelling and revealing here. Yellow is good for unravelling and revealing and leaving no stone unturned.

I was picking up that Paul had a great feeling of shame about his son. I felt sure that its origin was not entirely in this life. I couldn't get beyond his block – we had gone back to birth and the womb without anything enlightening showing up. At the beginning of the third session I suggested a regression technique where we look at a past life or two. Paul was one of those men who had not been particularly at home in the womb regression. But with the past life regression everything fell into place.

I prepared him by wrapping a sheet of deep, rich purple silk around his body. Then I darkened the room and flooded him with a deep purple light. Behind the purple, I put an indigo filter. Purple is the colour of prominence in society, while indigo is the colour of structure. I felt we were going to need to investigate both areas.

We went through several lives, interesting but without much emotional affect on Paul and not what I was looking for. Then we came to a life where he had played the role of a Judas. He had been in a position of trust and he had betrayed somebody he had loved and served. Furthermore, he had done it by the voice. He had spoken to the authorities and his words had betrayed his teacher.

Paul sobbed deeply through this, the dominating, self-confident businessman-Don Juan entirely gone. When he came out of the regression, he looked at me and said, 'I can tell you about my son now.'

Paul's son couldn't speak. He was autistic. The floodgates were open and Paul spoke of the shame and guilt he had always felt about his son's disability. He had been convinced it was largely his fault, although there seemed to be no objective reason why this should be so. He had never been able to talk about him, or to be a normally proud father. After this regression he felt that his son was silent because of his own outspokenness as a Judas.

I suggested to him that his son also had his own karma to work out and that it would almost certainly be the chief factor in his autism. Paul and his son were dove-tailing into each other's karma. I am sure that parents do have a real responsibility for their children. But this responsibility is for the flesh, not for the soul. I also indicated that he, Paul, might want to look at his need to control. Guilt and shame for another's condition or situation can be a hidden way of saying: 'I have control over you and your life.'

Other issues fell into place. Strangely enough, although Paul was a high-powered businessman, he confessed to having tremendous difficulty at board meetings. To stand up and say what he wanted or needed to say was terrifying. Now he understood why he had been so petrified of saying what he felt instead of what seemed acceptable. He was caught in a time warp. The belief his past life experience had left him with was: to speak causes disaster. The less he said, the less chance there was he would endanger anyone.

He had never been able to tell his mother what he felt, either. He was a dutiful and caring son, showing, by his consideration, the love that he had for his mother. But he had never been able to bring himself to actually say, I love you.

Paul came for six more sessions. It was touching how extremely vulnerable he became as he began to speak of his real feelings. Board meetings were still difficult, but, with my background in stage work, I was able to help him with speaking techniques.

We used a great deal of turquoise during this period. Turquoise unites the green of the heart, which is what we feel, with the blue of the throat, which is what we say. He needed to amalgamate these within him.

Turquoise is actually made of three colours – yellow being the third. In Paul's case, once the green of the heart and the blue of the throat were united, the yellow would give him the spurt of energy needed to say what he felt instead of what he thought would be appropriate.

> As you think, so you become.
> As you sow, so shall you reap.
> As is your faith, so is your fate.
> These are the principles of universal truth.
> *His Holiness, Param Sant III*

Regression should be treated with respect. I do not believe it should be used for entertainment purposes, such as 'I am Queen Afi Dufi and you are my slave'. Nor should it be used for spiritual ego trips. But it is extremely useful if the causes of the patterning, or limiting beliefs, cannot be found from birth to seven years, or from conception to birth, in this life.

We should be aware that the personality that appears in our past life is not important. Past lives give us access to our genetic and racial memory which will be a symbol for us today. It is the energy pattern of the past life that we must work with. For instance, I've had several Pontius Pilates turn up in my session room. What was significant about this for all of those who remembered being Pontius Pilate was the condemnation pattern. In this life they were either being condemned or condemning.

The past life that appears simply shows up the everyday patterns of behaviour that the person is struggling with in this lifetime. This is our karma. Colour helps us delve into our history. Through colour we can move from the bloom we are in the present to the roots beneath the earth of our past.

Whenever I ask someone what they understand karma to be they usually reply 'cause and effect'. Well, what does that mean? Does it mean that if I've been good before in previous lives I will have a good life now this time round? If I have been bad will I only receive bad in this life?

I personally do not believe that what happens to you in this lifetime is a punishment for what you did before, but you will bring in with you from birth your own personal essence, which is unique to you and is the blueprint for the learning that comes with you from your past.

In ancient Sanskrit writing, karma simply means *action*. To give an example of this, if I am a student with dyslexia I will find it more difficult to get through my studies. It will take longer and my disability will appear to be a nuisance. But there is also a plus side because I shall get a thoroughness and a more in-depth understanding of the subject because I have to take longer. It is the action of doing the studying that is working with my karma – the dyslexia is just the means to get me to work with my karma. Saying it's my karma to be dyslexic is only part of it, the main part is how I cope with the disability.

Karma should not be confused with fate. Fate rather smacks of 'Oh well, there's really nothing I can do about it, it's all mapped out for me so I may as well sit back, do nothing', which invariably means I stay stuck. But fate and karma go hand-in-hand. If inner or outer conflict is not resolved it is usually called fate. However, I can change my fate if I am prepared to put into *action* the learning I need to experience: to work through my karma from my fate.

You may well ask why should we have karma anyway? Grappling with karma, fate, eventually leads to enlightenment. Being enlightened means you are prepared to take responsibility for your own life and not remain a victim of fate. This to me is the growth of the self. You can only enlighten what you have and that is you. Karma is the light in our lives. Colour and karma work together. Our personal light affects everyone. When we come together in groups or relationships, we share each other's colours which means we always experience each other's past, present and futures.

The magic of past life work for me is that touching into the old life can dissolve the grip of the destructive behaviour pattern in this life – and often instantly. One observation I have made is that this past life colour technique can be invaluable in working with schizophrenics. You can talk to schizophrenics endlessly and you may not necessarily get anywhere. In my understanding, schizophrenics have subconsciously decided to cut themselves off from reality. When we lose connection with our inner self, we lose contact with the outer world. But I have found that if schizophrenics are regressed into a past life after giving them a colour drawing test and then asking what colours they see can be amazingly effective in bringing them back into their bodies. If they can see colours, I can quite often help them.

Seeing through the veil

THE LEGLESS VISITORS WHO COULDN'T
COME IN

As a child I used to see lots of people around that no one else seemed to notice. I did try to tell my parents, at first. My mother wouldn't answer me; in fact, she wouldn't even acknowledge that I had spoken. My father did seem to believe me – sometimes.

I had conversations with these people no one else could see. There wasn't much content in them. From what I can remember, they were always explaining to me that it was difficult for them to speak to me. It was mainly greetings, 'Hello, and how are you?' I used to tell them I was fine. They would tell me not to be frightened. In this, they seemed to me to be displaying one of the usual adult attitudes towards children. It generally means that the adult is afraid. I wasn't at all afraid, just curious.

I remember noticing that there was a whiteness about my visitors; their chests, particularly, seemed to be very white. I had the feeling that they wanted to connect, to be welcomed. That's why I had begged my father to let the man in.

The man who couldn't come in used to recur quite often. He would keep telling me that he couldn't come in to see me. Being a child, I thought, 'Well, it's so easy, I've only got to open the door and you can come in,' not realising, of course, that he didn't mean it in the way that I thought.

I never used to see any legs. It may have been because of the window sill and the wall. They used to come at night, mainly – perhaps there were more of them around after dark. I got great comfort and strength from them. They seemed to be letting me know that everything was all right. That may have been at least part of the reason for their visits.

I still see people. As a child I saw more detail but now I see a sort of dark shadow: 'Oh, there's somebody there'. I used to see their clothes and their faces much more clearly. Now, its more of an impression. Also, I sometimes smell a strong perfume. It's in the air – once I even followed it up some stairs. Psychics can often experience presences as a cloud of perfume in the air.

ON BEING PSYCHIC

Being psychic is dealing with space. We tend to regard space as empty, but it is not. In its 'nothingness' is everything. There was never a truer saying than 'out of the blue'.

Some religions believe that it doesn't matter what you do, it's all mapped out for you anyway. It's fate and nothing will change it. I have grappled with this idea for a long time. As often as I get an answer it moves on again. One minute, I completely believe that if I change my life I change the outcome. Then I realise that it is only my limited measuring of the mind that even believes there is an outcome.

When you look for the 'unseen' answer which is psychic-ness, you cannot perceive it as a form that the human eye can see in this world. Having received some information, if you start measuring it then you get into reasoning loops and it is gone. Reasoning loops get you nowhere. They are the unanswerable questions like 'Mummy, who made God?'

Being psychic is being a teacher. You get information and you pass it on. Sometimes the receiver understands it, sometimes they don't until much later.

I find it hard to distinguish one aspect of my work from another. I am a colour therapist, a palmist, a counsellor, regressionist, healer, psychic and clairvoyant giving consultations on drama role-playing, diet, dance exercise, bodywork, yoga and dream analysis. They all overlap through the psychic connection.

I don't get negative messages but I do get warnings which can help to avoid unnecessary suffering if taken notice of. It can come at any time and in any place and if I get something for a person it is always for a reason, like the young man and the lilac auric colour (see page 35).

Psychicness is something extra or maybe the beginning of it all. The palms, colour, etc., will definitely give you a lot of information but the psychic aspect goes way beyond. This mediating must only be used ethically. It must never be used for self-gain or manipulation. It never works if that is the motive. Psychicness has no religion. Religion is man-made. Psychicness is not.

It was once put to me that a psychic needs hurts to understand other people. Mediums have usually suffered in life, quite often physically. In the past they were social outcasts. We are usually scared of people who see life in a different way. We call it unacceptable behaviour. Why not embrace their richness? As I've said before, colour is part and parcel of the psychic make-up of human beings. It is as inherent as our eyesight or sense of smell. Colour is a psychic sense.

A psychic is someone who can see the whole. When you have a teaspoon of water from a lake, that's all you see. The psychic sees the whole pond. Being psychic means you can do it anyway. I was teaching a course on colour inter-pretation using colour as a tool. A participant on the course remarked to me: 'But Lilian, you can do it anyway'.

Being psychic means you don't have to take exams. Being psychic means every time is exam time. Being psychic means you never get to pass – you always have to keep sitting for it. Being psychic means: he revealed his word to my mind. He is spirit.

Psychic searchlight warning!

Beware of people who turn what I call the 'psychic searchlight' on you. They beam it on you and you are standing suddenly exposed in its spot. People like this can be found anywhere – in the office, at a social club or even your local shopkeeper.

They flatter you, they build you up ... and then they make their demands. They set you up, and then when you say, 'Well, no, I don't think that's for me', they flip the switch and you're in the dark. And they go off looking for someone else to beam on who might do what they want.

These are called psychic vampires; they are the negative psychics. They are working from the negative aspect of black, taking in everything for themselves and giving noth-ing out. It can be very seductive when they aim their searchlight at you. However, no matter what you think you are getting, what is happening is that you are being got.

SUSIE B'S BLACK WINDOWS

Susie B and I met each other when our husbands were involved with the musical show *Hair* in London in 1969. Her husband, Paul Nicholas, was playing the lead in the show and my husband was the producer.

Susie and I got to know each other very well as we were both getting divorced. We were just two more of the marriage casualties from that show. We decided to go to Paris for a holiday just to cheer ourselves up. It was a great break away and we shared lots of fun and laughter. Susie was ten years younger than myself and was full of the red rays of seizing the day.

We were close friends for about three years when suddenly we lost touch with each other. Following her divorce, Susie B had experienced great suffering with a relationship that did not materialise. She had been very much in love. After this disappointment, she moved into a way of life that I could not follow, so we parted.

One night, two years after our friendship ended, I had a dream. I dreamt I was sitting at Susie's kitchen table and as I looked out of the window into the garden my view was blocked. As much as I tried to see through her windows I could not see out of them – they were painted black.

'Why have you painted your windows black?' I asked her. She didn't answer and I woke up puzzling over this.

The next day a mutual friend of ours rang me up and said: 'Have you heard the news? Our dear friend Susie B has died. It was yesterday afternoon in a multiple car crash.'

I immediately knew what the dream the night before had signified. Susie had been showing me that she had died and that she would not be able to view her garden again from her kitchen window in her bodily form. My friend remarked that I did not seem surprised. I explained to her that Susie had already told me.

The following evening I could not sleep. Every time I dozed off, Susie would appear distraught and sobbing, asking me to help her as she didn't want to die. I woke several times. Each time Susie was sobbing. This also made me cry as I told her I couldn't help her, that she must go, she was already dead. Her sobs were so pleading and painful and I was caught up in feeling her distress. But I could only tell her gently over and over again that she must move on. The psychic healing she needed from me was to help to come to terms with moving over. She pleaded that I was her only link and please bring her back, as her children needed her. But I couldn't.

In the early hours of the morning, she finally departed. She realised that she had gone over and that there was no way back. Several years later, I heard through a friend that a relative of Susie's had visited a medium soon after her death. The medium had said that she kept coming back crying and crying.

Susie had a great fear of old age. She would often remark to me: 'I hope to look like you when I get to be your age.' I was thirty-four at the time. She died four years later aged twenty-eight.

Where is healing to be found? When is it time to die and let go of trying to heal? Sometimes there is no cure, only transforming.

Years before I joined the Psychic Circle, I would occasionally find myself staring at a person. 'Why,' I would wonder, 'am I looking at that person in this unusual way?'

I couldn't seem to help myself. I had to look – my eyes were drawn to the person as if by some kind of magnet.

Then I noticed that I would hear that the person had died a short time after this happened. I also realised that there was something different about the faces of those I looked at in this way. There was a particular pallor, a lack of colour. I could not see the life's blood under the skin. This was nothing to do with the person having fair skin. The human body alive reflects all colours, whereas death does not.

I knew that the life force starts to leave the body quite a while before the body is actually dead and finally I had to admit that what I was seeing was that the person's life energy had begun to go.

'THEY'RE HERE FOR YOU, AREN'T THEY, MUMMY?'

When I was eight years old, I was sitting watching my mother setting the knives and forks on the table for dinner. As I watched her moving around the table I saw her body change shape. It swelled and her flesh became bloated. It looked as though something in her body had blocked up and now it was going rotten. All the time her body was shimmering with light and I knew in an instant how she would die. I felt a deep sorrow because of what was to come for her later in life, and a loneliness as I couldn't share this with her. At that age I didn't know how to say 'Mummy, I've just seen how it will be for you when you die and maybe we should look at this.' My mother was twenty-seven at the time. Thirty-six years later when she was sixty-three, she was in hospital with terminal cancer of the lymph glands. It affected her body's drainage system and she did swell up because of her final illness.

I knew her time was near when I saw a halo of white mist that appeared to be escaping from her head. It was about a foot wide and like steam coming out of a kettle. I asked the nurses if they could see the white mist around her head? They said they couldn't. I thought I had better not say any more in case they wanted to put me in the bed next to her.

Up to this point, my mother had denied that she was going. For three years, she had denied that she had any kind of illness at all. After I saw the mist, I sat down next to her and gently took her hand. I said quietly, 'It's your time now isn't it, Mummy?'

A beautiful smile appeared on her face. She nodded her head. Then she turned her head away from me slightly as though to talk to someone on the other side of the bed.

I said, 'They're here for you aren't they, Mummy?'

She smiled again. I could see that she was listening to them. I leaned across her to touch them. As weak as she was, her hand came out and took hold of my hand and pushed it back to my side.

'They're not here for me, are they, Mummy?'

'No,' she said.

'Uncle Harry is here, isn't he?'

She nodded.

'He's waiting for you. He's going to take care of you, isn't he?'

She nodded again. There was such peace and beauty in her smile. The struggle was over. She was going, but she knew she wasn't going to be alone which had been her greatest fear in life.

My mother had sensed that she would be ongoing and that her 'self' would be untouched by the passing of her body. She was strangely confident and strengthened by the approach of a new openness. My mother had found the key to dying: if you let go of the mind and die into the heart, you will be free of your fear of death. It was the most perfect moment of total truth between my mother and myself. We had never been able to experience that kind of openness with each other during the whole of our lives.

What I see – or rather what I do not see – in the unusual look on the face of a person close to passing over is the lack of vital *colour*. The face becomes translucent, the features invisible. It is not the same as the pasty grey face of someone who may be rundown but who is definitely going to stay in the land of the living for some time to come.

I don't find observing this scary. It's a natural process. Just as you can see the coming birth of a child in the swelling of a pregnant woman, so I can see the face's change with the coming of death.

I know I am not alone in witnessing this, but we do not usually allow ourselves to know that we see it because of the sorrow we associate with death – this leaving of earthly existence to go into a new sphere.

We feel it perfectly natural to welcome and prepare for the coming of a birth. So it is, I feel, a pity that we ignore death and make little preparation for its arrival. Other cultures have dealt with this time of life differently. In his book, *Who Dies?* Stephen Levine writes of the way one culture brings even colour into their transition:

'In the American Indian culture at the time of death a naturally formed crystal is often offered for use as a meditation object. Gazing into the fissures within the crystal that create prismatic rainbow tones, one projects one's consciousness into the rainbow, letting go of all that keeps the mind from focusing beyond itself. At death, one is guided into the Rainbow body, melting out of temporal form with ease and preparation.'

Perhaps we try to ignore death because it represents a 'barrier' beyond which is a great unknown. Death is not the end as there is no beginning. Like the seed that blooms into a flower, where does it go from decline of blossom to seed again? Being psychic, I can see through this barrier between what people see as life and death without any fear.

IN STRANGERS' FACES

I am in the hands of the Unknown God,
He is breaking me down to his own oblivion
to send me forth on a new morning, a new man.
Shadows, D.H. Lawrence

One of my first experiences of seeing death in a stranger's face was when I was living in Barnes. There was a delicatessen I used to visit quite often. One day I went in with my daughter Louise in her pushchair.

I looked at the face of the man who owned the shop. His face seemed strange; it had an unusual look. There was a translucent quality. There was no pinkness; in fact, the translucency had a tinge of grey. It looked as though the blood had been drained away. Years later, when I discovered colour, I realised that this lack of pinkness was because the red energies were leaving the body. I kept puzzling about the man's face in my mind, I didn't know why. Two days later I found out that he had died suddenly of a heart attack. What struck me particularly was my complete lack of surprise!

Several years later, I was on holiday at Fort Lauderdale

in Florida. One morning as I was sitting enjoying the sun, I noticed a man come down to the pool with his wife.

They were middle-aged, in their early fifties. The woman was very beautiful and was wearing a white towelling robe with a hood. Why, I didn't know, but I kept thinking: 'When you take that robe off, you life will be different.' Then I looked at her husband. I couldn't really see him. It was as though he was behind a veil of some kind.

I began talking with the pool maintenance man. He told me that they were regular visitors. The wife had been a Las Vegas dancer and he was a high-powered business-man. They came here every year and were lovely people.

The woman moved away and her husband lay down on the sun bed. I watched him put his sun oil on and I thought: 'Why am I staring at him so? It's not as though he is very good-looking . . .'

About twenty minutes later I got up to go for a walk along the beach. I saw the wife again by the bar where she was speaking on the telephone. And she was still wearing the white towelling robe with the hood.

Again, I had the impulse to go over and tell her to take the robe off now, that if she did, maybe events could be changed . . . I didn't even know what the events were.

When I came back from my walk twenty minutes later, police cars and an ambulance were on the beach. Later in the afternoon I heard the white-robed woman's husband had gone down to the sea and there died instantly of a massive heart attack. I realised then that I had kept looking at him because I couldn't see him. His essence had left; he had already gone. And when his wife did get that robe off her whole life had indeed changed.

A MESSAGE FOR THE DAY NURSE

In 1978 I was in a London clinic recovering from a major operation made necessary by peritonitis. I was being cared for twenty-four hours a day by two nurses doing twelve-hour shifts. It was yet another of the illnesses that had dogged me from childhood.

Later, I understood how ill I had been, but at the time I wasn't aware that I was so close to the edge. I simply felt very removed from life, encased in a cocoon of warmth and very detached from reality. I was slipping away from life quite comfortably.

I remember waking up and seeing the back of a nurse at the foot of my bed tidying up some bottles on a table. And then I heard this strange noise getting louder and louder like a tube train coming out of a tunnel towards me. The noise became deafening, accompanied by a blast of wind.

I was aware of a shaft before me, a tunnel, and I felt acute discomfort as if I was being pulled out of my body through the top of my head into a boat or onto a platform. I felt like I was an inner tube being pulled out of a tyre.

Once on board, I looked down and could see my body spread-eagled on the bed below. As I was looking at the nurse (who still had her back turned on the whole proceedings), I thought: 'If she asks me to move in that bed she's had it as I've left! I'm not in it any more.'

I became aware that the speed at which I was ascending into the tunnel was becoming faster and faster, and that I was going further and further into space.

I eventually came to a halt. I could see the most amazing deep indigo sky. And everywhere darting and flashing about and whizzing by were these sparks. It was so alive, so full of electricity! I felt isolated and lonely and wanted to go into this beautiful indigo space. But I also felt that I was on hold, not allowed yet to fully join in.

I looked above me and I could see the outline of my body in gold. Rays of light were being poured into my abdomen. I knew I was being healed and I had an urge, a firing of the will, to live.

I realized that I must have been dying and that I had been brought to this place only as a visitor. I was not stopping, which explained why I couldn't join in with the other sparks and become one with them, not just yet.

The next thing I remember is hovering a few feet above my body in its hospital bed. The nurse was still in the same position with her back to me. As I was about to enter my body, a voice said: 'Tell this to the nurse'.

'You were brought up as an orphan. Your mother's sister brought you up. She was a spinster and her favourite dress was made of purple velvet. She wore a cameo brooch on a black velvet ribbon around her neck and wore her hair in a bun at the nape of her neck ...'

The voice went on to tell the nurse through me that her aunt had been a very strict disciplinarian who had loved her but been unable to show or express it. I had reached the point where I was telling the nurse details of her aunt's life when I heard a terrible crash of bottles and she fled from the room.

The voice said, 'It's all right, she'll be back.'

I slid into my body and into a deep sleep, knowing I would now get well. When I woke, I found the nurse sitting by my bed in a state of excitement. She told me she had been new on that morning. We hadn't even said hello before I began giving her her life's history as well as some messages from her aunt. She also said that the messages had made her feel content within herself.

For me, the communication from her aunt was the confirmation that my experience was not just a dream or imagination, but an experience of the ultimate power and caring of the Universal Intelligence that created, and continues to create, this universe.

Over the next few days, I could see that the doctors and nurses were very wary of me. I could see that they were thinking I might go off again. With a smile, I assured them that I would be staying.

From this time on, I could look forward to sleep at the end of every day knowing that I could visit that sacred temple in the sky and become a spark. As a spark I can receive any knowledge I need to know in purity and justice, knowing that come morning I shall be me again.

Colour yourself well!

A colour a day keeps the doctor away,
So colour yourself healthy, wealthy and wise.

My father had the power to heal. He was a Scot, a race who are said to be more naturally open to the psychic world than most. A long time after he died, my mother's cousin, Renee, confirmed a story from the time when he was lodging at my Granny Meyer's home.

My grandfather had extremely bad legs – they were covered in huge ulcers. For years, he had tried every kind of medical treatment. The doctors had given up.

One day my father said that he would heal Grandfather Meyer's legs. The family stood there amazed and silently wondered what my father thought *he* was going to do. He had only been in the house a few months and no one had noticed much evidence of his having any powers that would help his fellow man.

My father ordered a bowl of warm water, nothing else. After unravelling the bandages on Grandfather Meyer's legs, he scooped the clear water up in his hands and gently poured it over the infected ulcers. Then he wrapped them up again.

The family stood there waiting, and thinking, 'Is that

it?' Renee remembers her mother bending over to whisper in her ear, 'A fat lot of good that will do!' But within two days, the ulcers had healed completely. Now everyone was truly amazed.

I don't think my father ever realised the full depth and value of his gift of healing. It wasn't the kind of healer he had wanted to be. As a young man, my father's ambition had been to be a doctor but the Depression prevented him from going to medical school. I believe my father was a great healer. I've met very few people who could heal ulcers by bathing them in warm water. He had an uncanny knowledge of the human body. He seemed to know exactly how everything in it fitted together. When he handled someone's arms or legs, it was as though he could read them. He also had a great feeling for the state of balance of a person's body. He would often warn the person in whom he detected some disharmony that they would become sick or damage themselves unless they corrected it.

It gradually became known in our neighbourhood that 'John Grassom' could heal where doctors had failed – he was wonderful with epileptics. People would often turn up on our doorstep with just his first name: 'Is Jock the healer here?'

He was very proud of his hands. He would hold them out in front of him and say, 'Look at these hands, they're beautiful, they're really healing hands.' It was true, they were exquisite. My father was also a very melancholic person but in a strange, backwards kind of way, his melancholia taught me the power of visualisation. 'Life is not a bed of roses,' my father would say. 'It is, it is,' I thought, 'I can see rose pink petals covering my bed, I can smell them.'

Deep down inside me, I knew that life was magnificent.

MY FIRST HEALING

My first encounter with my own healing powers took place in the bomb shelter with Leslie, the boy next door. He was a year younger than me and my first love. It was his idea to play doctors.

Leslie had a keen sense of nature. He got a long twig from the garden for the game of doctors. He told me it was safe because the twig was natural. Furthermore, it was what doctors used.

He then dropped his short pants, exposing himself.

I saw that he did, indeed, have something that looked as though it needed healing. I knew it couldn't be right because I didn't have one.

'If you touch it with the stick, you will make it better,' he said. Leslie had said the right thing, he had spoken to the *healer* in me.

I thought, 'How can I get rid of it for him?' I wondered if maybe I did touch it with the twig, it might disappear. It was worth a try ... Just then, the shelter door opened casting a bright light across the scene. A face loomed through the glare – Leslie's mother.

Leslie got a good hiding immediately, and was sent to bed with no supper later. His protestations that we were 'only playing doctors' seemed to fall on deaf ears. Nothing at all happened to me. It was just like it was with the bombing. I also said we had been playing doctors. They just nodded. I couldn't believe it. Saved again!

There is always a way of healing. It may not be the conventional way. The way is not important. What does matter is that you find it.

It was Hippocrates who said he would rather know what sort of person has a disease than what sort of disease a person has. The first step towards healing is to be able to recognise patterns in our life that we act out. You are constantly living it if you don't relive it. To relive it you must experience the original pain. You have to get to the root cause. What we mean by this is if you are to become well, you have to relive your past hurts so you can release them. This is done in therapy or just by talking it through with a friend. If you don't do this, you will experience the pain every day until you do face up to it and relive it.

If you always do what you've always done, you'll always get what you've always got. People are generally what they think themselves to be. What is healing anyway? Is it just curing an organ in the body or making the person's life better? When you become ill, you don't believe in a future, and when you don't have a future, you don't take care of yourself.

Sometimes it is necessary to look at what the illness is; to look into the illness rather than follow the preconception of it. When we get flu, for instance, we expect to have a temperature for several days, feel off-colour, followed by catarrh, etc. This is our preconception about what flu is. However, we could look at the reason *why* we have it, what was the emotional cause – 'Why did *I* get the flu? Why was I vulnerable to it? Many other people around me could have got it but didn't. Why me?' They didn't get it because their particular personal pattern, which is their emotional make-up, didn't fit the energy pattern of the flu.

Once we have recognised our patterns – positive and negative – in our life, we will have to get behind them to find the person we truly are. Then we will have to see why we adopted the patterns or the role in the first place and what function they serve in the present. Usually, the reason why we adopted the role in the first place was fear. Peace of mind sends the body a live message while turmoil, conflict, fear, depression give it a die message. When we lose connection with our inner self, we lose connection with the outside world. What we create within will always be reflected without. Illness is seen as an imbalance of the forces within us. The only way to get out of our disharmonious state is by self-knowledge. This self-knowledge is available to us by several means, i.e. personal growth, which is the discovery of how we motivate which will show us who we are.

Regard your pains as a treasured wound. You either learn from them, or you treasure them as a means to manipulate other people.

Disease is war. It is you at war with yourself. Fighting with ourselves within causes war to break out – we get ill. Fighting with ourselves weakens our immune system. Disease is regarded as an enemy. The best way to destroy the enemy is to make it your friend. It can become your *best* friend. Disease is telling you the truth about yourself. It means that you have ignored the whisper; now your body will make itself heard by a loud shout called disease.

Healing aims for the union of self with the sound within. We think our body is silent, but it's not. Even when we sit still, our body is full of sounds and rhythms. It is very noisy. Taking your pulse is listening to your internal sound. When I listen to my pulse I am listening to myself. Each of us is a symphony of thought, form, colour.

To heal ourselves, we need to follow the thought-form-colour pattern being played within our body. Doing the processes (on pages 157–75) is a way of tuning in to this pattern. Dancing also connects you to your own internal rhythms. The heartbeat is time and the circulation is space. The body has rhythm and it beats to the melody of the heart. That's why dance and movement are natural healers.

When you start to resonate with your self, you start to resume responsibility. Then you start to have an influence on what is happening in your life. Only then can you be there for others as a healer.

Look to the kingdom in your own heart, your own personal kingdom where you rule supreme. Look for the gold that lies there within your own heart. When you are content within yourself, you will be free of the dark yellow of judgement and condemnation. Being in this healing space takes total acceptance of what is, which neutralises negative conditions. When you work with the gold of the heart, you are saying to the person who needs healing (and this may be yourself): 'I may not love what you do, but I love you anyway.'

THE GOLDEN TEARS OF FORGIVENESS

Life is a school, and a hard school at that, and whoever we meet during this learning period of a 'life span' acts as a mirror encouraging us to see in ourselves that which we need to know in order to progress.

I remember being eight years old and looking at my parents and thinking, 'they're so young and scared'. They were like children and I felt so old by comparison. I was full of compassion and wanted to comfort them as they naïvely struggled with life.

Since that time, I have come to understand from my own researches and experiences that I chose my parents before I was born, just as we all do. (This is called Karma see pages 69–70). I can see now that they gave me the perfect soil in which to grow and learn my life's lessons – if I chose to do so. They were my perfect teachers, the two people who would give me exactly the environment I needed to develop and become whole in this lifetime.

It is only recently that I have completed the particular

lesson that my parents embodied for me – which is that of the golden tears of forgiveness. Forgiveness does not mean that what has happened to you is all right. It wasn't then and it isn't now and never will be. Forgiveness means to have no energy still attached to what happened to you. You have no need to get even or resolve it. Forgiveness means there is no longer any anger or pain connected to it.

Forgiveness is the vehicle for correcting misconceptions. When we forgive, we let go of resistance which is fear, and give ourselves and others the opportunity to flow and move on. It is difficult to forgive and love others when we have not let go of the pain and hurt their behaviour and ours has caused us. It's usually when we have a limited understanding or perception of their behaviour that blocks us from loving them. When we realise what was done to us was an extension of love, then we can learn to understand it. It was love, but not as we know it. If we learn love in a painful fashion when we are young, then we will only be able to give love as an adult in the same way. The person receiving this love will not be able to receive it and will find it unforgivable. We only stay in a state of unforgiving when we need to keep that person attached to us. Forgiveness allows the hold we have on that person to slip away. It leaves a space for a new feeling to come in along with reconciliation. We also have to learn that other people do not have to change for us to experience peace of mind. You can also let go of beating yourself up. When we have touched another person with forgiveness we no longer need or require anything from them. It is over and done with, it is complete. Forgiveness is understanding. It is not just pity. Forgiveness allows life to blossom and unfold.

HEALING OTHERS

As a healer, you can give through yourself and not of yourself. I remember an American woman at a lecture by a famous healer asking, 'How can I be a healer?'

The reply was, 'You must open your heart, not think of yourself, and become humble.'

'How do I do that?' she said.

'You must not be selfish,' came the reply.

The woman looked perplexed. I spoke to her afterwards. 'When you've got your heart open and there is this great big space,' I asked, 'what are you going to put in it first?'

She said she had no idea.

'Yourself,' I said, 'because if you don't, you will not be able to get rid of all your negative ways, thoughts and hang-ups. You must be selfishly there for *you* first. Otherwise you will be so busy using your energy shoring up your lack of self-esteem and low self-worth. Your heart will be closed, of course, while you have to do this, and rightly so.'

Turquoise is the colour to help you focus on yourself. Only when you have put yourself in that healing space of the open heart and seen to your needs, can your heart then be free for anybody else.

The gold of self-trust is crucial to the development of independence, and for healing. It opens up the heart. When I vibrate to the gold of trust within my psyche, then I can surrender. Trusting does not mean that I become victim. It means whatever the world may throw at me (or put my way) I will have the confidence that I can deal with it come what may.

True healing takes place through the heart. When you can let go of the holding of the mind, then you can discover the healing of the body. As Dylan Thomas' poem about his father's death puts it, we 'do not go gently into that good night'. We have great anger at 'the dying of the light', i.e. our death.

When a person is very ill or in crisis, they sometimes ask 'Shall I live or die?' Only the heart can answer. Being in the heart is not about living or dying, but focusing on the moment to look beyond the mind and body and take a step into the unknown which allows the present to be experienced fully and naturally. Healing doesn't necessarily mean being physically cured – sometimes it is healing into death. We all look for a way to conquer death. The yogis of ancient times were said to have found a way, but it did not mean they would live physically forever. To have conquered death is when a person decides for themselves the right time to depart from this Earth. To decide consciously 'I will now leave my body', instead of being forced earlier than expected because of circumstances or disease.

To be in the heart is to be able to focus on the moment and look beyond the mind into the unknown without fear. When we can take the step of allowing ourselves to be in the state of healing, we allow ourselves to become whole again. The risk is are we going to be healed into bodily health, or healed into the next realm? Healing is taking the future into our hands. Something within the heart touches the disease and allows it to depart and wholeness to return.

Being in the healing space requires total acceptance of what the problem is. This is what neutralises and dissolves the negative factor. Nor is it necessary to appear spiritual – just *be* it. God appears in many guises.

As I said before when we go to a therapist, we are asking for support or assistance. We may not be consciously aware that this puts us in a state of humility – which allows us to be teachable. When we are teachable, we are ready to learn and grow. We tend to think that a therapist's support is going to be nice, orderly and comfortable. But support can also seem unreal, uncomfortable and unexpected. A therapist can help all aspects come together which can act as a trigger to move energy forward.

It is important to realise that the therapist is not perfect. No one is perfect, no one can be put on a pedestal. Perfection is in the moment – everything is perfect. What we have to realise is that there is no formula for life; there are no guarantees, even in therapy.

I believe it is important that a therapist/healer has been, or still is, in therapy themselves. After all, it could get difficult if your client is constantly pressing the buttons connected to your unresolved issues. When I am teaching or with a client, it often comes to mind who is the healer here and who is the client?

His Holiness Param Sant put it very neatly what healing work is all about: 'Because I give positive thoughts with a clear conscience, people have faith that whatever I say will happen. Thus, their faith works and they give credit to me, while I do nothing. I simply transform the negative into a positive. This is what I do.' This is a reminder of who we are as healers.

THE HISTORY OF COLOUR HEALING

'And life is colour and warmth and light
And a striving evermore for these.'
Julian Grenfell (1888–1915)

Colour leads us into virtually all realms of human life and culture. Colour healing is not a new idea, something that the 'New Age' has discovered. In 1937, M. Luckeish in his book, *The Science of Seeing*, wrote: 'One should not be surprised if it is revealed some time in the future when we know more about the human being, that all wavelengths of radiant energy from the sun are intricately entwined in the life and health processes of human beings.'

Kate W. Baldwin, MD, FACS, former Senior Surgeon, Women's Hospital, Philadelphia, also observed 'I can produce quicker and more accurate results with colour than with any, or all, other methods combined; and with less strain on the patient.'

There were schools of colour healing in ancient Egypt. In his book, *The Seven Keys To Colour Healing*, the famous colour researcher, Roland Hunt, writes: 'In the ancient temples of Heliopolis, Egypt, the force of colour was used, not only as an aid to worship, but also as a healing agent. These temples were oriented so that the sun shone through in such a way that its light was broken up into seven prismatic colours and suffering ones were bathed in that special colour which they needed to restore them to health.' In China, as well, many centuries ago, people found it worked when they wrapped their bodies in red silk and placed themselves out in the sun to stop scarring from chickenpox.

Our civilisation's temples of healing are its churches. In these, the memory of the ancient knowledge of the healing power of colour can be seen in the stained-glass windows. When the sun shines through the coloured windows and floods the congregation in healing light, they are being bathed in colour in just the same way as in ancient Egypt. Throughout history, healing always came from inspiration and intuitiveness, coupled with as much scientific knowledge available at the time. In the eighteenth century society changed its view and understanding of enlightenment – there was a sudden swing to intellectual consciousness and rationality. A new era, the Age of Reason, had begun. The local tea rooms were full of ideas and ways of thinking, poets wrote about the new trend and philosophers pondered on it. The new belief was that natural sciences held the key to understanding and intellectual consciousness. In other words, science was in and intuition was out.

As sometimes happens with radical change, the pendulum swings too far in one direction at first. We still suffer from the intellectual snobbery and narrowmindedness of that time. What we need to aim for, as in all things, is moderation or a balance of reason and intuition. We are coming round to this, but let's hope the pendulum doesn't swing too far the other way and we start to disregard science. I have always believed that science and intuition go hand-in-hand – the creative person's thoughts of today are the scientist's discoveries of tomorrow.

Today, because of the introduction in the last century of modern drugs, we have let colour lapse out of use as a healing agent. This is absurd as how can we ignore the sun and its light? We are now beginning to remember and appreciate the greatness and influence that colour has on human affairs. The rainbow truly is smiling on the universe. The rainbow can be seen in so many things – water, snow crystals – it's reflected everywhere. Colour affects our emotions which will be shown through our bodies. Man does not have to see or feel colour to be affected by it. Our interest is now returning to the realm of light and it's showing us that all our ills are because of a lack of harmony with nature's laws. We have lost our focus and the only way back into well-being is to read the bible of light. Colour is the affirmation of light. Light is truly celestial medicine.

Colour is an intimate part of our being. The body acts as a prism in the light. When we are truly well, all the colours shine out from us in an ever-changing but always rhythmically serene lightshow. Then we are being the light we truly are to one another.

Colour is the simplest and most accurate therapeutic measure yet developed. It is nature's healer. It can be prescribed just as drugs can. Don't choose to be ill – choose a colour instead!

The power of colour has always been about the application of various colours to affect the health beneficially on all levels. Whether we realise it or not, colour has an energy that affects us physically (red), mentally (yellow) and emotionally (blue). Every emotion and feeling that we have is related to a particular colour. We get angry and 'see red', for instance. Sometimes the colour comes first – we see red and feel irritable and hot. Colour association will also be attached to everything we do or have ever done in our lives, whether it be experience, behaviour, lessons we've learned or our surroundings.

As science has known for some time, everything in the universe is a certain combination of vibrations. All organs and parts of our bodies when they are healthy hold to a particular set of harmonious vibrations or, in musical terms, notes. From this point of view, we can be seen as marvellously complex and individual pieces of music. If we become ill or diseased, it means that disharmony has crept into the music – off-colour means off-key. Even thoughts and ideas are vibrations and can be as 'unwell' as the liver or pancreas or any other part of the body.

Colours affects man totally. Man uses colour as an experience of feeling. Colour has a quality of zinging out towards you. It vibrates and hums until it sings to you. The same as music, except that colour sings to the eye and not the ear.

Colour healing is a wonderfully direct way of working upon the body. Neither flesh nor mental attitude nor emotion is a barrier to colour. Colour can go to the seat of the problem instantly. We can eat, drink, breathe, visualise, meditate and dance colour. We absorb more colour when we are unwell and we can apply colour to restore the bank of health.

COLOURS FOR VARIOUS PROBLEMS

If you tell me – I will forget
If you show me – I may remember
But if you involve me – it will stay with me forever.

The medical profession is becoming more aware of natural therapies for healing and looking at health holistically. The colour therapist is not in competition with the medical world. Colour is an effective way of healing and complementing existing methods. But if you are on any medication or treatments doctors would prefer you to check with them if you are in any doubt about a natural healing technique, and rightly so.

What are the best colours to use for certain conditions? I can give you information gleaned from my own experience with colour.

There are various ways of working with colour that help prevent many of life's mishaps and used alone or with other methods and treatments can speed up the healing process. Colour puts another light on the matter.

First of all, let's look at white light that many followers of colour seem to advocate as though it were an antidote for all our ills. Agreed it does contain an equal measure of all the colours within it, but it can be too bright if used indiscriminately. Some therapists flood everything with it and then wonder why they have knocked everyone out. It can be too strong because of its powerful vibration. The white light should be confined to specific uses only. One of its most beneficial uses is protection – you can surround your house with white light to protect it from vandalism and keep it safe. You could visualise a streak of white light surrounding a family member or friend who is travelling by car to keep them safe on their journey. White light will always protect you from any form of invasion. I refer to it as the 'clearer upper'. It can clear the air if there are bad feelings or something that leaves a nasty taste such as the aftermath of a divorce. To clear the ground so that you can start afresh, just imagine a stream of white lava pouring from the top of a volcano, a beautiful, rich flow of light that will transform or destroy any ill feelings in its path. And when the ground has cooled after a flow of lava light it leaves a richness of soil that is just perfect to rebuild your life.

Another way to heal with white light is to visualise a beautiful rainbow surrounding your body so that you are within a circle like an egg yolk. Visualise the seven colours gently floating around you in their bands and allow your body to take the colours into yourself that you need for your well-being. Don't worry, your inner light will pull the necessary colours towards you.

White light is a potent force, never to be misused. Respect it as you would fire or electricity.

CHROMATHERAPY

As we become more aware of the influence of colour in our lives, the next step is to educate ourselves in the many ways of using colour to our advantage. I can foresee that in the future we may come to expect colour prescriptions for our ailments.

One of the techniques is called chromatherapy. This is the use of high-powered lamps and different coloured slides. The body is either flooded with an appropriately coloured light, or the light is pinpointed onto a specific area using a spot lamp. Chromatherapy should only be undertaken by a specialist or qualified practitioner. The timing and duration of the colour being applied must be expertly monitored.

The application of coloured lights to the body can bring about enormous benefit. Every organ has its own colour vibration and when we are 'off colour' that vibration has become dull. Applying the correct coloured light will restore balance – and it is a painless way to get well. After the First World War, shell-shocked men were exposed to vivid flashing coloured lights which broke through to them so they could be brought out of the trauma that had blocked them.

There is now a lot of research going on into the advantages of using colour, including investigations into ancient knowledge and how it can be brought up to date.

Unfortunately, medical researchers have not been able to agree on the effects of colour. The tests have been inconclusive or even contradictory. For instance, blue was used to lower high blood pressure. But it was found that if exposure to the blue was continued past a certain length of time, the blood pressure actually went back up again! This is why chromatherapy is such an individual treatment. No set formula of treatments does the same for everybody all the time – just as with pills. You will always find someone who will need a different combination. The art of the colour therapist is to first diagnose by the use of colour; and then find the unique treatment for that person. There is no format that applies to everybody. This, to me, is the beauty of colour.

COLOUR COMPLEMENTARIES

The simple chart below shows how each colour has an opposite or complementary. You can use this in your everyday life, so how does it work? Say, for instance, you have an appointment and you know you are likely to lose your temper, which is related to colour red, you can use blue to cool down by visualising that colour surrounding you. If you feel depressed, which is related to dark purple, then choose to visualise yellow to release the depression. To relieve pain which is dark red, choose indigo. The Colour Catalogue (pages 194–346) will tell you which colour belongs to your mood or circumstances, then you can check the chart for an instant remedy.

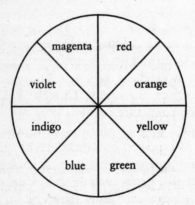

After the initial moment has passed and you have given yourself the correct colour for instant relief, it may be worthwhile to check out why you had the problem in the first place. The Colour Catalogue can be used to bring about a more permanent solution if you find the complementaries only act temporarily.

In healing, the pastel colours, which have the most light in them will have the most power in them. Simply check how much light there is in it. Pale blue will have more healing power in it than dark blue. The principal colour would be blue, which, of course, is therapeutic in itself. All dull shades need to be avoided when working for an alignment in the body. Until full health is restored, leave the dark shade alone.

FAVOURITE COLOURS

I am often asked what is the significance of a person's favourite colour. Does it automatically mean that it's the best colour for them? Is it their soul colour? The answer is 'no', not necessarily.

Your favourite colour may not be the safest or the best colour for you to use for healing, but it will be a key. It will give clues about your life and circumstances. It could be a colour you are addicted to, conversely it could be your soul colour – the colour of who you really are. Only a trained colour therapist could give you an accurate assessment after a detailed consultation.

Some people say, 'I don't have a favourite colour', but you do, we all do. If you have difficulty in pinpointing a colour, think back to when you were a child or a teenager. Maybe you had a favourite gold-coloured teddy bear – gold could be your colour so use it as a key to unlock some clues about yourself.

At first I was hard pushed to come up with my own favourite colour – I seemed to like them all. Then I remembered as a child I had a dance costume that was cerise pink and I instantly knew that that was my favourite.

A dislike for a particular colour is just as revealing as an attraction. The rejected colour will represent a challenge to you as it will point to a deep inner need. It reveals what is holding you back, what the stumbling block is – even if you didn't know you were stumbling. Some aspect of the colour has a message for you.

I have come across a few people who actually dislike all colour. They find that not a single colour appeals to them. When a person feels this way, what they are actually saying is that they don't like themselves. They feel life has not been very gracious to them. They believe it has given them a rough deal and as a consequence they have learned to hate it and themselves too, as well as colour.

COLOUR BLINDNESS AND BLINDNESS

Colour blindness affects males more than females, but is passed on from mother to son. You can be born with colour blindness or it can come about through disease, vitamin deficiency or exposure to a number of poisons. The person with congenital colour blindness will have a more serious defect in their vision. Their main difficulty is with differentiating between the shades. People who are colour blind from the other causes may only experience a dullness of colour.

Red and green are usually the two colours that help diagnose colour blindness. There is usually difficulty in differentiating between the two, although other combinations can also cause problems. Often there is an inability to separate light shades from dark.

I've often heard it said that a colour-blind person perceives colour on a different level – maybe they do, but they certainly have difficulty in distinguishing one colour from another on an Earthly level! A person may not be aware of the defect in their vision until someone asks, 'Why are you wearing a red tie?' when they thought they were wearing a green one. There is no known cure for colour blindness as yet.

People who are blind have an understanding of colour through vibration. In some houses, the doors are painted different colours. The blind person can feel the door with their hands for the vibration and then will know where the door leads to. An experiment was done in America where coloured spots were placed on a table, and every time a blind person put their hand near a particular spot they always could tell the colour by the vibration they received.

COLOUR RELATE READING

This is a way of giving yourself a colour reading. I use colour here as a tool to guide me. Just follow the instructions and go with your intuition. You can also use the Colour Catalogue to help you with your analysis.

When I give a private colour reading, I always use the Aura Soma bottles. These are bottles full of coloured liquid which Vicky Wall was inspired to develop by a vision received in meditation. You could use coloured card or pieces of material, but I love to use Vicky's 'jewels' as she called them, because they are such a wonderful focus on colour. They also have the added advantage of containing more than one colour in a bottle which means you can give a more precise and intricate reading. There are many ways to read the colours and it is important that you know what your intentions are for the reading.

This set pattern is what I call a Colour Relate Reading and it covers everything generally in our life from past, present and future. You will notice that the way the bottles are set out on the page represents the pattern of a snake (see page 107).

In ancient teachings, the snake signifies wisdom.

The method is simple. All you need is to have a selection of colours available and then interpret them. It's interpreting them that can be the problem! I have said before that colour never lies – it is only the interpretation that can be at fault. By following the simple pattern opposite, you can become your own healer and therapist. As you may not have Vicky's jewels at hand, just colour in the squares provided. Start at number one and proceed until you have completed all the squares. You are allowed to use two colours per place or you can colour them both the same. You can, if you wish, leave a space clear and this will be counted as Brilliance. You can use whatever colours you want in whatever combination in any of the places.

I won't give an example of a colour for a certain place because if three people choose the same colour for a place, the meanings for each can be different. All that is needed is for you to colour in the places and then with your intuition, check the Colour Catalogue to find what the colours are saying to you.

The language of colour is a tool of self-discovery. If you feel drawn to a particular colour, it probably indicates a deep need within you for something that colour vibration holds within itself.

Colour in the chart now, before you read any further. Having coloured in your places, we will now take the interpretation step-by-step.

Karma colour

The first place you have coloured in is your karma colour. This place tells you what memories you brought in with

Colour Relate Reading

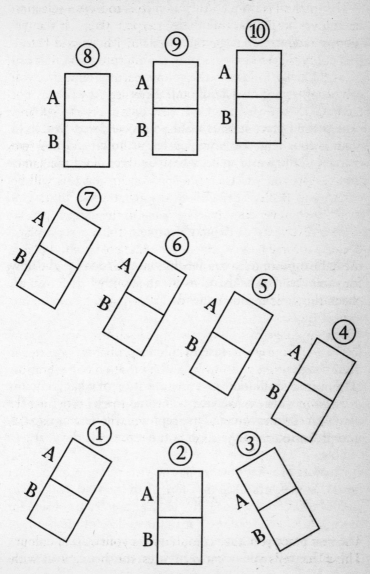

you at birth. Each person has their own individual essence which makes them who they are. It is an important place as it gives an indication of why you live your life the way you do, and in turn why your life is the way it is.

Childhood colour

The second place tells us what you were doing as a child. This colour tells you how you felt at home and how you perceived the world to be, what you were developing in or not.

Today's colour

The third place tells you where you are today, right now, this minute. This is useful as it can show whether you are preparing for the future ahead.

Insight colours

The next seven colours give an indication of what is coming for you in the next five years. The first three bottles are the first year. Bottles four and five represent the year as two six-month periods and the sixth bottle represents the year as a whole.

Aspects of what you see in one year may run into other years. Sometimes I see the start of the second year in the sixth bottle, for instance. If you have used two colours for each bottle, you read the line in the middle of the bottle as a division between the body above the waist (A) and below (B) in the physical body and between the conscious (A) and subconscious (B) in the mental and spiritual realm. In other words, A shows us what you are consciously doing in life, and B is what you might like to do. If you use the same colour for a bottle you are working on the same aspects consciously and subconsciously. If you find your subconscious colour is negative it probably means you need quite a lot of therapy to change core issues and the structure of your life.

Never forget that colours have many meanings. You will know intuitively when you read the Colour Catalogue what the colours mean for you. For instance, your combination may be yellow (A) with mid-blue (B) which for you may mean that you need to think through (blue) your actions (yellow) – or it's about time you thought before you leapt.

You can, of course, go on and colour in more places to get an even longer term view. Now you have your whole evolution before you and you can glimpse into the years ahead.

INSTANT COLOUR CHECK

Everyone is born under a particular colour ray. There may be a strong second colour, or even a third. But there is always a dominant colour. My dominant ray is red. But I often work from a very strong yellow influence, and sometimes violet.

Once you discover what colour light you are working with, you will understand better your relationships with others, work and life. The next question, of course, is: how do I find out what ray I am under? It would take even an experienced colour therapist some time to track this down. However, by reading the Colour Catalogue, you may find that you have a feeling, an inclination, an understanding, for one colour above all others. The 'That's me!' effect. Everybody is different. Different colour strokes for different folks.

But everyone also has three colours that influence them and will be around them in their everyday life. To do this instant colour check, write down on a piece of paper the first three colours that come into your mind. Label them in the order that they appear to you.

The first is your personality colour, so check its characteristics in the Colour Catalogue for an understanding. The second is your work colour and will show your creative abilities. This is the colour to surround yourself with at work as much as possible as it will support you in your endeavours. The third will be your social colour and how you interact with other people and the world. It is the colour you motivate from in relationships in every area.

When you know your three colours, you can use them to recharge your batteries. A few minutes in your three colours does more than any other booster programme to strengthen your system and constitution. For instance, if your personal colour is blue, why not put blue sheets on your bed. If your work colour is orange, why not choose this shade for your desk equipment and stationery. And if your social colour is yellow then wear yellow clothes at parties, at work or even when you go shopping.

Check the complementary colour chart on page 102 to see how your three colours interact with each other. For instance, if your personality colour is violet and your social colour is yellow then your personality has a good chance of attracting the relationships it wants. But if your personality is red and your social colour is orange, there may be friction between the two and your personality may find it difficult to get on with people in your relationships.

COLOUR YOUR NAME

This colour chart is for those of you who like to put things down on paper. It is a way of working with colour that incorporates numbers and the alphabet. Numbers are symbols which represent structure. Life is mathematics in vibrational form. One of our basic needs is structure. Structure gives life form and form gives us safety. By giving ourselves boundaries of form to work with, we can use our energies more efficiently.

Each name has its own colour. This process enables you to discover what colour your name is. At birth our name is fixed. When our name is called, we recognise the sound, it has its own vibration. As sounds vibrate when our name is called, so our names vibrate to their own colour. A person's name is their colour credential, a colour tag. Our name will have distinctive colour characteristics. Even when our name changes with marriage, etc, the name we were born with will continue to vibrate in conjunction with the new ones. The original colour will always have a spiritual bearing throughout our lives. In the Orient, a lot of emphasis is put on the name given to a child. The child's life will be lived trying to become the name. We, too, will vibrate to the colour of our name. All life is vibration.

Use this chart to find your personal name colour and then check the Colour Catalogue to understand what your name means and how you can see if you are working in harmony with your name vibration.

In the chart, I have given nine colours. Add numbers over nine together; for example, if you get ten, add one and zero to get one which is red. I have chosen rose pink for number eight and sun gold for number nine. As number eight would start the beginning of the spectrum colours again, I chose the rich pink as a positive aspect of red and sun gold as a positive aspect of orange. This will cover a wider range of colour meanings to work from. Turquoise will be represented by the blue and green of the principal hues.

First, write out your name. I have chosen David Brown as an example here. Using the table below, find the appropriate number for each letter of your name. Add the numbers together, and keep adding them until you end up with a number between one and nine. As you can see, David's first name adds up to twenty-two, which, by adding two and two, leaves us with four. Now check which colour relates to your number. David's first name is green. Do the same with your surname. David's surname is gold. Then adding the numbers for his first name (four) and surname (nine), David's overall number is thirteen = one + three = four. Check against the table to find your own overall number.

```
D A V I D                 B R O W N
4 1 4 9 4=22 =4=green     2 9 6 5 5  =27=9=gold
David Brown = 4 + 9 = 13 = 4 = green
```

Spectrum colours/principal hues

Red	1	A	J	S
Orange	2	B	K	T
Yellow	3	C	L	U
Green	4	D	M	V
Blue	5	E	N	W
Indigo	6	F	O	X
Purple	7	G	P	Y
Rose pink	8	H	Q	Z
Sun gold	9	I	R	

Name colour deficiency

The next stage is to find out which colours are missing from your name. With David, as you can see, I have written the appropriate number and colour against each letter, so D will be 4 which is green.

D = 4 = green   B = 2 = orange
A = 1 = red   R = 9 = gold
V = 4= green   O = 6 = indigo
I = 9 = gold   W = 5 = blue
D = 4 = green   N = 5 = blue

Now check how many of each colour you have in your name. David's is shown below:

Red = 1
Orange = 1
Yellow = 0
Green = 3
Blue = 2
Indigo = 1
Purple = 0
Rose = 0
Gold = 2

David is lacking in yellow, purple and rose. He will need to pay attention to these three colours and incorporate them into his body such as through his diet, decor, visualisation or any other way that is appropriate for him. The energies these colours produce will be absent from his system which will affect his daily life. These missing name colours can give you clues as to why you are not getting what you want from life. They can have an effect on all levels – physical, mental and emotional.

Birth date colour

Our birthday is another fixed aspect of our lives. We also have a birth date colour. It quite often turns out to be the same as our name colour. If not, check to see if the name colour and your birth date colour are compatible. You can always change your name. I have had a client who says, 'I've never been happy with my name,' and on working out their name and birth date colours they have seen the reason why.

To find out your birth date colour, simply add up the numbers that make up the date (don't forget to add the '19' to the year) and refer back to the colour/number chart on page 102.

You may find your parents' colour vibrations were just perfect for your name colour – or not. It's fun to check out your partner's or friends' names or even a company's name vibration or that of a business colleague to see if they're compatible with your colour. In fact you can check out any word with the chart.

The clown process

The circus of life – a multi-coloured experience.

'Who is more foolish – the fool? or the
fool who follows him?'
Alec Guinness in Star Wars

Several years ago, I devised a process of self-discovery that combines the language of colour and the language of the body. Not only that, it also bypasses the conscious mind which often distorts or totally suppresses the information we need in order to know ourselves. Most important to me is the fact that this process allows the child in each of us to come out and play with colours and shapes. All you have to do is draw a clown and then colour it in. So I call it the Clown Process.

Clowning comes from the heart. You are born a clown. Even the child in the high chair clowns around to get attention. Clowns make you laugh, make you cry. They have an effect upon the heart. And the nervous system. For a start, clowning around releases stress. Clowning allows you to act out and release emotion that you do not normally display. We tend to get sick when we have bottled up in us emotions that cannot be released. Clowning helps keep you healthy. Clowning opens you up. The clowns speak to us through our feelings. But both sides of our feelings, the sad and the happy.

The clown, the court jester, the fool and the joker all have one thing in common: fooling around. They have a mood for every moment. You never know what is coming next with a clown. Like life, he is unpredictable.

The joker in the pack of cards has two faces, like the roman god Janus, the god of beginnings. The month January was named after him. These two faces are the happy and sad aspects, the theatre's two masks of comedy and tragedy, the two sides of life's coin.

It is very basic: when we are well we are wearing the happy mask; when we are ill we wear the tragic. We all want to wear the white mask of happiness and avoid the black of tragedy. But, of course, this is an impossible quest; in reality we must take the good with the bad. All healing, physical and psychological, comes down to this. Comedy and tragedy in life walk hand-in-hand and we are free when we are not attached to either.

The clown, the fool, the jester know this. Their significance lies in the fact that they wear both masks, and by doing so, they can reconcile the comedy of life with the tragedy. They know that to be truly happy, you have to find the Golden Medium. As the Chinese put it, the middling path is the way of life.

The clown agrees with Buddha: life is a joke. So it can only be understood, and truly lived, by a joker. Because the clown–jester–joker knew and operated from this basis, he could perform antics as wild and as irreverent as those of life itself.

The fool can be easily confused with the buffoon. The buffoon resembles the fool in his absurdity, but he is mischievous rather than insane, whereas the fool is essentially a real or pretend lunatic. In imperial Rome fools were kept in wealthy houses, courts and taverns. Archibold Armstrong, fool to James I and Charles I, made so much money he became a landowner in Cumberland. Masks were used and the fool could be the witty fool. They used certain tricks of their trade, i.e. practical jokes and burlesque. Often the fool, thinking he had tricked the clown, had the tables turned on him by a rustic wit as clever as his own. The clown fools around. He usually follows a permanent routine which most commonly is to fail miserably in all that he does. August clown is the German word for fool. The Altura clown, which is the classic white-faced clown, sets up the situation for August the fool. This can be much like life for some people.

The clown, fool or jester at the courts of kings was the psychologist. He dared to act out a scene in which the king could be shown his own follies, or what was going on around him that he might not be aware of. The king could then take the advice or not. The court jester's performance was something like a cross between a gossip columnist, the modern therapy session and a stand-up comic. He had to be either the clever fool or the buffoon, the fool's fool. Everyone at the court would be there in a state of fascinated trepidation as the jester took them along a knife's edge on his wild roller coaster ride through the twists and turns of the truth of the matter. The court jester often sailed very close to the wind of the king's displeasure. His only protection was in sticking to the truth. How he presented it was his skill.

Our problem is how first to discover the clown–jester–joker in ourselves, and second, how to find the nerve to listen and look at what he is saying about us and our situation – and then to have the courage to act upon that information. If we can let him play in us, in the court of our self, our clown–fool–jester can show us aspects of ourselves of which we, like the king, might not otherwise willingly become aware.

The fool in the Tarot pack is depicted as a someone starting out on a new path. We start out at birth – the January of our life – on such a path, seeking experiences, going into the world light-heartedly.

But there is a Wise Fool and a Blind Fool. The Blind Fool, connected to the dark yellow colour is summed up in the word 'folly'. He is terrified of his own desires. What we aim for is to reach, at the end of our journey, the state of the Wise Fool who has struggled with existence and finally transformed himself from the Blind Fool into a consciously perfect spark of brilliance.

Another aspect of the clown process lies in this: the fool is sometimes shown risking his life by walking along a tightrope or the edge of a precipice. In the Tarot pack, the dog, Toby, is depicted tugging at the fool's leg to make him aware of the danger. The joker is always stepping out carelessly. He is supposed to ignore the material world and be concerned with the journey of life. He could bring bad luck but armed with spiritual sense he could protect himself from all evil.

Your clown can draw your attention to where you are heading. He can show you where your relationship with the material world is out of balance, or in danger of diverting you from the real purpose of your journey through life.

It is often very difficult to know whether things are real or some form of play-acting. Like the Blind Fool, we can be deceived by others and by ourselves. So something that can give us clear, unbiased knowledge of ourselves and our situation is priceless.

I have learned that colour does not lie. Colour just *is*. Each colour has its Wise Fool and its Blind Fool aspect – the positive and the negative of the colour. It is not that one thing is 'right' and another 'wrong'. What the fool knows is that nothing of itself is the right way or the wrong way. He understands the very important principle of reversal: he knows that the trick is to be able to go both ways, from the top down, as well as from the bottom up. The aim is not to end up on top or at bottom. The game is to play freely between the two extremes and not be caught anywhere.

Madelaine, a very successful businesswoman, explained how she felt at parties that she was always the court jester, making everyone laugh: 'It's as though I always sing for my supper.' Madelaine had come from a very deprived background but despite her great business success she still carried internally a very wounded child. A child will always think it's their fault if parents are hostile and will do their best to put it right. In Madelaine's case this was to entertain them, to try to put it right. Part of her therapy was to go out to dinner and shut up and see how it felt. The feeling she experienced was deep fear. She felt if she didn't say something it would fall apart. This of course was her little child's belief. We worked on her little child by getting it to realise that it didn't have to be the super-fixer – or supper-fixer – any more.

The clown is the little child. Watch how children react to clowns. They love them. Children want to see clowns. Adults ask for clowns. Children can be the little child they want and adults seek their lost childhood. The clown is the little child which was never allowed.

Never forget: your clown has a mission or serious reason. His battle takes place between the two faces of the real and the unreal, the top and the bottom, the in and the out, the comedy and the tragedy, the acceptance and the rejection. This is the battle that takes place within us all, that *must* take place if we are to reach the cosmic maturity of the Wise Fool. Finally, this maturity is simply knowing that the more we know the more we realise that we do not know. As my father was often given to saying: 'It's a wise fool who knows his own father.'

Enlightenment is knowing and believing who we are. We can only enlighten what we have, and that is us. Learn to love your clown. Have fun and also cry, like the two faces of life. Even pulling a Christmas cracker is a symbolic way of releasing tension. So crack a cracker! Blow your bugle and get some custard pies! I certainly did.

CYCLES OF COLOUR

In ancient Roman times, colour was used in the circus ring instead of words to say what was happening. The crowd could read the changing colour relationships that the performers, animals and circus vehicles wove in the magic circle in front of them.

The *Encyclopaedia Britannica* states that 'The modern circus came into being in England in 1768 when Philip Astley (1742–1814), a former Sergeant-Major turned trick-rider, found that if he galloped in a circle while standing on his horse's back, centrifugal force helped him keep his balance. In doing so, he traced the first circus ring.'

The circle is a shape of harmony. Everything is equal. Nothing is no more or no less. Once you step inside a circle, you are in a different kind of time.

Just like the circus of life, we go round and round in circles – it's the same circle but with different people and places. The circle represents the wheel of fortune – it takes you into the ups and downs of life. In therapy, I look to the repeating Circle Patterns.

WHEN THE CIRCUS CAME TO TOWN

When I was eight years old I went to my first circus. It was on the Leyton village green behind the children's playground. I didn't breathe deeply all week for praying that my mother would find the necessary cash for the tickets.

Saturday arrived and in great excitement my mother, sister and I went off to see the circus. My anticipation was a little dampened as we drew near as the tent looked much smaller than I expected. It looked so much bigger in the movies.

We queued up to go in, accompanied by the loud putt-putt of the generator puffing away to supply the lighting. I was aware of the circus people. They seemed darker-skinned, poor and surly – not at all like the adventurous gypsy people I had seen in the film *The Greatest Show On Earth* with James Stewart. It looked to me like the circus was hard work. Where was the colour? The thrills? The glamour? The sequins?

During the evening a few fat horses galloped around the circus ring going nowhere and a couple of elephants trundled in. For all their size the elephants seemed weak and resigned. They lifted their legs up on demand in a bored manner. I thought they were such lovely, powerful animals, but they seemed so sad, and so gentle despite their size and suffering as they performed in the damp sawdust. The animals were trapped and defeated with no way of escape – like us at home – but I also recognised in them my own rebel spirit.

At last what I'd been waiting for happened. The lights

went up, the drums rolled and *she* appeared wearing a long black cloak ... The tightrope walker!

The drums rolled again and the Ringmaster stepped forward swirling his big red cloak and announced: 'Madame Zita, Queen of the Skies!'

She had masses of frizzed blonde hair and seemed ancient – all of thirty. Just as she was about to step onto the tightrope she dropped her cloak to reveal a bright blue sequined bathing suit. I went numb with the glamour of it! (My sister and I had post-war maroon woollen knitted bathing suits that stretched down to our ankles every time they got wet!) The sequins shimmered and sparkled in the lights as she danced high above our heads.

Soft music began ... Madame Zita twirled and ran from one side of the tightrope to the other. Such poise! Such elegance! Such control of the situation! She stopped and opened an umbrella ... and casually did a few more pirouettes in the middle of the wire. One last pose and it was over.

Why were my mother and I drawn to the tightrope walker? It must have been her blue sparkling costume that was welcoming. It struck a chord of truth within us. We were drawn to the colour because we subconsciously recognised that it reflected the rut we were stuck in at home. The positive aspect of the colour also gave us healing and urged us to use higher thoughts. In other words, it stretched our minds to considering how we could escape.

In between these events the clowns appeared. They came tumbling into the ring shouting and biffing, throwing chairs and squirting water on each other and us. All sizes, tall on stilts, dwarfs, fat ones, thin ones. My mother let out a groan. 'I hate clowns,' she said, and refused to look at them.

The clowns did seem rather aggressive and not at all funny. They kept bashing each other and laughing about it.

Other people laughed, too, but I saw the clowns as a grey mass of bullying unpredictability. I felt fearful every time they appeared and grateful when they went off. I felt guilty that I didn't enjoy them like everybody else.

My mother had no time at all for the clowns. I think that on some level they reminded her of the fool she must have been to have ended up with my father. Their random bashing, bullying and larking about made us both uncomfortable as well. It was too close to home.

She also hated the clowns' joy and sheer exuberance. My mother had a fear of emotions. Hers were locked away and she couldn't face looking at them. Like the clowns, they were a threat. Clowning around without thought or restriction was liable to let them loose. Then they would come tumbling out and set everything upside down in a moment.

In one and a half hours at the circus we had experienced cruelty, boredom and faded beauty and on reflection it had given us a wealth of information about us as a family and it had depicted the climate of the times.

I grew up hating clowns, too. I only understood why much, much later when I began to realise how for years I had ignored my own little child within, just as my mother had ignored hers. It was only then that I finally let my clown emerge.

I had to learn to love my clown. And, as usual, I had great help from circumstances. When I was twelve and in my first part in West End theatre in *Rainbow Square*, the biggest scene I was in was a circus scene. I played a kid going to the circus. I had to show great enthusiasm for the circus performers, particularly for the tightrope walker whom I instantly had a crush on! I was beginning to love my clown.

The clown appeared again when I was eighteen and in my first major film. I explored it while playing the ship's nurse

in *The Captain's Table* at Pinewood. There was a party
scene involving clowns, kids and custard pies. I spent three
days having custard pies thrown in my face. But I learned to
enjoy it and even to throw a few back! They call it
synchronicity. It was terrific!

First Draw Your Clown

1. Find a good-sized sheet of paper.
2. Using a pen or pencil, draw a clown. It doesn't matter whether you know how to draw or not. All you need to do is to imagine a clown and put it down on paper. Don't think about it too much. Be as free and spontaneous as you can. And try not to copy 'Janine's' clown as it is drawn on page 147 – it is only an example.
3. The next step is to colour in your clown using coloured pencils, pens or paints.

To fully experience the process, *complete your drawing before reading further*.

We can fool ourselves consciously, but drawing, which is nature's pencil, can bypass the rational mind and express our deepest inner feelings. In drawing, you are drawing yourself out.

Your Clown & You

In drawing your clown you have really drawn you! The state of your physical, emotional and mental self, your beliefs, how you relate to other people, how you feel about the parts of your body, how you view the future and much more, can be read in your clown's body and colour language. Have you, for instance, drawn a full clown or only half? What colour is your clown's hair? Legs? Which parts have you given the most prominence to? Which parts have you left out entirely? What you have left out is just as telling as what you have drawn. The missed-out parts will relate to areas in your life that will need attention right now.

When we draw, paint and colour we are working closer to the gut level, the level of instinct (the orange within us) and intuition (violet). We may be able to hide much of the truth about ourselves with our mental apparatus, but the body and colour do not lie or play games with us.

In interpreting our drawing, we can learn to become nobody's fool! Least of all our own.

READING YOUR CLOWN

The three main ways your clown is speaking to you are:

1. Interpretation of your clown as a whole.
2. Through body language.
3. Through the language of colour.

THE FIRST LEVEL OF MEANING –
THE WHOLE CLOWN

This is a first level of interpretation: your clown as a whole. What its *presence* is saying to you. How does the way it is drawn on the page strike you?

A person is made up of physical, mental and emotional parts. But we are all aware that each of our friends is more than the sum of his or her parts. So is your clown. So let yourself hear, see, feel and generally sense what the whole clown is saying.

One way to look at this first level is that it is the *being* of your clown (which, remember, is you) communicating itself. Try this process at regular intervals. The clown drawn at the moment will indicate how life is for you right now. The next clown you draw may be very different. The

Clown Process is a good DIY way of assessing yourself and monitoring how life is for you.

So to work!

First, place your Clown in front of you. Look at it as a whole. Try to get a feel for what it is saying, what its overall attitude to life is ... Don't hurry this. Let yourself slip into a slightly meditative but attentive state, as though you are listening to a friend trying to tell you something personal and important.

Now consider – how much detail is there in your clown?

If there is not much drawn in your picture, if it has an empty feeling as though something is missing, this could indicate how little you know about yourself. Parts that have been entirely left out – a leg or hand not drawn in at all – would show that these are parts of yourself that you do not know anything about.

If one part of the body or clothing is extremely prominent, this is drawing your attention to the fact that you need to look at that section immediately.

A drawing that is generally over-elaborate – everything, including the kitchen sink! – would show someone who has an overload in life. It may look like a bountiful life, but it isn't always so. It can show the person who has been swallowed up in the trappings of life.

The next step

Fold your picture in half down the centre. Open it out again. What is the left/right ratio? Is there more of your clown to the left or right of the centre crease? Or is it centred?

The right and left sides of the body indicate the masculine and feminine aspects of yourself. The ancient Chinese called these yin and yang. The crease you just made in the paper will also indicate the backbone. Look and see if your clown's body is centred exactly on the fold. If it goes to either side of the fold, that's the side you mainly motivate from.

If your clown is mostly to the right side of the page, there is an emphasis on your masculine energies. If there is more on the left side, you are working more from your feminine energies. If it is centred it shows that you have a good balance and can move easily between the masculine and the feminine.

When you are looking at your clown, remember to take this into account: the fact that you have drawn your clown with more of its body on the left side of the page than the right also shows that your masculine half is suppressed or not allowed its true importance. Suppression of the masculine drives us into the feminine. And vice versa.

Note: When I look at the page with the clown drawing before me, the *right* side of the paper will represent the *masculine* aspect. The *left* side I read as the *feminine*. I have interpreted Janine's clown (on pages 147–55) in this way.

However, you may, after a few moments, have a sense that you should read it the other way round – that is, the *left* side of the paper *masculine*, the *right* side of the paper *feminine*. If you decide to do this, do it consistently all the way through. Neither way is right or wrong. It just depends on what feels right for you.

In the film *Tootsie*, Dustin Hoffman plays a man who has to play the part of a woman in order to get work in a television soap. No one in the TV series is aware that he is actually a man.

Towards the end of the film he is attempting to explain himself to a young woman in the cast with whom he has fallen in love. The trouble is that she has only known and loved him as a woman and a friend and is not sure she wants him as a man and a lover. In a moment of great insight into the male/female dilemma that we must all grapple with, Hoffman says ruefully: 'I was a better man to you as a woman than I ever would be as a man.' It applies both ways. We experience the opposite gender when we have a relationship with our partner. But we also have both masculine and feminine energies within us. However, they are not always working in an atmosphere of equal opportunity.

The male side of us is the driving energy, so when we are very forthright and strong, we know we are acting from our internal male. The nurturing, safer side of us is our female energy working. Sometimes, these energies are at war with each other within us. When we have unity with these two energies internally, we will experience the joy of compatibility. A balanced person is able to use both sides and is dominated by neither. There is no greater love affair than that between our own male and female within.

We usually draw genderless clowns. This confirms the clown's ability to slip from the masculine to the feminine and back again. This is a valuable aspect of drawing our clown as we don't get caught up in sexual roles.

Some keywords for the male/female polarity are given here. It is not an exhaustive listing. You will probably be able to think of many more yourself. Also, remember that each side will have a positive and a negative aspect. For example, while 'firm' would be the positive on the masculine side and 'yielding' its feminine opposite, the negatives would be 'rigid' and 'weak'.

Feminine/Moon	**Masculine/Sun**
(Left brain controls right side of body)	*(Right brain controls left side of body)*
Feeling	Reason
Yielding	Rigid
Gentle	Strong
Weak	Harsh
Pliable	Determined
Obedient	Commanding
Loose	Tight
Scatterbrained	Calculating
Curved	Straight
Fickle	Reliable
Red	Blue

A few hints on right/left

If both sides of your clown are about equal so far as the sides of the page are concerned but one has much more colour, or brighter, lighter colours, than the other, you could still be looking at a masculine/feminine imbalance. The brighter side is the more dominant in a person's life.

Look for right/left colour combinations. If your clown's left trouser leg is brown and the right trouser leg orange, for instance, this shows that your female side is passive and dormant (brown) and the male side is getting all the action (orange).

Remember to add whether you are a man or woman to the equation. If you are male and you have drawn this colour combination (left brown, right orange) on your clown, you are inclined to be a rather macho male – tough, active, no time for frills. If a female uses this colour combination, it shows a very tough, strong, perhaps even unfeminine woman.

And while you're considering colour, look to where you

have put the most emphasis on colour. Is it on your clown's head, chest, or legs? Or all over? Just consider the colour pattern overall at this point, don't get into the colour of particular parts yet.

Now fold your paper once more

This time, fold the top down across the middle to meet the bottom edge. The centre fold represents the waistline of the body. Now your clown is spread across four squares.

How does the top/bottom ratio look? Is there more Clown above the centre fold? Or below? If your clown has more of itself in the bottom half of the page, you are very earthed. Your feet are firmly on the ground. Congratulations. However, it could also show that you may be a bit of a stick in the mud? Particularly if it has big feet! You could profitably consider looking upwards from time to time. Even aspiring to new heights. Set your goals a little higher . . .

The clown that is way above the line probably needs to come down to earth, to introduce a sense of reality into his or her ethereal view of life. On the other hand he, or she, may also be a suppressed pilot!

Just as there is a left/right imbalance, there can be an above/below imbalance. Is your life being run from down in the dumps or up in the clouds? The aim is the happy medium. But remember that the medium is not the absence of either but the harmonious mixture of above and below.

THE SECOND LEVEL OF MEANING – BODY LANGUAGE

A guideline to interpreting the parts of the body is given on page 133. Treat these as pointers to get you started in the right direction.

Remember, some part of you did draw and colour the clown, so it knows what everything means. Your problem is how to interpret and let yourself understand what that part is telling you. And in this journey into yourself, your own feelings and intuitions are worth a thousand pages of any list.

The Chinese Masters of Siang believed that a good life was one which was stable, that travelled along calmly without extremes of high or low in health, wealth or emotions. Confucius called this 'the steady, smooth path of good fortune, the "Golden Medium".' He urged all to seek it. An uninteresting life was also considered fortunate. I'm still pondering that one!

While you are considering your clown's above/below relationship, look to see what is happening with its feet. Does it have feet? If not, you probably suffer from a lack of grounding. Your family roots may be weak. Perhaps your childhood environment was not so good and you found that you could not escape. No feet shows you were unable to run away.

Keep it light! Clowns do!

You can see that it would be very easy to make the Clown Process complicated and difficult. It's not meant to be that way. In fact, it doesn't really work like that! It's meant to be fun! This doesn't mean that it can't be serious in the best sense of that word. If you have ever watched children play, you will have seen the serious and the playful perfectly combined. Children learn this way. So play with your clown. If you do, you may find it is playing with you!

Starting at the top ...
symbols, parts of the body and their associations

The head

Does the head lean to one side or the other? This shows which gender you relate to most. To the right, masculine; to the left, feminine.

As you consider your clown's head, some useful questions to ask are: Are the features more prominent on the right or left? – masculine and feminine again. How does the size of the head compare to the rest of the body? If it is over-large in proportion to the body you are likely to be 'in the head'; feelings would not be trusted. If it is small, you have a tendency to be all emotion and not have much sense of reality.

The face

You show how you feel by the look on your face. What is the shape of your clown's face?

- A long, narrow face is masculine.
- A wide face is feminine. This is an ancient teaching. The vertical is the masculine, and the horizontal, the feminine.
- A square face shows someone who is down-to-earth, business-like.
- A large round face shows neediness – the 'please give me' face.
- A small face says 'I have no needs, I can get along fine by myself. I don't need anything from anyone. Get lost!'

Eyes

Eyes reveal how you see things. They are the windows through which life is viewed.

- The larger the eyes, the happier the person. They have more fun – but they can be impulsive. There could also be shock in childhood; a pleading look.
- Small eyes show unease, they are fearful of the impression they give. They are suspicious, the fault-finder, and misunderstood by others.
- One eye higher than the other shows a displacement at some time in a major area of life, problems with parents – right eye = father; left eye = mother.
- No eyes suggests something is too painful to look at. This often goes back to a painful experience in the womb. Reluctant to see the truth.
- Eyes present but shut suggests you are looking for a clue to your life, probably in the womb.
- Narrow eyes show neglect.
- Beady eyes show mistrust.
- Protruding eyes show shock. Also they could indicate extreme wilfulness.

Colour of eyes

- Blue is a free spirit, fun loving, cool, moderate temperament.
- Sapphire blue is a deep thinker. Calculating. Truth-seeker. Honour. Discriminating.
- Pale blue is gentle. An eye for the main chance. Ambitious. Can't transmute.
- Brown is loyal. Studious. Frustrated. A doubter. Strength and determination.
- Hazel brown is uncommitted. Discontented. Either can be a vice or a virtue.

- Green is stabilising. Easy mixer. Adaptability. Has to learn to cope with conflict.
- Grey is service. Active. Idealistic. Endurance. Critical.
- Violet is majestic. Individualistic. Seeks adoration and fame. Single-minded.
- Black shows higher intelligence. Foresight. Dead, blank look. A truly black eye is very rare.
- If each eye is a different colour it shows changing outlook. Double values. A dual understanding of life. Neither one or the other. Consider the colour of each eye and come to your own conclusions from the section in the Colour Catalogue!

Whites of eyes

The positive eye white glistens and is free of all colour and blemish.

- Yellow is liverish. May be an indication of jaundice.
- Grey shows catarrh or mucus somewhere in the body. Congestion.
- Red shows irritation. Inflammation.

Eyelashes – the eyes' curtains

- Long eyelashes can make a person blind to their own faults. Generous disposition.
- No eyelashes shows there's not much hidden away. Doesn't like cover-ups. Bares all.

Eyebrows

These reveal how well you can organise your thoughts.

- Short brows show impatience.
- Knitted brow shows emotional turbulence.
- No eyebrows suggest you are not master of your own

life. No thoughts. Cut off.
• Vertical lines up between the eyebrows show struggles in childhood.

The ideal brow is curved and extends longer than the eye. Preferably, the colour is a shade lighter than the hair.

Nose

This points to the direction you are taking in life.

• Big nose shows you put great energy into whatever you are doing. Have good fortune.
• Small nose shows you are low on luck. You only gain by your own endeavours.
• No nose shows a lack of leadership. Aimless.

What colour is your clown's nose? The colour tells you what you are presenting to the world as your aims. It is your front. It can be misleading. In fact, just the opposite may be hiding behind your clown's nose!

If your clown has a red nose, it could indicate there is little pleasure in life. You will be misunderstood. A saying goes, 'A red-nosed man may not be a bully, but he will always be considered to be one.' Red seems bold, strong and powerful, but it could be hiding vulnerability – a sweet but insecure little child. If the nose is large and red, you get by. Red shows a need to be rescued at times. You can always rescue yourself by using red.

Whatever the colour of your clown's nose, read the opposite or negative aspects of that colour in the Colour Catalogue and see if they apply to you. Furthermore, if you have a dark shade of the colour, read the pale shade. This will give you an idea of what you are aiming for.

Nostrils

- Large nostrils show the meddler. The wheeler-dealer.
- Small nostrils show loneliness.
- No nostrils show impaired sensing.

Mouth

We communicate by the mouth.

- Open mouth is inviting.
- Closed mouth says 'Keep out!'
- Large mouth shows confidence. Happiness. Can communicate emotionally. More at ease with your sexuality. Particularly if coloured red.
- Small mouth shows difficulties coping. Unexpressed feelings, a holding back. Has to work hard in life to achieve.

Lips

- Full lips are generous. Spontaneous. If over-large, may need a little checking in sexual areas.
- Thin, tight lips show tension and held-in anger. Emotional coldness. May take out own childhood hurts on others.

Teeth

The ability to break down the substance of life.

- Big teeth – this person likes a big bite of the apple. Expects to receive.
- No teeth shows you can't get a hold of life. Lack of judgement and discrimination. No bite. Can't chew anything over. Unable to break down.

Jaw

- Wide jaw shows strength and power.

- Small jaw is less ambitious, restricted. Lack of safety. If the jaw is tight, it indicates unexpressed feelings – repression.

Chin
- Jutting chin is pushy, ambitious.
- Receding chin is retiring, no will power.

Ears
It's best to draw big ears. They show the most self-worth. In fact, some tribesmen still continue to stretch their ears with weights. The bigger the earlobe, the higher the sex drive. They also signify abundance. The only time big ears are not so desirable is if they are on a small face, which can show a lack of character. Big ears manage to get things easily but may find it hard to keep them.

- Big ears show great self-worth. Abundance. This includes sex energy!
- Big ears on a small face show lack of character. Irresponsible.
- Small ears show lack of confidence. Unable to rely upon others. Always comes up short of expectations. Although ambitious, there can be a gap between getting what you want and what you actually achieve.
- No ears show you're not being heard.
- Ears covered by hair shows maybe you don't want to hear!

What colour did you draw your clown's ears?

Hair
Your clown's hair represents your thoughts.

- Thin or no hair at all shows it's hard for you to have your own your ideas.
- Thick hair shows a very busy mind.
- Curly hair shows you go round and round in circles with people to get to the point. You tend to manipulate to get what you want rather than ask for it directly.
- Long hair is free and easy. Wild.
- Short hair is a neat and controlled personality.

What colour is your clown's hair?

- Red shows sexuality, zest, life's energy force. Power for growth or destruction.
- Grey hair shows pressure, anxiety, a belief you can only get your needs met if you struggle. No more juice.
- Silver hair shows you can be at ease and allow others to have their opinions even if it differs to yours. You do not have a need to change others. Unbiased.
- Blonde hair could show lack of confidence in your own thoughts and ideas so you resort to being in the head and not feeling because of fear. Intelligent, working from head only. It rather squashes the stereotype of the dumb blonde! Maybe not so dumb after all.
- Gold feels good and everyone knows it. At ease with success. Rich.
- Black shows all or nothing. Could be extremely powerful, or in decline.
- Brown is undiscovered as yet. Steady, reliable, and too understanding.
- Multi-coloured shows a multitude of ideas. Look to the colours to see what subjects the ideas cover.

Moles, beauty spots
- Woman: left side of her face, she outlives her husband.

On right side of face, her children have problems.
- Man: right side of face, he outlives his wife. On left side of his face, his children have problems.

Neck
The neck is the bridge between the head and the body.

- No neck shows you are not connecting. Like a threatened turtle. Deep insecurity.
- Long neck is searching. Likes to go with the flow if uncluttered by clothes. Prepared to stick your neck out.
- Medium neck shows compatibility between head and heart.
- A neck covered up with clothes shows emotions are being hidden.
- Stiff neck shows inflexibility – unable to see other side of things. Stubborn. Whiplash injury – I've got to have a look.

Shoulders
The carriers of happiness and burdens.

- Broad shoulders show you are able to take care of yourself and others.
- Small shoulders need protecting. Not able to take any pressure.
- Sloping shoulders are sliding away from responsibility
- Shoulders leaning backwards say 'I don't want to cope'.
- Shoulders drooping forwards say 'I can't cope'.
- Raised shoulders show tension and fear. If the left shoulder is raised, you have female issues. If the right shoulder is raised, male issues.
- Square shoulders show confidence in the world.

Arms

Arms represent reaching out for life. The arms have the ability to hold and hug. When you cuddle someone you form a vessel, a container shape. This symbolises the womb, the place of fruitfulness that can multiply. Every time you enfold or embrace with your arms, love increases.

- Long arms say 'I must have it at all costs.'
- Short arms say 'I know I won't get it, so I won't try.'
- Folded arms protect the area they cover.
- Arms behind the back, suggest you don't want to be involved. A loner who prefers not to relate.

Elbows

- Curved, bent elbows show flexibility. Able to change direction easily.
- Straight, rigid elbows show you are unable to express desires and feelings. Stuck.

Hands

The ability to grasp what is ours in life.

- Open hands are able to give and receive.
- Clenched hands in a fist shows apprehension, clutching at straws. Self-protection, ready to fight.
- Hands in pockets show you don't want to show your hand or intention.
- Clasped hands behind the back say 'No one is going to lead me on'. Preference for isolation. Don't touch.
- Clasped hands in front of body shows self-protection. 'Don't come too near.'
- Big hands (compared to body size) looks at the splendour of the whole. Can envisage the grand outcome of projects. Big plans.

- Small hands show a great eye for detail. Will be looking at the name plaque on a building rather than the building itself.
- No hands shows you are not expecting anything.
- Hands holding each other create a continuous circuit, as hands in prayer or meditation.

Fingers

The ability to feel and touch. The fingertips have extreme sensitivity. Touch picks up information as well as leaving an impression behind. Touch can give us pleasure or alert us to danger.

- Spread fingers means you need freedom. Must not be confined.
- Fingers extended and close together show you are not about to reveal anything or let anyone in.
- Bent fingers show you are feeling victimised.

Knuckles
- Large knuckles show intelligence.
- Small knuckles show impatience.

Thumbs
- Large thumbs enhance a hand. Show you believe you have the strength to pull through.
- Small thumbs show diminished strength.
- No thumbs shows you are not using your logic or strength of willpower.

Chest
The chest is the presentation of the self. The way you hold your chest indicates how you feel about yourself.

- Drooping, concave chest shows a lack of self-worth. beaten by circumstances.
- Big, overpowering chest shows conceit and arrogance, even the bully. An upstart.

Breasts

The female bosom represents nurturing, tenderness and caring.

- Small breasts are careful, cautious.
- Large breasts are the flowing milk of kindness.
- Over-abundant breasts show extreme giving; lack of self-control.

Solar plexus (midriff)

This area absorbs and takes the brunt of all our experiences. Frustration, humiliation and similar feelings affect the solar plexus. It is the seat of anger (liver). It often indicates the ability, or otherwise, to get things in life. It shows how kind you are to yourself. Emphasis on the waist:

- Thick waist shows repressed emotions and feelings, anger. Humiliation.
- Straight waist shows you go your own way.
- Small waist shows the follower 'I do as I am told'.
- Curvy waist is flexible. Can give and take easily.
- Belts: When we put belts around the waist, we are protecting this area. A need to keep everything under control. Great fear of letting go. Resisting the flow of life. A cutting off from above and below. Monks wore belts to cut the above away from the below – the dividing line between earth and heaven. Extremely large belts could suggest not wanting to look at your sexuality.

Hips

The hips are where our life is balanced. The pelvic girdle is the cradle, the vase, that holds who we are.

- Heavy hips show the vase is too big for the flowers (you) to grow from. Static in life. Not able to shift. Immobile.
- Narrow hips suggest not enough sustenance for growth. Meanness in support. Often, narrow-hipped people are very tall — like seedlings that have bolted. Subconsciously, this means that the person had to get out of the restricted circumstances of the vase.

Legs

Our legs connect us to our feet, our earthing and security. They are our supports in life. The right leg and right side of the body relate to action. The left leg and left side of the body relate to passivity.

- Short legs (in proportion to the body) usually indicate a bad start in life.
- Over-long legs show a fear of adulthood. Growing to get away. Weak foundation.
- Heavy thighs show childhood shock and trauma. Victim as a child. Disempowered. Suppressed anger.
- Thin thighs indicate growing too fast. No encouragement from environment.
- Short lower leg shows you are unsure of next step forward. A belief that nothing good ever happens.
- Long lower leg shows you were pushed to develop too soon.

Knees

The knees represent the mechanics of moving forward.

- Big knees show a fear of the self. Untrusting.
- No knees show an inability to bend.
- Bent knees show you are flexible, versatile.

Feet

Making a stand. The feet represent the ground we stand on
– how we stand in the world. Our feet ground us, enable us
to connect.

- Feet off the ground shows an idealism that cannot
  materialise. Up in the air. 'I cannot connect.' 'I'm not
  clear about life.'
- Right foot forward shows you are inclined to intellec-
  tualise.
- Left foot forward shows you are more creative and less
  structured in life. You feel before you think. Maybe a
  dreamer.
- Feet parallel (but on the ground) shows you meet life
  squarely.
- Big feet show you are weighed down in life.
- Small feet show you don't want life at all.
- Heels off the ground (high heels) shows a refusal to
  co-operate. 'I'm not going to do it.'

Toes

Toes are the antennae of the feet, feeling the ground out
before you. Trusting the future to take care of itself.

- No toes show no anchorage.

Chakra buttons

Buttons indicate the chakras in the body. Where they are,
what colour they are, how many of them there are, are all
to be taken into account. Each of the body's chakras has

one of the colours of the rainbow associated with it. When you work with these centres, you are working with your palette of psychic colours. You put your brush into the chakra pots and you stir them up. As they mix and swirl, they generate great energies in your body and psyche.

THE THIRD LEVEL OF MEANING – COLOUR LANGUAGE

The colour aspect of this process usually appears in your clown's clothes. I haven't found anyone who drew a naked clown as yet, but I am willing to be surprised. You will find that the colours bring another point of view to the picture in addition to that of the body language. The body language given here provides a tool to broaden the information from colour and includes a guide to the colour of the parts of the body you are likely to have coloured, such as the hair and the eyes. But if you find you have coloured a part or used a colour not covered here, work it out from the Colour Catalogue on pages 194–346.

For clues to the meanings of the colours you have used on your clown's clothes, again consult the Colour Catalogue. As an example of colour interpretation if the clown's trousers are blue, this would indicate someone who has difficulty expressing themselves. They would be likely to spend much time going round and round the verbal mulberry bush. Their voice would be in their pants! The larger the pants, the greater the problem. It would also show a very physically inactive person. He or she might eventually become a couch potato!

This is the more negative aspect. On the positive side, such a person would probably be a deep thinker. They would think before acting. They would also be very aware of the underprivileged. They would be the first to donate to charities. Animal welfare would also be close to their hearts. But don't ask them to compete in a marathon for animal rights!

INTERPRETING JANINE'S CLOWN

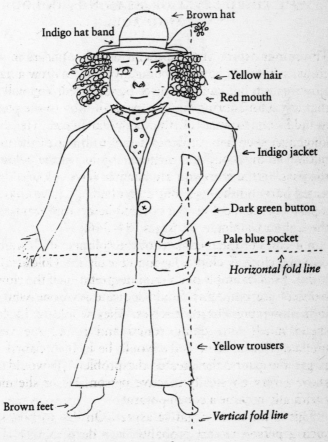

Janine's Clown

Janine drew her clown on her first session. I asked her to draw the clown because I intuitively felt that it would be a very quick way of discovering her basic life patterns.

The commentary below on Janine's drawing is given to help you interpret your own clown. I have given a colour analysis with Janine's body language plus comments on the placement of her clown so that you can see how to combine the three when you come to interpret your own clown.

Face

Janine drew a large round face for herself, which was a clue to her neediness. It said 'Please give me ...' Janine could not function unless someone else gave her motivation and support. She was not a self-starter. She did a lot for other people – and practically nothing for herself. This was shown by the way she placed herself on the page, working a lot from the negative female which was 'victim' – just the same as her mother who Janine later revealed, was dominated by her father.

Hair

Janine drew thick, dark yellow, curly hair. This told me that she was someone who found it difficult to get to the point. Lots of ideas, but a lack of confidence. Her fear of being wrong made her think very carefully before she said or did anything. But she has a quick mind.

Hat

A hat represents keeping the lid on things. That Janine's is coloured brown indicated that her thoughts and feelings had gone underground. She was not yet ready to take the lid off.

You will notice that as we go down the body of Janine's clown colours begin to appear. These are a sign that Janine was becoming open to change. Even the flower attached to the hat has many colours in the petals. Each represents a creative ability that she has.

The stem of the flower is painted green. The stem of the flower always leads down to the root cause. In Janine's case the key was the indigo band around the hat that the flower is attached to. The indigo means that Janine's structure of life was rocky. It also signifies intuition beginning to develop.

All bands on heads and hats represent psychic development. However, the colour of the band is a significant clue. Because Janine's was indigo, I understood that her intuition was working strongly.

Ears

The ears are invisible, covered by thick hair. This says, 'No one listens to me.' Also, that, as a child, there were things that Janine did not want to hear. What these were appeared in later therapy.

Eyes

Janine drew large eyes. These show that she loves to laugh and have fun. The eyes are rich blue, which indicates that she is a deep thinker and also that she does things with discretion. In fact, she could be a bit calculating.

The large eyes also revealed that there had been shocks in childhood. The furrows between her eyes confirmed that childhood had been a struggle for her.

Eyebrows

These are short, which indicates that she is impatient by nature. That she coloured them black indicated that she was trying to curb this. If they had been red, her impatience would not have bothered her, only other people.

Eyelashes

These are not too long, so Janine was aware of her short-comings. That she coloured them brown indicated that she had a tendency to believe that she was always in the wrong.

The right eye has more lashes. The right is the male side of the body, and in this case indicates someone who had episodes occurring in her childhood with her father that were hidden.

Nose

A small nose, so Janine will not have been a lucky person up until now. And whatever she does have will have been gained by her own efforts usually at the expense of herself. She intended to become money-wise, however, because she coloured her nose green, the colour of prosperity.

It is a small nose with large nostrils. The large nostrils indicate the wheeler-dealer. Strangely enough, Janine was a croupier in a casino at the time. She did deal with luck and money but it wasn't her luck and money. As her small nose revealed, she had to earn whatever she got.

Mouth

A small red mouth and shut tight. Unable to say what was going on at home. So some secret in Janine's past – a tendency to hold back.

This small mouth was another indicator of a difficult life. It turned out that Janine had had to be the breadwinner for the family early in life. Her home environment left a lot to be desired and in therapy revealed abuse from her father. This was shown in the red of the mouth as well as the brown eyelashes on the right eye. This was not something Janine felt safe and at ease to speak about. At ease with speaking would be shown by a full, free, even slightly opened mouth.

Janine's clown also had no teeth, which showed that she had never had anyone with whom she could talk over her past. Nothing with which to chew the problem over. The red lips also revealed her anger about the past.

Neck

Janine has drawn no neck. The turtle response: retreating from an impossible (for a child) situation.

She has also covered up her neck with clothes, which means that she has hidden her feelings. The knotted tie around the neck would have helped her keep these tied up and buried. The tie was coloured black with spots of different colours. The black also indicates something hidden. Each coloured spot reveals a happening from the past.

Shirt

The colour your clown has on its chest area represents the feelings in your heart.

Janine's clown is wearing a blue shirt, which is the colour of truth. It is also – most significantly in her case – the colour of the father. As the blue is close to her heart, it shows that she needed to understand what had happened between her father and herself. To be able to think about it.

Jacket

The shoulder on the right-hand side of the page is drawn higher than that on the left. This points to issues with her father which had caused her to be full of fear and tension when she was around him. It shows a holding back – her relationship with her father had forced her to cut off communication with her mother. She could not show her hand and tell her mother what had happened.

The shoulder on the left-hand side of the page is sloping,

which shows that Janine's mother took no responsibility, although Janine's hand is stretched out asking her mother for support. Unfortunately, this had slipped through her fingers.

The jacket is coloured indigo, which is the colour of structure. Janine's structure of life needs reassembling – but it will have to be taken to pieces first. As it is involved with structure and support, indigo here could also signify back problems – which Janine had.

There are no lapels on Janine's jacket, which says 'I have no self-esteem. There is nothing in me worthwhile decorating.'

Arms

The clown's short arms tell us that Janine's childhood conditioned her to believe that she could never have what she wanted – and so she has given up trying. The bent left elbow shows she was good at evading her father. She may not have been able to escape the abuse, but she became agile enough to keep herself out of his grip as much as possible.

Hands

The hand on the right side of the page is hidden in the pocket. Pockets represent treasure troves. They can be full or empty. They are rescuers – somewhere to hide. Janine had never been allowed to express her desires, feelings and intuition. It also indicates hiding feelings about her father. There is no pocket for the left hand to hide in – this shows no rapport with her mother. But as this hand is outstretched, Janine was still looking for the care and nurturing that she never had. The spread fingers also indicate a need for feminine freedoms. It also indicates that part of her was determined never to be trapped again.

Midriff

The clown has no waist. The thickness of the solar plexus area shows the humiliation of past hurts and repressed anger. The waist balloons out when holding onto repressed emotions. The dark green button on the midriff indicates resentment for what had happened. Only one button is drawn which singles out fear and resentment as being the main issue for Janine to work with at this stage.

Hips

The hips are rather large. It had never been safe for Janine to move, psychologically or physically, and she has become rather immobile.

The pale blue pocket in the hip area shows that Janine was in the process of struggling to reach maturity. Pale blue can also signify that a person has done a lot of work without much to show for it. But pale blue is also the beginning of ambition. The fact that the pale blue pocket is on her hip, the area of mobility, says, 'Right, I'm ready to break loose. I'm ready to move on.' Her pocket also signifies creative gifts. It shows that she expects to get something to put in it.

Legs

The legs are short. Janine had a bad start in life. That they have no knees shows she had difficulty with anything new and in moving forward. Loose trousers are often used as a cover-up. Janine had never been able to be flexible.

The trousers are coloured a dark yellow which meant Janine was wondering what her next forward move should be. She wanted to do what yellow does best: unravel the past and reveal herself to herself. Imminent activity in these areas is signified.

Yellow is the colour of elimination. There would be

much elimination to be done if Janine was to gain freedom from her past. But the signs were good: the yellow also indicated that she had confidence in her ability to stand on her own two feet. Not afraid to ask questions any more.

Feet

These showed that Janine had a lot of hidden potential to unearth. However, the heels up off the ground signified that she had to come down to earth and face whatever it was she needed to face to be free.

Small feet said that she was on shaky ground as a child and had preferred not to face life at all. Notice that her clown's feet point in both directions. This was a very good sign as it meant Janine was seeking the truth in both directions – about both mother and father – and that she was willing to reason and feel. However, the toes are very narrow which said that she did not yet trust that the future would take care of itself. She was still limiting her view of herself and her future; still afraid to feel the ground or the future before her. No trust of life as yet.

Summary of Janine's clown: 'I don't count. I want to count.'

Janine's picture has two distinct psychological moods or levels. One is that of the past, a kind of 'pardon me for living' feeling in which she has been trapped all her life. This had been ingrained into her personality by her experiences in her home as a child.

Her parents didn't get on well and had 'only stayed together for my sake'. This had made Janine feel that she was a burden and so did her best not to be any trouble. She kept quiet. An interesting footnote to this 'I don't count' aspect is that her job as a croupier meant that she spent her working life counting! A clue to this is her clown's green nose.

Janine's clown is also a picture of someone who has begun to reach out for help; who is ready and willing to bring the male and female parts of herself into balance; and who is not going to stay quiet any longer. Janine was ready to let go of doing things at the expense of herself and ready to reach out and claim her own. She was ready to prosper.

First, she would have to get rid of the ghost of her terrifying father. To do this, she would have to bring the secret of his abuse out into the open and release the pain and anger associated with that. Then she would be able to restructure herself, cease being trapped by the situations that inevitably arise in life, and move out into a far more balanced future.

JUGGLING – A QUICK AND EASY REMEDY FOR STRESS

Because of her life circumstances Janine suffered from stress as well as other problems. So, as the Clown Process had given us information on Janine's life I decided to use a clown's technique to help release the stress.

Juggling is a quick and easy remedy for stress. The act of juggling uses both sides of the brain. We are usually stressed about the past and future. Juggling balances both sides of these so that you can feel at ease with being in the moment of 'here and now'. It cuts across anxiety. Start with using two objects – apples or oranges will be fine to work with. Just get into a natural, even rhythm of throwing one ball to another in each hand. While juggling, you will be able to concentrate on now. It's also fun!

After juggling, follow it with a nice relaxing process. I refer to this as the 'Western worry beads'. Rub two small balls in the hand in a rotation movement. Marbles will do perfectly. This is hand reflexology which helps to remove stress.

Colour healing processes

This is a wonderful way of topping yourself up with one or more colours. It is something you can do on a regular basis just as you might jog two or three times a week. It comes under the heading of taking care of yourself.

A good time to do this process is whenever you have to wait somewhere, or when you are travelling home from work in the evening, or on a long plane or train journey, etc.

Among other beneficial effects, the regular use of the Rainbow Tonic exercise helps you to be receptive to colour. It actually raises your colour absorption level.

1. Make yourself comfortable in a chair. Close your eyes and relax. Focus on your breathing by taking in deep breaths and exhaling slowly.
2. Remain in this relaxed state and visualise a sky of pale blue. Across the sky stretches the arc of a rainbow.
3. Focus on the red band of the rainbow. The red band now starts to vibrate. Be conscious that the red vibration is now leaving that band and coming towards you like a rich, red cloud. As the colour gets near you, it disintegrates into a million fine ruby crystals. These shower all over you!

4. As the crystals touch your skin, they become very fine ruby red droplets of water. This water sinks through your skin and into your body. Your body fills with this colour, being gently warmed, rejuvenated and regenerated.

5. When your body has absorbed enough of the red vibration, the pores of the skin will gently open and the excess will escape as a red mist that swirls softly around your body, gently touching your face and skin lightly. Within a few minutes, the mist will evaporate.

6. Repeat this process with the next colour band in the rainbow, which is orange.

7. Continue until you have absorbed all seven colours of the spectrum – red, orange, yellow, green, blue, indigo and purple.

Note: It is perfectly all right to use just one or more colours rather than the whole seven. However, if you do this, make sure that you use the magnetic colour or colours (red, orange, yellow) before the electrical (blue, indigo, purple).

Another point: this process can be used for colours that do not appear in the rainbow such as turquoise, gold, lemon yellow, jade, etc.

One thing to notice is the difference in your absorption times for different colours. If one takes longer than most, check the positive aspects in the Colour Catalogue to see what you were replenishing.

THE STAR BREATH PROCESS

With this technique you can relieve pain with three breaths wherever you are. Or if you are feeling depressed, anxious, stressed, lethargic – whatever emotional state or mood you want to change – you can breathe in the colour antidote.

Before you begin the actual process, you need to work out which colour will best counteract the particular emotional, physical or mental state you are suffering from. Use the Colour Catalogue for guidance, or just go with your intuitive feeling for the colour you need.

This is a visualisation process. Don't worry about visualising – if you are able to imagine then you can visualise. To prove you can imagine, just think of a time when you were happy. Picture the scene, whether it was a party, a wedding or whatever. A mental picture will come into your mind and that is visualisation.

1. First, sit comfortably and relax. It is better to sit up with your spine straight. If you decide to lie down you may go to sleep! To prevent this, just keep one arm raised in the air, so if you do fall asleep your arm will drop and wake you up. Now that you are relaxed, you are ready to concentrate on your colour visualisation. Now clear your lungs by taking three deep breaths, inhaling strongly, exhaling slowly.
2. Visualise an indigo sky full of silver stars.
3. Choose one of the stars as your star – one of them *does* belong to you. Once you have found your star, you will use it every time to carry out the Star Breath process.
4. Choose a colour that you need for your healing.
5. Switch your star on so that it beams down a ray of the colour you have chosen. This ray should be broad and powerful. See it filling the air around you with its colour radiation.
6. Breathe in for the count of three, visualising yourself inhaling the colour as you do. Visualise this strongly. Actually see yourself pulling the colour in through your

nose out of the air and watch it going away into your body.

7. Hold your colour breath for the count of three.
8. Exhale for the count of three.
9. Repeat 6, 7 and 8 twice more. This completes the three in-breath, out-breath colour cycles.

It is important to take the in-breath through the nostrils. Exhale through the nose – unless the pain or condition is acute, when the out-breath should be through the mouth. This applies particularly for severe pain or any kind of shock.

You can use the colour breath to fill the whole body, or if you are attempting to remove a particular pain, direct the colour breath to whatever organ or part of your body is in pain. If the first three breaths do not achieve the result you want, continue the process for two more sets of three breaths. Once you have established your colour breath star, you will find that you can turn it off and on at will.

The Star Breath Process is invaluable for situations where other help is not immediately available. It is also a good process for childbirth, using a different colour for the three stages of labour – these vary depending upon the delivery. It can be used in many ways throughout pregnancy as well. For morning sickness, for example, try having your star beam jade or emerald green.

It is also a very useful technique for calming the nerves before going on stage, lecturing or before an interview – for any situation that is unusual or creates stress. Try turquoise for this. On the other hand, someone who needs to be energised to meet the demands of an important business meeting where they will need facts and figures at their fingertips could try breathing one set of three green breaths for the memory, and one set of three scarlet breaths for impetus.

Children take to this process easily. Orange and peach, for instance, will help the child regain his or her lost appetite after illness.

If you find the colour fades after a few breaths, note that that means your body has absorbed all it needs of that colour and has automatically shut off.

A night variation

Visualise your star in the indigo sky just before you go to sleep. Turn it on and allow the colour to beam down on you. You will be inhaling it as you sleep. Your star will fade away without your conscious control when you have had enough.

Once again, have the star beam whatever colour you wish to work with. Indigo would be a good choice for insomnia, for instance, or for acute pain. Indigo is the strongest colour to relieve pain. This is a wonderful technique to use for people in hospitals or hospices. It's a way of controlling the pain.

If you're lonely or restless, a warm pink would be comforting. Just flood yourself with pink and away you go into dreamland, safe, secure and nurtured.

If you have a trying day coming up involving facts and figures, leaf green would help prepare your mind for this kind of work. Once again, to choose the best colour, work with both the Colour Catalogue (pages 194–346) and your own intuition.

It is probably best to avoid the bright magnetic colours – red, orange, yellow – for night-time use. Tints of these colours such as pink, peach, primrose would be safer. Whether using this process awake or asleep, use only one colour at a time for each set of three breaths.

THE ICE WALL – A BRILLIANCE TECHNIQUE

This meditation/visualisation process is designed to help you remove inner blocks that restrict you in life and relationships. In terms of colour, it works with Brilliance, the pure light (see pages 200–207).

Emotional experiences and mental attitudes that we took on board in our distant past often create blocks to our enjoyment and freedom today. And it is frequently the case that no amount of realisation or intellectual understanding, or dramatic emotional catharsis seems to shift them. A deeper level of our psyche must be brought into play.

This process is in two sections: the first part is a meditation. The second is a visualisation of dissolving of the Ice Wall.

The Crystal Breath Bath

This is the melting ice process. Frozen thoughts create immobility. You become stuck solid – it's called a 'safety stand'. The attitude is, 'At least I know where I am.' The only way to free us from these ice blocks is to melt away frozen ideas.

1. First, find a comfortable place where you can be alone and undisturbed.
2. Sit in a relaxed position. Close your eyes and concentrate on your breathing. Notice the coming of the in-breath and the going of the out-breath. Become very aware of that small space that occurs between the in-breath and the out-breath. What happens for you in that U-turn space? Do you go anywhere? Just observe and let go.

When you are breathing gently and without strain,

body relaxed, mind at rest, go on to the next step.

3. Visualise yourself warmly dressed in white clothes sitting in a sleigh at the North Pole. White snow and ice stretch away to the horizon all around you, yet you are not at all cold. The sun is shining and the snowy expanse sparkles beneath the crystal-clear air. The skin on your face tingles from clean, crisp, cold air. Establish this scene and your place in it strongly.

4. As you sit in your sleigh in this scene of purity and light, feel yourself drawing in through your nose the sparkling crystal air with every breath. Be aware that the air is filled with light. You are bathed in Brilliance, inhaling Brilliance.

   Allow yourself to stay in this meditation state for several minutes. Let whatever arises in your mind come and go without interference – there are no 'right' or 'wrong' thoughts or feelings. Simply notice what it is coming up in your mind and body.

When you are ready, proceed with the second part of the process:

5. Still sitting warm and comfortable in your sleigh in the snowy Brilliance, visualise a wall of ice slowly rising from the ground in front of you. This wall contains your inner block or blocks.

6. Look at the ice wall closely. Is it cloudy or clear? How high is it? How thick is it? Is it thicker in some places? Is it thicker at the bottom of the wall? Or towards the top? Do not worry yourself with what these features mean. It is not necessary for your conscious mind to know – something deeper has taken over.

   Notice that the bright, warm beams of the sun are shining strongly on your wall. Its beams are directly focused on you.

7. As the sun shines visualise the wall of ice starting to melt. Be very aware that your inner blocks are this wall of ice. Watch as it melts under the power of the sun – drip, drip, drip. This may take some time. It can also be somewhat uncomfortable. Strong feelings may come up. If they do, simply acknowledge them and let them go.

8. When your ice block has melted away, let yourself feel a warmth spreading in your body. That particular block – or blocks – has gone forever!

9. Look at the water from the melted wall. See it as slushy ice. As you look at it, forms start to take shape. These become strong, friendly, white husky dogs shaking their bodies free of old slush ready to pull your sleigh onwards. Take a deep breath and, as you release it, feel the pull on the reins in your hands as the dogs start to pull your sleigh forward. Let the pure, clean air brush your face and body as you go faster and faster. Feel the exhilarating life coming back into the newly created spaces in your body.

10. Take in a deep breath. As you let it out, begin to visualise your sleigh pushing you forward to break through to the consciousness of now. Take several more deep breaths and, as you exhale, begin to come out of the process.

11. Come out very slowly, like a cat having an after-nap stretch.

As well as being used to clear old blocks, this process can also be used any time you feel your energy has become blocked in your system.

THE TOWEL TECHNIQUE – A BRIGHT RED ANGER RELEASE

Because the body is always giving out colours, when I read

someone's hand I can see not only lines, mounts and markings but also a display of colour. Its significance depends on the colour and where it appears on the hand. For example, the colour red (not to be confused with the natural flesh colour) will indicate repressed anger, anger that remains in the system. It is like a can of worms with the lid kept on.

You may well ask why the anger shouldn't stay in. Do you tire easily? Is your energy used up quickly? If so, you may have repressed anger that needs to be released because it uses up a great deal of our energy to keep it down. High blood pressure and angina caused by a tired heart can come about because of repressed anger. You may say, 'But I don't feel angry at all!' But of course you won't feel it if it is deeply submerged. A simple process to start to release this anger is the Towel Technique. This technique frees the energy so that it can be harnessed for the individual's benefit.

1. First of all, find a hand towel, preferably red but any colour will do. Sit in a chair and make sure that you are really slouching so that your bottom is near the edge of the seat. Your legs should be apart and your back should be curved with your stomach concave.
2. Hold the towel at arms' length with your elbows straight. your hands should be about four inches apart. Do not curve your wrists underneath or around the towel. Keep the top of your hands facing up and only let the fingers curl round.
3. Now feel your feet securely placed on the ground and for a few moments just look at the space between your two hands because you are going to wring the living daylights out of that space.
4. Now take a deep breath and hold it, then bear down into your body so that you can feel a pressure in your lower

abdomen and bowel area. It's a feeling of strain in the lower part of the body as though you are constipated and having to push hard to pass a motion. At the same time, wring that towel. If you want to you can let out a grunting sound as the breath releases.

5. If you don't feel angry, just fake it and you will find that sooner or later you will get immense action both physically and vocally doing this process. Try thinking of someone who upsets you and shout, scream or growl at them. Swear if you wish. It's much better to do it this way than wring their neck!

This process takes only two and a half minutes a day and you will start to release your repressed anger. It could even have been there since birth and babyhood. Repressed anger will not allow your body to relax fully, so go wring a towel and give your circulation a treat. Just one super wring is enough to change your body's energy. If you feel depressed, wring a towel and after just one breath it will start to spring you out of it and you'll begin to feel better immediately.

Another aspect of anger is boredom which is also related to the colour red. The bright red of anger is active, whereas the dull red of boredom is lethargic. The person who is bored is also tired and listless. Underneath boredom you will find there is repressed anger. When you take the lid off boredom it allows the bright red of anger to come to the surface. A good old anger release will work wonders.

Wringing the towel is a very useful training action to help you learn how to feel angry. Often, when we were children, we were not able to express our anger or to experiment with it and know that when it comes it can be released to quickly blow away. We were told 'Don't be angry, it's not on.' We learned that this is one undesirable emotion so we block it and repress it. We will always experience it but will not know what to do with it because we have not been trained to use it appropriately. The towel process allows you to practise with your anger and it's great fun. You can give yourself permission to be as angry as you like, no other reason than just to feel anger. You will find it's not a taboo feeling. Appropriately used it is as important as all the other emotions, but you can't use it effectively unless you've had some practice – after all you wouldn't go on stage without rehearsing first.

A SUNSHOWER FOR THE MIND – A YELLOW VISUALISATION

The mind is the composer of the body's activities. This is a colour cleansing process for the mind. It makes use of yellow's richness, the colour of the mind's mental processes. Like the Rainbow Tonic, you can use it anywhere and anytime.

To escape the domination of the mind can be a Himalayan task. Part of the purpose of this process is to experience a mind bubbling with joy rather than irritation. By using it over a period of time, you will be able to have the joy-filled mind as your natural state.

It is also a process that enables you to be receptive to the power of love and desire. It clears the mind of shadows. When the mind is shadowed and blocked, the power it has to have your desires fulfilled is also inhibited. Whatever your needs, the sunshower brings you closer to being able to allow the Universe to meet them.

1. It is preferable to do this process lying down. Make yourself comfortable, close your eyes and begin a pattern of deep, slow breathing. See yourself inhaling long, slow

breaths of goodness into your body and exhaling all negativity.

2. Now turn your thoughts to your mind. See it as a room. Note what is in this room. Is the room cluttered up? Is there a colour to the clutter? Are there any grey or dark patches?

3. As you continue breathing gently and slowly, allow your mind to become very still and very quiet. You may actually feel it settling down. This may take a few minutes to happen – the mind sometimes resists slowing down because it is used to being busy. Be patient with your mind in this part of the process. Just be aware that you are letting go of all thoughts so that your mind can become still and very calm. It is like a liner coming into the quayside after a long voyage. You may even feel a slight jolt when your mind finally comes to rest.

4. When you feel your mind has come to rest, imagine an opening appearing in the top of your head. A soft, warm, yellow ray of light is beaming down from an indigo sky above. It pours through the opening in the top of your head and streams into your mind's room bursting into a million sparkling gold stars.

5. Let this light fill the mind. Let it seep into every space and every corner. Fill your mind's room with this liquid sunlight.

   As your mind fills with this lovely yellow light, it becomes buoyant and cheerful. Any black-spots or grey areas will be cleared as the light filters through them. And, as your mind becomes clearer, so your body becomes lighter and more joyous. You can stay in this state for as long as you wish. But when you decide to return . . .

6. Gently close the opening in your head. As you do, become aware of your breathing again. Take several deep

breaths to bring you back into the world. Wait a few minutes before moving because you may experience a light-headedness.

This is a good process for those times when your mind is full of fears, of dark thoughts and black places. It is excellent for depression of any kind. When a person is sad, they are full of feeling. But when they are depressed they are empty. I call depression a colour drain. I see it as a black rainbow – the dark, desperate side of the soul. The sunlight has gone behind the cloud but light can break through where no sun shines. This is why gold is the great healer for depression.

What is behind that cloud? Usually there is anger and sorrow. When a client visits me in deep depression, I am careful not to tell them to be positive. Obviously, a person in such a depressed state feels they have nothing to be positive about. What the person needs is tools to work with. I encourage a person in depression to go into that dark cave. What the person will usually find when they get in there is only what they took in with them – which is themselves.

The nature of depression is that the person tends to become very inert. But there is always a funny side, even for someone in depression. As one optimistic but depressed client once exclaimed to me, 'At least being a depressive you get your rest!'

The root of depression must be grasped, taken in hand. When the dark and hidden fear that is the heart of depression is in the person's hands, it can be dissolved. Always wear colours if you are depressed. Light can enter and the dark rainbow be transformed into its spectrum of colours. Gain access to peace of mind through the gentle sun shower.

'Tears have washed the colour from my light.'
Elizabeth Barratt Browning

THE LITTLE CHILD PROCESS – SPRING GREEN

This is a technique by which you can reconnect with your own little, abandoned child who lives within you. It is the one I used with Maria (see pages 52–3). Though there are many other little child processes, the effects of this one are so deep and moving that I would recommend that it be the first one used for inner child work.

1. Take one of your jackets and roll it up into a bundle. It is important to use one of your own.
2. Put the jacket bundle close at hand and sit on a chair with your feet firmly on the ground and the lower part of your back firmly supported by the chair.
3. Take the jacket in both hands and, keeping secure hold of it, place it on top of your knees.
4. Look upon the bundle and be very aware that you are now holding yourself for the first time as a small child.
5. You are now going to talk to this little one who has never heard from you before. When I use this process with a client, I have the person gaze upon their child and repeat the following words after me: 'I will never, ever leave you again.' Pause ... 'Not ever. You are always coming with me. Do you hear me?' Pause ... 'I will never, ever leave you behind again.' Pause ... 'Not ever. You are always coming with me.' Pause ... 'Always.'
6. Repeat this until you *know* your little child has heard it.
7. Finally, draw the little bundle into your arms. Hold it and cuddle it close against your chest and rock it gently.

You may need to repeat this process once a day for as long as it takes for your little child to fully understand. Remember, he or she has been living in a state of fear of being left behind. Its experience was that it was always left behind. And you as the adult are the one who is leaving it behind and ignoring it now.

When we grow up, we take over parenting our little child from our parents. As we were parented so we parent our inner child. The inner child stays with us until the day we die; the child is who we are. I feel our child is within our abdomen; we carry it around with us.

The magic of cuddling with our inner child is that we as parents can now give it anything it needs or wants. Thus, we can ourselves become whole and well again instead of a victim and always incomplete. We cannot change the happenings of childhood, but we can certainly release any painful energies that remained with us.

I have found that people I am doing this process with will often cry with relief at the reunion with their lost child who has been wandering around for years, ignored and alone. The release can be so great that body changes appear – the person becomes softer, and a contentment enters their presence. So often people go around searching for something all their lives. What they do not realise is that what they are looking for is their own little child that they lost so long ago.

TUMBLE ROLL – THE VIOLET-ORANGE BACK-TO-THE-WOMB PROCESS

This process/exercise is to help you release any negative experiences you may have had while you were in the womb. The fact that you do not consciously remember these is not a problem – your body does and it would love to let them go.

1. Lie flat on the floor, with your eyes closed. Your body and legs are relaxed, your arms lying loosely by your sides, your palms facing up to the ceiling. This is called the Dead Man's or Corpse Pose.
2. Begin breathing deeply, consciously relaxing every part of your body. Begin at your feet and move up the body until you reach the top of your head. Imagine each part becoming heavier and heavier. This may take you some minutes, but it is an essential part of the process.
3. Having completed 2, visualise the air around you filled with violet. You can use the Star Breath technique given on pages 158–61 if you wish.
4. After five minutes of breathing in violet, sit up. Keep your eyes closed and your back as straight as possible. Keep breathing in the violet light. Next, bring your knees up to your chest, cross your ankles (it doesn't matter which ankle you cross over which) and fold your arms around your knees, clasping them to your chest. You should now look like a little foetus curled up in the womb. Finally, let your head roll forward and come to rest on your knees. Do this position as well as you can. But do not overstrain.
5. Imagine your arms holding your knees filling up with orange light. Some people find that being in the foetal position brings up fear and they immediately want to come out of the position. Traumas in the womb always put the foetus into fear, particularly of moving forward. The orange arms absorb shock and support you while you carry out the process. If you experience feelings of fear coming up, just acknowledge them and say, 'Yes, I feel fearful' and then let them go.

6. In this position, start to gently rock backwards and forwards. Let yourself fall into a rhythm of slow rocking – backwards and forwards, backwards and forwards. There can be a tendency to hold your breath at this stage, so keep breathing! And don't worry if you fall over. Just keep your eyes shut, sit up again and keep going.

7. After five minutes of this exercise, let your rocking gradually come to a halt, release your arms slowly and, still keeping your eyes shut, lie back on the floor again in the original Dead Man's Pose. As you do so, let the orange that filled your arms drain away out through your fingertips.

8. Continue to breathe in the violet light deeply for two more minutes. And then let that light fade away also.

9. Lie still for a further five minutes. As you do, be aware of the sensations passing through your body.

You may, at first, find this a long and quite complicated process. So you may want to have a friend talk you through it. In fact, two people can take turns.

It is most important during the Tumble Roll exercise to be aware of your breathing. Keep breathing all the way through it, try not to stop. If you have a friend with you, have them remind you to keep breathing. You may find you want to breathe faster or slower. If so, be aware of it and then go back to your regular breathing.

Several things may happen during this exercise. You may have a rush of intense feelings. Or you may find that you seem to go numb or blank. Crying, coughing, shaking, yawning deeply, even laughing at nothing at all, are releases of energy. Whatever form the release takes, you can be sure that you are getting in touch with your birth trauma and that the experience you are having is perfectly appropriate. This process is using the power of colour to heal simply and quickly.

Once you start this exercise, it is better to continue with it on a regular basis until only pleasure is experienced while rocking. People who have persisted with it for some time report experiencing a feeling of joy and lightness within their bodies. Until our pre-birth traumas are released, we cannot feel truly at home in the world. Or experience our life as the truly wonderful adventure it can be.

LISTENING BELOW THE WORDS – THE TRUTH, THE WHOLE TRUTH AND NOTHING BUT THE BLUE OF TRUTH

One of the techniques that my inability to read as a child led me to discover is what I call Listening Below the Words. To understand I had to look 'under the stand', as it were. It is not a process in the usual sense of the word – more of a psychic scan – but it has served me well and I would like to pass it on.

I was at a conference and a rather dominating woman was telling me something for my own good about my life and how I was about to make a mess of it. She had been engaged in this for some minutes with absolute confidence in the rightness of her perception of me: 'I really don't feel that you should be going into this avenue of work, this would not be the best for you . . . I am quite sure that you will . . .'

I could see she was quite sincere, but something inside of me made me increasingly uneasy. I felt very uncomfortable. My gut instinct, the orange area, was on full alert. I am sure you have experienced in your life feelings of 'I know this is supposed to be for my own good, but it doesn't feel right.' Suddenly, I remembered what to do. While she was speaking I turned my eyes to the area of her throat and the top of the chest. I tuned, as it were, into that area. I was aware that I could see underneath the words and then I could hear her hidden message.

Although she consciously believed she was giving me sound advice, her unconscious motive was that she was afraid that I was going to develop too quickly in my work and maybe become more well known than she was. It was her fear, disguised as concern for my welfare, that was talking to me.

I thanked her very much for her advice and went away from there knowing what had been going on. I didn't have to spend the rest of the day in a state of confusion and self-doubt as to what I should do. I had not been undermined by someone else's opinions and well-intentioned advice.

You can see how simple the technique is. Remembering that you have it when you need it is the main difficulty. Just let the words the person is saying go on without attempting to understand or consider them on the level of their apparent meaning, while you actually look at the speaker's throat and the upper chest just below. Tune into this area and connect to the vibration coming to you from here. You hear the words as sound, but what the speaker thinks they mean does not distract you from the real meaning hidden behind their subject.

This process is an intuitive use of blue and green. Blue is associated with the throat chakra and the truth. Green leads you to the heart of the matter. A really useful process, it lets you see whether the story you're hearing is the whole truth or not.

The colours we eat

WHY LIFE IS NOT JUST A BOWL OF BLACK AND WHITE CHERRIES

There was a report in *The Times* a couple of years ago (August 1991) about some of the hostages in the Lebanon who were given a bowl of red cherries. They had not seen colour for three years and they just sat and 'looked at the cherries for a whole day in spite of an overwhelming desire to eat them'. The report said that they could not take their eyes off the red.

Colour is, I believe, an essential food. There is such a thing as colour starvation. Colour is as necessary to us as is food for our stomach, or air for our lungs.

Red, for instance, is the colour that connects us to life and life's energy force. It directly affects the blood and the circulation. It gives us zest, moves us forward. It gives great courage and it is expansive. These were just the qualities that the hostages most needed after three years of imprisonment in a small room. They had been literally starved of the red vibration. They needed to soak up the colour of the cherries more than they needed to eat the flesh of the fruit.

Furthermore, colour tells our body what kind of nutrients a specific food contains. The nutrients are colour-coded.

One day we will find ourselves drawn towards red foods, another day green. The colour vibration tells us which food has the nutrient we need.

Understanding the connections between colour and food offers a key to remaining healthy. We are all sensitive to the colour of food. Our appetite will be increased or decreased by its colour. Why are foods coloured anyway? Why aren't they all just black and white like old movies? The answer is because there is an essential connection between the vibration rate that is a particular colour and the pattern of nutrients a particular food provides.

Different coloured foods are a good way of putting the colours we need into the body to improve and maintain health. Each food has its own vibrational rate. Red foods fuel and charge the body; they fortify the blood. Yellow foods are the natural laxatives and citrus fruits – the colours orange and yellow – are the stimulators and eliminators. They are the most highly vibratory coloured foods we have. Orange juice first thing in the morning can help to remove undigested food left over in the system from the day before. Green foods cleanse the system. Green herbs represent the bloodstream or circulation of the plant kingdom. The bright green chlorophyll that comes to us in green plant life is the greatest rejuvenator you can put into your body. Green is the sunshine vegetable. Green food is loaded with sunshine, that's why it's green. Even if a person doesn't like vegetables or salads they have to admit that the food looks appetising. The added bonus of green is that it puts you off white sugar. We can get natural sweetness from vegetables and fruit.

Food is another way of introducing sunlight into the body. The natural juices of the fruits and vegetables we eat are the plant equivalent to blood in the human system. But they must be fresh. If food is picked before it is ripened to its full time, it is robbed of sunlight and will not develop the full range of minerals and vitamins.

Light is a nutrient and like food is necessary to health. Foods eaten that grow above the ground carry imprisoned sunlight – they are suncharged. Vitamin D is derived from sunlight so when we sunbathe, we are sun-charging our bodies. It is advisable to eat three parts of vegetables grown above the ground to one part grown below for the maximum health benefits.

Some foods can be disharmonious with our body rate – in which case it is likely to cause imbalances to occur in the body. And watch out especially for junk foods that have been chemically treated or processed in some way.

Furthermore, our emotional state can turn food into this kind of unbalancing energy. If we are angry or upset, the vibrational rate of the food we eat is upset. Food should be eaten in an atmosphere of calm and harmony. We need to be aware that there are calming foods and stimulating foods and foodless foods. Overcooking of food can also cause the vibrational rate to be changed. We can kill the vital colour.

Foods exposed to different coloured lights will also be affected. Red light seems to lighten heavy bread – it seems to expand it. Any food or water that is passed under the sun seems to be lighter (enlightened?) and has a marked quality about it.

We must be aware that we can create different colour combinations with the food we put on our plates, so if we have green, blue and yellow foods, for instance, they combine to make the colour turquoise and we will receive the vibratory action of that colour. Likewise, red and yellow foods will produce orange vibrations.

If there is an overload of any particular food, you can always balance it by using the complementary colour (see chart on page 112).

Depending on the choice of foods you make, you can

build disease or health. Understanding this could give you the answer to various ailments, the commonest being indigestion – after all we cannot have sweet thoughts with a sour stomach. All our bodily functions will try to maintain us in a state of well-being. As long as the law of nature is in force, which is an input of decent colour coordinated food, we will remain in perfect harmony.

In short, be aware when cooking that you create a meal in which you have combined the colours for balance. A plate of food that is all one colour is not balanced.

If a certain colour is missing from the food itself, supply it by the table decorations, the flowers, the napkins, etc. Then at least the colour can be taken in by the eye if not by the mouth.

So, understanding the connection between colour and food offers a key to remaining healthy. We are all sensitive to the colour of food. For instance, it will always be stimulated by red foods – they will make us eat a lot. White and brown foods are found to be the most popular coloured foods eaten in restaurants. This is because the brown represents the goodness of the Earth and white represents mother's milk – nurturing. Being drawn to white is putting us in touch with our emotional connections to security while being nursed as a child. I personally feel that we don't need milk – like other animals, I can see no reason for humans to have milk once we are adults. We are definitely not drawn to food that is blue, perhaps it is because we get the blue vibrations from the sky.

But, as so often happens with us human beings, there is a complication: we can also be attracted towards foods that we definitely do not need. These foods, while trying to restore a balance to the system, actually create a further imbalance. Why, for instance, should a person find himself or herself eating chocolate at every possible opportunity?

Consider it from the point of view of colour, consider the colour brown.

Brown is the colour of a person who is inhibited, who does not want to be all that they are, who wants to hide their light under a bushel for some reason. Being attracted to brown often indicates someone who is insecure, frightened to expand to their full potential. Such a person lives their life like a little seed in its brown husk in the ground, afraid to take in the life nutrients around it which would cause it to explode into growth, rise up through the ground into the air and break into bloom.

One of the well-known side-effects of chocolate is that it makes a person fat. Being fat is an excellent way to be unattractive in a society that worships slimmers. Being unattractive is a way of avoiding our sexuality because we are frightened of it. In other words, the brown chocolate helps the person keep buried their power to attract others. Why they are afraid of being attractive, and where and when they learned that fear, is something that colours can also reveal. Fat is fear. Continual fear causes a person to be fat and weak. There is a lack of firmness in the person's life.

Another reason why we may over-indulge on chocolate is because somewhere in our lives we are not getting our own way. Eating chocolate is getting your own way – it may be the only area in your life where you can fulfil your own needs. 'I need chocolate. I'll have it. I can't get what I want anywhere else in my life, but this way I get my will fed.' That's why it's so hard to give up chocolate or any other food that substitutes as a nurturer. Binging literally fills a gap. The problem is the food can never be enough because it isn't appropriate for the food to fill an emotional need. It has been proved that 97 per cent of people on a diet today will be on a diet next year and some will be more over-weight!

This is not to say that the fat person consciously does not

want to lose weight. They often do, desperately. But the person who is imbalanced – which simply means unable to be his or her real self – will often choose the foods or colours that will tend to keep them in a state of imbalance. Those who crave white chocolate are likely to be expressing the extreme frustration that white denotes. White represents our mother's milk which gives sustenance, so when our addiction is to white chocolate we are saying that our feeding times as a baby were not satisfactory. We do not blame our parents for this, they did their best. It's just how our child perceived it. Unfortunately, if the mother for some reason is under undue pressure she may become hostile to parenthood. Her mother's milk for her baby will then be 'poisoned'. This can lead to eating disorders in the child. Distrust sets in which leads to the non-absorption of food syndrome, anorexia, and to food allergies. The same is true of those of us who over-eat, as it is of addictions or eating disorders of any kind. In over-eating or bulimia – a binging and purging illness which is a self-hatred syndrome – the colour of the food the person over-eats will often give a clue to the deeper problem.

Another addiction is caused by brown alcohol. Brown makes you want to shrink away, to hide or go to sleep – which is just the way you feel the morning after a drinking session. As brown comes from a mixture of the warmer colours, use the opposite end of the spectrum, the cooler blues or green the great neutraliser to conquer the effects of alcohol.

I find it interesting to notice the colours of the foods people choose when I am out to dinner. If you have a knowledge of the psychology of colour, you can always see where a person is by the colour of the foods they choose. For instance, if you are having a business lunch and you are considering employing your guest for a job, and you need a quiet, reliable and unassuming person for the role, if they assure you they are of a retiring disposition and then choose a lot of red food, forget it! They'll no more stay in the background than fly to the moon. Brown or indigo food, however, would be entirely another matter.

Understanding the connection between colour and food offers a key to remaining healthy. We are all sensitive to the colour of food. When the Indians in Peru found that they had fallen out of balance – which is another way of saying fallen ill – they would put themselves in a state of great receptivity and then go out and walk quietly through nature. It is said that, in this state, they were able to hear the herbs or grasses or leaves that they needed to correct the illness speak to them. It's a lovely story, and it is more than just a story.

We have the same abilities. The same intuition – which simply means 'in-knowing' or 'in-teaching' – lives within us. But we have lost our connection with it. For a long time, its value and truth – even its existence – have been denied in our society. I am sure that our health and well-being, both as individuals and as a society, depend upon our recovering that lost connection so that we can once again hear what nature is saying to us.

Quite often, though, we go in exactly the opposite direction: we drown out the inner voice and steer 180 degrees away from what we need to restore our well-being. We can be so imbalanced in ourselves, physically, mentally and emotionally, that we are unable to recognise the foods and the colours in life that would help us recover that lost balance. We have forgotten that it is wiser to first eat what we need and then, if we must, eat what we would like.

Our body will actually be drawn towards what it needs to restore its vitality, but we will not be able to hear the quiet voice, or feel the gentle impulse, that is our intuition – so weakened by the prejudice and ignorance of our society and education – urging us towards the balancing corrective. So often we are given whispers telling us that we have to look at something, change our ways. But we ignore them, we don't listen. It is only when we get a great big shout – which is called 'illness' – that we take any notice. To maintain our health, maybe we should follow Hippocrates' advice from 2,500 years ago: 'Let your food be your medicine, let your medicine be your food.'

This is one of the uses of a colour reading: to help us restore our damaged intuition. The herbs we need, the foods and the right colours, even the right course of action are out there. We just need to identify what exactly we need for our particular situation now. One sure way that we can, like the Indians, hear them speak to us is through the language of colour.

WATER SOLARISATION – THE SUNSHINE DRINK

This is a simple way of drinking sunlight-charged colour! The sun purifies the water and instils the sunlight. You can literally bottle the sun's force. Just place a bottle of clear water in the sun for one day. Sip this slowly. It is a wonderful natural rejuvenator that revitalises you. It's a way of drinking the Brilliance. You can separate the individual colours of the spectrum too, and this is an excellent way of drinking colour. Water solarisation can be used at any time on its own, but it is also a fine way to boost other colour treatments. The effects may be slow, but they will occur.

One advantage of this way of absorbing colour is that there are no complications from over-dosing which can happen if you are exposed to a colour for too long.

A basic guide is to drink the red, orange and yellow water in the mornings, and the blue and the violet in the afternoon and at night. Green is best at lunch time – but it can be used at anytime.

1. Fill a clear glass tumbler, glass jug or bottle with pure spring or filtered water. It is important to use a vessel made of glass.
2. Wrap the container in a sheet of cellophane, a spotlight filter or gel, or even coloured perspex, in the colour that you want the water to carry – the top does not have to be covered. Some colour therapists use more sophisticated coloured wrappings, but for home use, cellophane and the spotlight gels you can find at theatrical lighting stores are perfectly adequate.
3. Leave the glass in a position that allows the sunlight to fall upon it. Even thirty minutes will make a difference to the water. However, I recommend that it be exposed to the light for at least six hours before drinking. The longer the time it is exposed, the stronger the energy of the colour becomes.

Red, orange and yellow water should be sipped slowly. (Yellow should not be taken after 6 p.m. because of its elimination effect.) Greens, blues and the colours above these in the spectrum can be drunk somewhat faster – but never gulped.

A good way of discovering your level of sensitivity to colour is to shut your eyes and taste a glass of solarised water. Then take a sip of water from the same source without solarisation. See if you are able to notice a difference. (Just because you do not detect a difference does not mean that you will not benefit from the solarised water.) Some sensitive people can detect a difference after the water has been instilled with a colour for five minutes. Try it yourself. Then try after twenty minutes exposure, and so on up to twelve hours.

Do not solarise water for longer than twelve hours. One experiment showed that when the water had been solarised with a colour for two days it 'burned' when tasted.

Note: It is possible to charge water using an artificial light – particularly useful in northern winters! To do this, you will have to find a spectrum electric light bulb. Once again, it may be easier to find this in a theatrical lighting store.

Food can also be solarised

Wrap the food in the coloured cellophane, or put it in a bowl with the colour gel over the top, and expose it to the light for some hours. A red apple can be made even redder this way!

THE RAINBOW DIET

The Rainbow Diet is simply a support system, enabling you to harmonise within. We often do a great deal of work on ourselves spiritually without using or harmonising our physical stamina, which could aid us and supply us with vitality and energy. The body is our temple, and as such it must be attended to. Use food – regard it as having come from the divine light that became the ultimate spiritual nutrition. By using the Rainbow Diet we are working with nature, which will only encourage our endeavour to become fully aware.

The Rainbow Diet is also a way to treat yourself to a colour holiday. Regard it as a trip to a health farm, only you can do it at home. You can have either a one-day treatment, a two-day or weekend treatment, or take a whole week.

Whichever treatment you choose, clear the day so that you do not have to go out or rush around. Use the day to relax totally so that you can receive the benefits of colour. Get an easy book to read or some magazines, and take the phone off the hook – you're not at home. This day is yours.

These treatments help your body clear out toxins (the negative of colours). As well, your body will be receiving the pure hue of positive colour. It will be both detoxified and regenerated. Check the Colour Catalogue for different coloured foods.

Note: If you have a medical condition, are taking medication or are in any doubt as to whether you should embark on these diets, please consult your doctor before you begin.

The one-day treatment

1. On rising, drink a glass of warm water with a slice of lemon in it.
2. Take a sea-salt bath. Put two large spoonfuls of sea-salt into a warm bath and soak for at least seven minutes. You can take a sea-salt shower, if you prefer. Wet the skin first, and then rub the sea-salt all over your body ... and rinse.

   After your bath or shower, smooth on clear oil, the purest you can find, one with no added perfume. Any good health food shop will advise you on this.
3. *Rainbow Breakfast*: This is a deep cleanser and rejuvenator. Prepare a rainbow fruit salad for yourself. Use any mixed fruits that are available – preferably fresh. Dried prunes, apricots, figs, etc., are perfectly acceptable mixed

in with the fresh fruit items. Try to incorporate a coloured fruit, including skin, from each colour of the spectrum in your Rainbow fruit salad. Remember, each colour in the Colour Catalogue includes a list of foods. Red: strawberries, raspberries. Orange: apricots, oranges. Yellow: bananas, pears. Green: kiwi fruit, limes. Blue and indigo: plums, blueberries. Purple: grapes, passion fruit. Any white fruit can also be included. White fruit represents the Brilliance from whence all coloured fruit comes. In white food you have a small but equal amount of every colour in the spectrum. 'White fruit' refers to the colour of the skin and flesh.

4. Lunch and dinner? Have the same as breakfast. If you need a snack mid-morning or mid-afternoon, have a banana and a glass of warm water.

Your clothes for the day should only be white – a white dressing gown or track suit. When you wrap a white robe around yourself, you are swathing yourself in sunlight.

Before retiring at night, bathe again in sea-salt to wash away the toxins that will have emerged onto your skin. Your nightwear and bed linen should also be white.

This day is not only a cleanser, it also attunes your body to the Brilliance I have written about in the Colour Catalogue. By the end of the day your body will feel lighter. The Rainbow fruit salad has introduced all the colours that are hidden in the white light.

Throughout the day, drink as much pure water as you can. At least eight pints!

The weekend or two-day treatment

The best time for this is over a weekend unless you are lucky enough to have some days free during the working week!

This treatment is the same as the one-day cleanse. However, in addition to the Rainbow fruit salad, a green and white soup has been added to lunch and dinner. This soup is built around green vegetables and herbs. It can also include potatoes and onions. Potatoes, onions and garlic being white represent the Brilliance. These are the only white vegetables allowed in this green soup. Use a vegetable stock, not a meat stock, for the liquid. If you just add water only it will make its own stock. Onions, garlic and white pepper can be used freely. Use sea-salt sparingly. Help yourself to this on both days.

The complete one-week treatment

Every day in the week has its own colour. Taking each colour in turn, start with red Monday and follow through to purple Sunday. Each day is given over to the appropriate colour plus green and white. Green is included because it goes with every colour. You are less likely to over-dose on a colour if green is incorporated. It balances and maintains a stability within the system. While the body is working with the colour vibration of the day, green is detoxifying. It is also a great tonic. Make sure each day's food consists of 75 per cent of the colour of the day and 25 per cent of green and white. If you want to reduce the colour of the day, just replace it with green or white. You may notice that you just don't want to eat a lot of one day's colour because of physical or emotional imbalance. You may just want to try one colour day, which is fine but make sure that you do it on the appropriate day, i.e. don't do a red Monday food on an indigo Thursday.

Day 1 – red Monday

Wear only red clothes. Eat only red foods. These can include anything from bright red apples through the pinks of pomegranates and prawns to the dark red of beetroot. Every meal must incorporate the red colour. But no red meat, please! You can get your protein from red beans and fish such as red salmon. Green food must be incorporated in at least two meals.

1. Have a breakfast of red apples, raspberries and green grapes etc.
2. Lunch and dinner: peppers, tomatoes, beetroot, red cabbage, red lettuce, radishes, seafood (pink/red only) and add a green salad or green vegetable to one of these meals at least.
3. Use the Star Breath technique (see pages 155–61) with red at least three times daily.

Make yourself a green and white soup. The one-week green and white soup has more white vegetables added than the two-day soup. Any green vegetables, potatoes, leeks, onions, celery, garlic, green or white herbs and seasoning can be added. Use sea-salt sparingly.

The green and white soup can be eaten every day in unlimited amounts.

Beverages Do not drink tea or coffee. But fresh mint or Japanese green tea is fine. Do drink as much clear water as feels comfortable. The water you drink up to midday can be red solarised water (see page 184). After midday return to the clear water. Also, take one glass of freshly pressed fruit or vegetable juice in the colour of the day (beetroot, tomato, raspberry or redcurrant). This can be bought – make sure it contains no sugar or additives.

Day 2 – orange Tuesday

Wear only orange clothes. Eat only orange foods. These can include peach-coloured foods. Remember to have your greens as well, and your green and white soup if you are feeling really hungry. Proteins must be orange in colour, such as pulses or tofu.

Again, no tea or coffee but green or mint teas are allowed. Drink plenty of water. Orange solarised water can be taken up to but not after midday. And have a glass of freshly pressed orange or carrot juice.

Use the Star Breath technique with orange at least three times a day.

Day 3 – yellow Wednesday

Wear only yellow clothes. Eat only yellow foods, plus the green foods. Have yellow pulses or tofu for protein. And, of course, follow the liquid diet component of a glass of freshly pressed yellow fruit or vegetable juice, clear water, and the green or mint teas. Yellow solarised water can be taken up to but not after midday.

Use the yellow Star Breath technique a minimum of three times a day.

Day 4 – green Thursday

Wear only green clothes. Eat only green foods, no other colour, i.e. green fruits, green vegetables or salads. For protein, eat lentils plus tofu. And, of course, have your green and white soup.

Follow the water, juice and green or mint tea programme. Green solarised water can be taken all day.

And use the green Star Breath technique.

Day 5 – blue Friday

Wear only blue clothes. There are few blue foods. You can have a fruit salad made up of white fruit only such as lychees, pears and apples (skins removed) plus any blue fruits. Have any amount of green and white soup plus green salad.

This is a fruit and vegetable day – with white tofu and fish for protein. To incorporate the blue hue in your system, drink only blue solarised water from morning until bedtime. No tea or coffee, and green or mint teas only.

Use the blue Star Breath technique.

Day 6 – indigo Saturday

Wear only indigo clothes. Eat only indigo foods, plus green foods and the green and white soup. Eat protein in the form of oysters, white fish, caviar. Plus the clear water. Indigo solarised water can be taken from midday onwards until bedtime. No tea or coffee, and green or mint teas only.

Use the indigo Star Breath technique.

Day 7 – purple Sunday

Wear only purple or violet clothes. Eat only purple foods – plums, aubergines – plus green foods and the green and white soup. Eat protein in the form of fish and tofu. Plus the clear water and green or mint teas. Purple solarised water can be taken from midday onwards until retiring.

Use the purple Star Breath technique.

Don't forget to use the Star Breath meditation with the colour of the day.

The Colour Catalogue

*The psychology and language
of colour*

The language of colour

Brilliant!
There's a bright spark
Red rag to a bull
As red as a beetroot
Feeling blue
Once in a blue moon
In a brown study
Green with envy
A greenhorn
Salad days
Yellow-livered coward
Tickled pink
In the pink
Golden handshake
The Golden Age
As good as gold
Clouds with silver linings
Little white lies
Things are looking black
Put it in black and white
In a purple patch

- The stepping stones of colour.
- Colour yourself healthy, wealthy and wise.
- Colour is information. It sends signals.
- We can use colour to navigate the uncharted territory of ourselves.
- Colour is a code. It is read and understood throughout the animal kingdom and insect world.
- Colour is a problem solver.
- Colour is white light broken up.
- Colour is an intimate part of our being.
- Colour can bring order out of chaos.
- Colour points the way.
- Colour is living energy.
- A colour a day keeps the doctor away.

This section is an ABC of colour. Most of us have not been fortunate enough to be taught the language of colour as we were the alphabet and words at school. However, I know that the alphabet and words of colour can be learned. Of course, what you create with them is where the art of colour enters.

I have never seen anything like this section attempted in any colour book I have read. It is not a scientific analysis. What I have tried to do is to use words to create a wash of colour that will draw you into its magic.

Each colour has many facets. In fact, this section could as well be called 'The Many Faces of Colour'. Each colour in the spectrum has its own level of consciousness. As we go up the spectrum (taking red as the base colour), we leave the slower, denser vibrations of the material world (reds, oranges and yellows) and enter the finer, quicker vibrations of the mental and spiritual world (blues, indigos and purples). Green is the balancer, the divider between the two. It is made up of aspects of each side – yellow from the magnetic end and blue from the electrical end.

Blue is often thought of as being more 'spiritual' than red. This is a misunderstanding. The person who climbs to the top of Mount Everest has just as much spirituality as the priest in his church. All colours are spiritual. Each colour has a different way of manifesting its spirituality.

Every colour is strong, but each colour's strength differs from that of any other colour. Each colour has a different wavelength and frequency. Like television, each colour has its own channel. Only when the appropriate wavelength is tuned into the correct station can a clear picture appear. It's called healing or synchronisation. Blue's strength lies in the fact that where red, for instance, will charge in without a second thought, blue will consider the situation first. Blue looks before it leaps. The green channel will tell you about one aspect of yourself, the yellows about another – furthermore there are no commercials!

The point of working with colour is to seek out the positive aspects of each hue and aim towards the desired effects. You need not be afraid of or shun the negative or lower aspects of a colour, they are there to help you. The dark aspects show what needs to be attended to. The aim is to achieve a balance. Colour is liberation from black and white thinking.

Each colour section is arranged in the same way giving the principal colour's polarity, positive and negative keywords, general qualities and characteristics, how the colour connects to parts of the body, the uses of each colour and information about its different shades. Every colour also has a story. The first section on Brilliance is presented differently from the colours *because it is* the light from which all the colours come.

So be aware that your introduction to the colours will be the experience of feeling pure sunlight physically on your body, but on another level you will be tapping into the Universal Intelligence. It may be the closest you can get consciously to feeling cosmic force. The Brilliance is transparent and you may ask, 'How can I see anything if there is nothing?' The clear message from the invisible light is, 'In everything there is nothing and in nothing there is everything.'

You can just dip into a section to get an instant aspect of a colour. So, for instance, if you see someone wearing red shoes at a party you could go to the red section and get some red meanings as to what that person was saying about themselves. You could also check the body sections of the clown process (page 145) to see what the feet symbolise. Or you could try to guess the colour of the person sitting next to you. Or check what colour dominates your wardrobe at the moment. Understanding the language of colour can save you money. You could avoid buying that red jersey you absolutely *must* have, by buying a red light bulb and flooding yourself with its light instead. Although the skin will absorb very little of the vibration from the clothes we are wearing, we will be affected psychologically by them. Colours in our wardrobe reflect who we are. If your wardrobe is full of 'off' colours for you, empty it and start again. If life is stagnant, get rid of your old clothes.

It is possible to discover your physical and/or psychological history through the language of colour. One way to do this is to chart your favourite clothes for as far back as you can remember. From sixteen to twenty-one my wardrobe was full of blue. In my case (it won't be the same for everyone), the negative aspect of blue indicated that I was in a deep rut in my home environment during this time. The positive side was that I was looking for a way out.

The other way to approach the colour sections is to read them from beginning to end to get a total experience. The language of colour is a tool of self-discovery. If you feel drawn to a particular colour it probably indicates a deep need within you for something which that colour vibration holds within itself. Light is the whole; the colours it diffracts into are individual personalities and each speaks with an individual voice. Each colour has its own voice and point of view. There are blue statements and green statements, orange statements and black statements. This is the language of colour that you need to listen for – with your eyes! No colour is 'right'; no colour is 'wrong'. By learning the language of colour, you will be able to appreciate the entire spectrum of meanings and information the intelligence of Light is giving you through colour. Just reading the pages on each colour in this way is to open yourself to the influence of that vibration. Think of the colours you are reading. Suspend the critical faculty and let the colour permeate your being. Colours reflect to you fine inner echoes of yourself. Close your eyes and visualise the colour you are about to read. Swamp yourself with this colour and breathe it in. Open your eyes, and as you start to read keep the colour in mind so that it stays with you while you read that section.

This would be the way for the colour student or anyone serious about achieving an overall understanding. By reading a section you not only gain knowledge but will actually begin to experience a feel for the colour. Try smelling and tasting the colour. While reading red you will become red, while reading blue you will become blue. This will enable you to recognise the subtle and obvious differences on a psychic level. Remember, colour is experienced directly. It does not have to pass through the intellect and be scrutinised to see if it makes 'sense'. It is an immediate experience.

So, let your imagination wander into the land of colour. You will find that the sun paints its lessons on all things.

Brilliance

'When you can see the nothing then you can see everything
because nothing is something.'
The Art of Happy Living, *His Holiness, Param Sant*

Transparency
Brilliance is the supreme ray;
the Ray of rays.
Brilliance brings all rays of colour
into perfect balance.
The number of Brilliance is thirteen,
which shows that it has the power
to pierce through death
and resurrection
Many people mistake Brilliance for white.
Brilliance is the light from whence
all other colours spring,
and return into.
Light is the whole.
The colours it diffracts into are individual personalities
and each speaks with an individual voice.
Brilliance is not
actually a colour: it is the Original Light.
It is not an Earthly colour: it is Cosmic Light.

Brilliance represents the Universal Intelligence.
It has the purity of the trinity of Love,
Power and Wisdom.
Brilliance's positivity is simplicity in all things.
It is just being.
Brilliance's negativity is when we feel lost, invisible or in a
vacuum.
The complications of life.
Our local source of Brilliance is the sun.
Without Brilliance there is no vision.
Brilliance cuts directly through to the truth.
It clears the way for necessary actions.
Brilliance clears any cloudiness in a person or colour.
When we say that a person is brilliant.
we are acknowledging his or her
purity of vision and action.
Brilliance is transparent; it can see
right through you.
Brilliance adds lustre and beauty.
Look at the light coming from a diamond.
Add a touch of Brilliance to any colour
and it will become brighter.
Brilliance is the hard light that exposes all
flaws, shams and corruptions.
Brilliance is the reality of life.
Brilliance contains the essence of all qualities,
both positive and negative, sparkling
in the brilliance of
perfection.
Light
sustains our life.
Our expression of someone
being 'off-colour' is literally true.
We can see that the light in the person

is muddied or diluted in some way.
If the light disappears entirely,
the person is dead.
No Light, no Life.
When I want to restore a person's vibrancy,
I will put them in pure light.
Or simply tell them to go for a walk in the sunlight.
Two weeks on a Greek island
being flooded with the sun's Brilliance
does wonders for body,
soul and psyche.
A little touch of Brilliance goes a long way.
And we will go a long way for a
touch of Brilliance.
Light is a nutrient and it is vital and necessary for
perfect health.
Brilliance is there in the wisdom that brings the
Universe into a state of perfection.
It is pure Spirit and Conscious Perfection.
Brilliance
is the Clear Light
that *The Tibetan Book of The Dead*
advises the newly dead person to head for . . .
Brilliance is the Clear Light
at the end of the tunnel
that people report from
their near-death
experiences.

Brilliance and parts of the body

Brilliance is the aura which is life's energy force that reflects
the inner light of a person. This luminous glow can be seen
around the outside of a person's body by sensitives or
psychics.

The use of brilliance

We use Brilliance when we want to bring about change, major or minor, in our lives. Brilliance allows us to wipe the slate clean, to start again, to recycle. The shaft of pure light gives us a new page to write on. The old blots have gone, together with all tears and regrets. We can turn that page and move on in a new direction. The new direction can mean a change of house, career, partner, even to emigrate. Or instead of outer change, we may notice subtle shifts within us so that people say: 'I don't know you any more. You seem different.'

Healing makes use of the Pure Light. Many colour therapists consider Brilliance to be a 'cure-all'. Brilliance has the power to modify any condition. Exposing the body to a spectrum bulb in a darkened room can begin the process of clearing things up, clearing allergies, chronic conditions – whatever offends you.

Florence Nightingale understood the value of light. Sunlight is a great antiseptic. When a room has no sunlight, it becomes filled with bacteria and has a musty, putrid smell. The first thing she did upon entering any sickroom was to have the windows flung open to let the sunlight in. The Italians have a saying 'Where the sun does not enter the doctor does.' You can do the same with any room that you feel needs clearing: just visualise sending out a flash of Brilliance to whip round the room.

Try a sunshine bath. No more than ten minutes' sunbathing in the sun is so beneficial and so pleasing as the sun gently kisses your skin. Sunlight is forever renewing growth. Eskimos seem to survive very well in their winter wonderland, being exposed as they are to an equal balance of colour all the time. A snow-flake shower is, after all, a fall of brilliance. The Ice Wall process given on pages 162–4 uses the power of Brilliance to clear away old blocks.

I used Brilliance techniques such as these to break through my reticence. That is, my fear of giving out what I saw and knew. By flooding myself with the Clear Light, I was able to wash away all the fear and prejudice of using my psychic perception for other people that my childhood and social environment had instilled in me.

Light absorption process

Seers have always used the Brilliance to foretell the future, whether gazing in a pond or a glass of clear water or a crystal ball. People often ask me how do I get answers for questions. I reply 'Use the light and it will tell you'. To be able to see anything, you have to gaze into clear space. A simple process to help you start your development along these lines is an absorption of the light technique. It is a fascinating way of training you to become sensitive to the Brilliance. The method is to look into an electric light bulb and stare without blinking for thirty seconds (not longer than this) and immediately close your eyes and see where it leads you. Just look at the pictures, colours and shapes, etc., that have come through. This is a very positive way to start training your psychic powers by working with the light. A word of caution – *do not* use this process by looking into the sun, use only an electric light bulb.

The Brilliance positivity is simplicity in all things. The Brilliance is transparent and you may say 'How can I see anything if there is nothing?'

I had an experience while I was attending a course. My mind wandered from the lecture and I felt myself gazing at the tree tops through the window. Immediately I was on a rainbow and whizzing through space along it. My heart leapt. I was going to find out what was at the end of it. After travelling at great speed, I came to a halt and knew I was there. I looked and I went into total shock as I couldn't see *anything*. As I was being engulfed in disappointment, I was jolted and could feel myself spiralling down when a voice said, 'Look again'. I did and what I saw was space. It was the most beautiful thing I've ever seen. I only saw it for a few moments, but it was totally packed with activity and translucent colours of all kinds, all mingling with each other but at the same time transparent. I have never seen on Earth such vibrancy and aliveness. The next thing I knew I was clinging onto the back of someone's chair in front of me. I was breathing heavily and gasping, and as I looked around I saw a few pairs of curious eyes staring at me with a look of 'What on earth is she doing?' The clear message that had come to me from this experience of the invisible light is that 'In everything there is nothing and in nothing there is everything.'

To clear and recharge yourself at any time, simply visualise a cascade of sparks of Clear Light pouring down through the top of your head and into your body and on out through your feet. Jewellery gives us a constant reminder of our source in the perfection of Brilliance every time it sparkles and flashes light. Men and women have always adorned themselves with precious stones. Every time a flash of light sparkles from a jewel it reflects its owner's own relationship to that Original Light that is the essence of each of us.

Brilliance can be seen in a spark, in a burst of high thoughts, in a moment of ecstatic understanding. As a spark, I am part of the whole, a tiny, tiny part of the Brilliance that fills all levels and planes of consciousness with purity and justice. As a spark, I am part of the whole, hence the saying: 'There's a bright spark'. We are all sparks buzzing about, coming originally from the Brilliance and the first point of light. A spark represents perfection and we are perfect just as we are.

Nature's way of having us take in Brilliance is by providing us with streams of pure, clear water. Water is liquid Brilliance; bathing in a waterfall is the equivalent of standing under a cascade of Clear Light. My father knew this when he healed with water. Baptism can thus be understood as healing the separation between us as sparks from our home in the Pure Light. Drinking clear, clean water especially during fasting is a practical application of this cleansing aspect of Brilliance – see the water solarisation technique on pages 183–4.

Brilliance puts a crystal cloak over the Earth as the dew every morning.

The clear message from the Brilliance is 'In everything there is nothing, in nothing there is everything.' Brilliance's transparency can see right through.

A BRILLIANT STORY
The Healing Light

One day when I was feeling low and very unwell – I had a severe attack of mouth ulcers – I suddenly got this urge to unplug the phone and lock the door – which I did. I would take half an hour's rest. It was a compulsion. I had to go to bed.

I lay on the bed and started to relax ... I remember thinking: 'I'm going to have half an hour and when I wake up, I am going to be well. I do it for other people, why can't I do it for myself?'

I lay on my bed and consciously allowed myself to open up. The thought came that sleep would make me better. I let myself drift into the blackness. There was a jolt and I was suddenly in another state of consciousness – not awake, my eyes weren't open. I was flat on my back, my arms and legs straight. A great energy was streaming through me. It was as though my fingers and toes were plugged into electric sockets. The energy was the Clear Light, and it was surging through me. I felt plugged in and switched on. My body was vibrating.

I was quite scared at first. I thought of moving but a voice said, 'stay still'. I knew it would be unwise to move.

I was experiencing the power of the Clear Light. Of Brilliance. It is a perfection state, a state of wisdom and understanding. It gradually receded, and after a few minutes, I opened my eyes and woke up. Then I realised that I had been receiving a healing. I moved my mouth – no pain, the ulcers had entirely gone.

Through this experience, I had a personal understanding of Brilliance as the Healer. Brilliance makes whole, makes perfect again. Brilliance, I realised, was there in its wisdom to maintain the Universe in its state of perfection.

I was left in no doubt that Brilliance is the Supreme Ray. That Brilliance maintains the perfection of existence within the limitless boundaries of the Universe. It can enter any part of the universe effortlessly. It could even come right down to me to heal my ulcers. In that experience, I saw that I was a spark of that perfection, of that Universal Consciousness.

By using Brilliance we can keep a balance between the world of restricting form that is the material Universe and the formless Spirit that it emerges from and returns to. A balance between creativity and science, between the heart and the head.

'(Man) is an object which views the light while in light.'
His Holiness, Param Sant

White

'Cleanliness is, indeed, next to Godliness.'
John Wesley

White polarity:
Virgin – Sullied
Positive white keywords:
Pristine; completeness; all-giving; openness;
unity; lightness; multitudinous;
exposes the hidden and untrue.
Negative white keywords:
Isolation; sterility; stark; frustration,
starchiness; prissiness
boring.
White is a denser Brilliance.
White is what is left when
the Brilliance has been taken out.
White has a density.
If you hold up a transparent crystal,
you are looking at clear Brilliance.
If you hold up a white cotton sheet you
cannot see through it.
White has just stepped down from the
ultimate purity of Brilliance.

Thus the Bride wears white at her wedding
to symbolise purity in human form.
White contains an equal balance of all the
colours of the spectrum.
White is a combination of all the colours.
As such, white can show both a need to,
and be used to, combine.
Hold a handful of snow up to the sunlight and you
will see minute flashes of all the colours
of the rainbow sparkling away.
White's fundamental quality is equality.
All colours are equal in white.
In mythology white is a symbol of unity.
White seeks to be fair.
The Judge's white wig on his head
symbolises his impartiality.
White is the spiritual saver.
All will be well when white is about.
The white knight
on his charger rescuing maidens ...
The doctor in his white coat rescuing
us from Dragon Death ...
Hopalong Cassidy wearing his
white hat and riding his white horse ...
White shows up in the nick of time.
White encourages.
It helps bring us through times
of stress and strain.
White is next to the cosmic intelligence of Brilliance.
So, while white has faith, it is not blind faith.
White derives its faith from reason;
even when it cannot explain
the reason for its faith.
As the French philosopher Blaise Pascal put it:

'The heart has reasons that Reason knows not of.'
This is the faith of the missionary who
continues his divine mission
against all odds, and
even unto death.
White is expansive and creative.
It is the perfectly fair field against
which all things may manifest.
White is efficient.
It is clean and unruffled.
However, too much white causes frustration,
isolation and a feeling
of emptiness.
All white decor creates an atmosphere of sterility.
It provides little stimulation for the senses.
Hospital rooms should never be all white.
It may get rid of the germs,
but it also bleaches
the human psyche.
For the same reason, a baby's nursery
should never be just white.
The pastel tints of cream, lavender and
peach make the occupant feel
relaxed and welcome.
White reflects all the colours, therefore
it is the coolest colour.
The empty pot is the lightest.
So tropical countries favour white for clothes
and the interiors of houses.
White is the perfection of all colours.
It is completeness; yet it holds nothing in.
White is the great opener.
White clears things up and out.
Because white is closer to the Brilliance than

any other colour, it has the ability
to bring hidden things
out into the open.
'Pure as the driven snow.'
There is something inhuman about white.
The two whitest places on Earth are
the North and South Poles.
Their pristine purity is legendary.
But they are also the coldest and least
populated places on Earth.
White is so close to Brilliance that human life is unable to
survive there comfortably or for long.
And yet human beings are drawn to
return to it again and again
for its purifying power.
White conjures up hope.
White is tranquillity
because everything is equal in white.
So white is the symbol of peace.
When someone raises the white flag of surrender, the
fighting ceases.
The first step towards living in that harmony
that the colours symbolise living
side by side in peace, is white.

White and parts of the body

Each gland has a specific colour of its own (listed in each
colour section) but the collective functioning of the endocrine system is governed by white. White also represents the
eyeball. The colour that is reflected from the eye white is
used in diagnosing physical health.

White keeps the skin supple and moist. A masseuse in a
Turkish bath in a tropical country noticed a marked
difference in the quality of the skin of women who wore

mainly white clothes. Their skin was softer and moister. The skin protected mainly by dark clothes was more wrinkled and pinched.

The use of white

White is primarily a carrier: it is host to every colour and favours none. When it is used for healing, it is most beneficial when combined with another colour or colours. The reason for this is that every part, organ and gland in the body has its own individual colour. White, containing as it does equal amounts of all the colours, does not discriminate between one organ and another. This is an aspect of white's fairness and impartiality. White does not address itself to the particular colour need of a specific part of the body. Trying to heal with white alone is like eating a small amount of every known vegetable when what you really need is carrots.

It's good to wear white when the sky is cloudy. Our vitality drops on a dull, grey day. White can be used as a tonic to top up all the colours in our body's system. Wearing a white dressing gown is a simple way of swathing yourself in the healing white light. Use white to restore anything that's faded.

It can also be used in interior decoration which is like giving your room an antiseptic wash. White sheds light in dark corners.

I sometimes use white with clients when they are having trouble opening up. If I see that a client is rigid or frozen, or has a one-track mind in some area, I will often use white so that they get a small amount of each colour. White helps them become less dense. It begins the process of cracking the ice; the blinkers begin to come off. In some cases it is as though the person has become snow-blind, in which case white acts homoeopathically and opens the person to the whole spectrum of colours.

White can be taken more directly by using the Star Breath technique (see pages 158–61).

White foods

The white food par excellence is sea food. But also white radish, parsnips, Jerusalem artichokes, lychees, garlic, onions, cauliflowers, leeks, celery, potatoes, rice, tofu, egg white and rare white truffles.

A WHITE STORY
The Little White Lie

Sally was forty-seven and still a virgin. She was also very attractive.

She arrived for her first session wearing a white cashmere coat, white blouse and a navy blue skirt. She told me later that she loved white and wore it all the time.

Sally said that her problem was that she had fallen in love with a man at the office. She talked about this for some time. Then I asked her when she had begun going out with this man.

'Oh, I've never been out with him. He doesn't know,' she said. It turned out that this was a recurring pattern in Sally's life. There had been other men who had never known either. She had come to me seeking a technique for letting this one 'know that I like him'.

In the third session I broached the subject of Sally's father. The navy blue skirt had given me the clue that there might be something profoundly wrong with the structure of her relationship with her father. It turned out that Daddy, in fact, was even now trying to get her to go back and live with Mummy and himself in the family home. She also confirmed that there had been sexual abuse as a child, but it was 'all right now' and Daddy was an absolute darling. Whatever she wanted he would make sure she got! And he had never minded her having a male friend.

'Daddy has never had any objections to me having a boyfriend. In fact, he shared them! On my first date ever, he ran out into the street and pulled the young man in by his coat tails to have a cup of tea ... As soon as I met a possible boyfriend, Daddy would insist that I brought him home so that they could make him one of the family.'

Sally had, in fact, got as far as the bedroom several times. However, she told me that when it came to making love she 'just could not do it'. Finally, I was able to get her to see that she was still remaining faithful to Daddy. For Sally, sex with anyone else was adultery. The tears streamed down her face as she had an emotional understanding of the truth of what had been happening: her little child's heart belonged to Daddy. The pain was in realising that it had been stolen, not given willingly as a mature woman gives.

The white coat that Sally had been wearing in her first visit was like a flag signalling her frustration and the sterility in her life. Even so it took her several sessions to uncover Daddy's little white lie: he wasn't at all in favour of Sally having boyfriends and his love was dependent upon her remaining true to him.

From the inner light of rest,
all colours are rising in white hope.

Red

The Red Badge of Courage
Title of a novel by Stephen Crane

Red polarity:
Growth – Destruction
Positive red keywords:
Leader; tenacious; fights for the right; creative;
dynamic; perseverance; gratitude; multiply;
reviver; cheerfulness;
pioneer.
Negative red keywords:
Physical violence; lustful; intolerant; cruel; destructive;
warmonger; bullying; stubborn;
graceless; shame;
guilt.
Red is the spirit of physical life.
Red is the colour of the base chakra – the will to live.
Red is power.
Red is fire and drive.
Red is adrenalin and willpower.
Red is going to get its own way, come what may.
Red is tireless energy.
Red likes to keep moving.

Red is the survival of the fittest.
The red signal of pain is Mother Nature's warning.
Red is territorial.
Our evolution on Earth would have been
impossible without red.
Red likes to be first.
Red is the liberator.
Red is courage.
Red's motto is: 'We will overcome'.
Red alerts you to danger.
Red is passionate.
It believes with a passion.
It loves or hates passionately.
When red defends, it defends to the end.
Red is exciting.
Red is quickening.
When the mother feels the baby quickening in her
womb for the first time, this is a red action
on the baby's part.
Red is practical.
Red believes in action.
It hates to hang about.
A red statement is: keep moving.
Even when it speaks, red speaks towards action.
Red gets the blood up.
It is essential for the circulation of the blood.
'The body is the blood thereof' – *Leviticus*.
Red has a burning desire to get somewhere.
Red can tend to act without thinking.
Red rag to a bull in a china shop.
Red is the pioneer.
Red pushes forward against all odds.
Red is the irritant that keeps you moving
no matter what.

Red helps break the patterns of rigidity
that block our path.
Red puts you in the hot seat; it spurs you to get up and go
for it.
Red stimulates you and gives you the willpower
to continue.
Red recycles and renews the enthusiasm
to carry on.
Red is the conqueror
Red is power, and the power to direct
the power.
Red was the colour of the Roman legions.
Rome's law and order marched across the world
behind its legions.
Red is sexuality.
Red is the mating energy and governs sexual relationships.
Red is amoral – all it is concerned with is
reproduction, continuing
the species.
In its sexual aspect,
Red rather than religion is the opium of the people.
Red has sex out of true sexual desire.
Red at its best will give a
satisfying and passionate lovelife.
Red at its worst becomes bestial and perverse.
Red is goodwill to all men.
Red is a great rescuer.
It is the cavalry that charges in at the last minute
to save the wagon train.
Red believes in survival – self-preservation.
Red seeks to make up for all that is missing.
Red has a desire for justice.
But it is practical and will ensure that
justice is seen to be done.

If necessary, red will go to war to achieve justice.
The 'Just War'.
Red brooks no obstacles.
Red is the reformer.
Red is the fiery force; it burns away impurities.
Red redeems.
Red can mean war.
Red is a great fighter.
Red must win.
If necessary, it will go to war to attain supremacy.
War can be red's answer to an argument.
Particularly if red tempers are lost –
which easily can happen.
Red takes no prisoners when
its back is to the wall.
Red can become dictatorship.
Too much red can make the will
over-ride the heart.
Red can be the warmonger with no
compassion for the loss of lives.
Red at its worst is the tyrant and
brutal murderer.
Red at its best is a fine leader of men.
Red is a born strategist.
Red is a lover of mankind and
will sacrifice itself for its
fellow human beings.
The soldier who sacrifices his life for his comrades.
Red is the ego.
It loves having the red carpet rolled out.
Red has no hesitation in going public.
Red ego in its positive form is the belief
in the worth and value
of the self.

Red ego in its negative form is the inflated ego;
the bullfrog.
This red seeks advancement no matter
who or what suffers.
Frustrated, red ego can become extremely harsh,
rebellious and destructive.
Negative red can be pushy,
domineering and defiant.
If someone tramples on your toes to advance
themselves, they are likely to be working
in the negative red.
Red is insecure.
Negative red is shame and guilt.
Shame means 'I am faulty'.
Guilt is 'I am never going to be good enough'.
Red can be a show-off.
Red is a very noisy colour.
It wants your attention.
Science has shown the human
body to be a noisy vehicle.
Where the circulation is
good, the blood literally
sings through
the veins.
If hindered by disease, it becomes
a sad, sullen murmur.
Red is a good colour to help someone face death.
It removes fear.
Red overcomes lingering and reluctance
to move on.
'Time to move on' is the red view of dying!
Red encourages the person to see death as the
door to the new adventure.
Beautiful red flowers for the dying person

to gaze upon would be ideal.
Red has a burning desire to probe deeper.
It is the explorer with the energy of the
life force at its command.
Red is zest, energy and drive.
Red builds great things from very little.
It is the constructor.
From little acorns great oak trees grow.

Red and parts of the body

Red in the body refers primarily to the genitals and reproductive organs. The glands in the body connected to the red are the gonads and the ovaries. Red also prompts the release of adrenalin into the bloodstream when there is danger, aggression or pain – thus its connection to fighting or fear. The blood and circulation are a focus of red. Muscles, which give the power to act, are also a red concern. Primitives regard red as the life force.

We even go red in the face when embarrassed. Red also controls the body's temperature. The lack of red in the blood causes anaemia. Anaemia emotionally signifies the loss of power somewhere in our lives so the blood becomes weak. Another area of red focus in the body is the genitals – the reproductive organs. Sexuality gives us the experience that there is 'other'. Sex has the power to enable us to become one, albeit briefly. At the moment of orgasm, a couple split into infinity. Nobody knows where they actually go at the moment of climax. Sex is a spiritual unity through physicality. Nature has used red to attract the opposite sex and ensure the continuation of the species by reproduction. Red is nature's sexual signal. We flush when sexually aroused, our lips go redder – which is why women wear lipstick!

Irregularities in the red will show up as a clogging of the circulation or irregularities in the blood supply, blood clots, furring up of the arteries, heart attacks, strokes, anaemia, etc. Also sexual and reproductive malfunctions.

The use of red

Red's polar opposites are growth and destruction. Neither is 'bad' nor 'good' of itself. It depends on the situation and use. For instance, red's destructive quality could be used to destroy that which is holding up growth. One could see all illness as the attempt to destroy that which is holding up growth, including the body itself. Thus, death is part of the order of life's continuity.

Red is a good detoxifier. Red gets rid of rubbish from your life and psyche as well as your body and removes negativity.

The muscles, the power to act, are also a red concern. Red will ease stiff muscles and joints. This is particularly true in the legs and feet, which come under the root chakra that red governs. Red is useful in cases of paralysis – particularly combined with physiotherapy. It stimulates.

Red is good for anyone who catches colds or chills easily. The chill is the blue – fifth chakra, the throat – which the red warms. Red controls the body's thermostat. Use to counter-act hypothermia. But remember, red can cauterise inflammatory conditions but if used incorrectly, it can irritate and aggravate all inflammatory conditions.

If someone is stressed and irritated, avoid red.

Use red in a positive manner to focus your mind and go with the flow of this colour. Red has thrust that drives you on to achieve greater things. So if you have something you are dreading doing, or are feeling low or sluggish in any way, just apply a little red for support and quickening. To do this, you could wear it or put it about your house in the form of flowers, furnishings, decorations, red lighting, etc.

For absorbing red, or any tint or tone of red, use the Star

Breath (pages 158–61), Rainbow Tonic (pages 157–8) and Solarised Water (pages 183–4) techniques. Do not use dark red, maroon or russet red with these techniques. Because these colours have black in them, the red will be inhibited.

Just as red lifts, so red encourages shy people to come out of themselves. If you are somewhat backward in coming forward, add red to your wardrobe. It doesn't have to be much – like all the strong colours, a little goes a long way. It is a good colour to start a business with as it puts you in the hot seat. Red roots you, it brings your efforts to fruition.

Red is for danger – warning! **Do not use red lighting (chromatherapy) above the waist for heart conditions**. Professional colour advice should be taken for any heart problem.

Red foods

Another way to incorporate the red vibration into the system is to just eat it. Red meats, red peppers, red-skinned apples, tomatoes, radishes, red lettuce, beetroot, red currants, raspberries, strawberries, watermelon and red spices.

THE MANY MOODS OF RED
The shades and tints

There are many tones of red. They all have red's basic qualities, but modified by whether they are a higher or lower octave to red itself. Red is the most dominant colour of the spectrum.

Scarlet, crimson and flame are all higher octaves of red. In general, they are the most active of the reds. After these, brown begins to enter the red and we have the shades russet red and maroon. These are more subdued and cautious. Then come the pinks. There are a host of pinks. They are worthy of a book of their own. I can only sketch in a few here: cerise, rose, soft salmon pink, orchid and pink. The pinks are, as their hues suggest, much lighter and gentler than red. One obvious characteristic of the pinks is that they are extremely feminine. The last of the red hues here is magenta, red plus blue.

It is important to be aware that the tints of any colour are considered to have positive characteristics. However, it is my experience that an overload of a tint can have negative side-effects. For instance, an overload of pink can produce the dominance of red again. On the other hand, the shades of any colour are considered negative. But the negative can be useful! It tells us what we need to look at.

The difference between a shade and a tint is that a shade has *black* mixed with a colour, whereas a tint has *white* mixed with a colour. The shades are darker and the tints are paler.

Scarlet – love of life, enthusiasm

- Scarlet is the highest octave of red.
- Scarlet red seems brighter and richer than the pure red.
- Scarlet is red with bells on.
- Inspirational entrepreneurs, speculators and originators work with scarlet in their make-up.
- Scarlet-driven people not only climb the mountain, they must climb the highest mountain.
- Scarlet has a strong sexual drive.

Good examples: Edmund Hillary (first climber of Mount Everest); St Joan of Arc; Boadicea.

Problem: More inner conflict than most; lack of scruples; fanaticism.

Crimson – peaceful strength, determination, liberation

- Crimson is also a high vibration of red.
- Crimson has a touch of blue in it.

- For the crimson, life is to be loved, not overcome.
- It does not believe in struggle – it believes in going and getting what it wants.
- Nothing daunts crimson.
- Concerned with the individual rather than the mass, crimson is extremely forthright. It believes in speaking up.

Good examples: Moses; Duke of Edinburgh.
Problem: Impulsiveness and unpredictability.

Flame – cauterising

- Flame is a medium octave of red
- It has licks of bright orangey yellow in it.
- Flame generates new life by force or fury: 'I burn through'.
- It cleanses by fire.
- Great zeal.
- Flame red keeps going no matter what.
- Probes deeply.
- Guts and fire.
- Begins a new spiritual phase in life, the whole being having been regenerated.

Good examples: The Avenging Angel; Winston Churchill.
Problem: Too hot in its zeal; leaves the ground scorched and barren.

Russet red – knowledge with wisdom

- A mixture of brown and red.
- Russet red has a quiet confidence, an enthusiasm that does not draw attention to itself.

Good examples: The backroom boys; the inventor; Jane Austen.
Problem: Lack of direction; impractical in worldly matters.

Maroon – deep concern, breaking through

- Maroon has the will and power from the red plus the deep thought and quiet understanding of the touch of brown.
- Maroon shows endurance and overcoming of a time of great sorrow. It is saying 'We have come through' and it is now prepared to turn the painful experience into useful learning.

Good examples: The Beirut hostages.

Problem: Can stay stuck in old sorrow; feeling persecuted.

Dark red – the vampire, the lecher

- Dark red can become inert through hopelessness. They believe in the old Arab saying 'God gives nuts to monkeys with no teeth', so 'what's the use' is the familiar cry of the dark red.
- Dark red can be over-indulgent on all levels, particularly in sex.
- The ambitious bully.
- Dark red can be brutally cruel, even murderous when thwarted. One aspect of dark red is that it can be cruel to animals.
- This colour is connected to congealed blood.

Good examples: Pimps; sex molesters.

Problem: Stagnancy.

THE PINKS

Cerise – womanhood; ripeness; friendliness

I have noticed that whenever I wear cerise, a blend of rich rose and lilac colours, everyone comes and talks to me and becomes very open, warm and friendly.

- Cerise is the woman who has got it and knows she's got it . . . and everybody else knows she knows she's got it.

- The woman in cerise separates the men from the boys.
- Men don't wear cerise – at least not on the outside.

Good examples: Sophia Loren; Joan Collins.

Problem: Too available; flaunting oneself.

Rose pink – spiritual beauty; universal love; compassion

Rose pink prepares the way for all treatments. It relaxes the physical body and helps us to receive. It prepares us to respond.

- The essence of rose pink is full bloom; maturity.
- A very feminine colour, rose pink states that a woman is ready to have what a mature woman wants. When a man is in his rose pink stage he is 'distinguished'. Not a colour for the teenage girls.
- Rose pink has healing beauty. Beauty that expands, that extends beyond the physical.
- It is the in-breath of the breathing cycle.
- Rose pink is a constant affection, faithful, forgiving: the true love that we are all searching for.
- It is fulfilment of potential.
- The colour of support when betrayed or let down.

Good examples: The Madonna. Barbara Cartland.

Problem: Immaturity and blind trust; impetuousness.

Soft salmon pink – love of humanity

- Salmon is a combination of pink and brown.
- The pink side of it is very concerned with love, and the brown puts a curb on the pink.
- Salmon is high affection – affection without ulterior motive.
- It is sensible love.
- The man in the salmon pink shirt is saying: 'I am sensual'. But a lovelife with him may be on ration ... salmon pink doesn't give it away easily.

Good examples: The bachelor at fifty; the sexual tease.
Problem: Over-cautious in love – 'I'm not ready yet' syndrome.

Orchid – individual; rare; unconventional

- This lovely lavender-blue-pink indicates the one and only. Individuality. Thus, the significance of giving an orchid to one's beloved.
- If you are drawn to orchid, it shows that you are doing things your way and that it's a 'one-off' course. But the negative side is you must take care not to become waxen and immobile.
- No one else does anything quite the same as an orchid pink person. They are rare, just like the orchid. You stumble upon it in a jungle and just one word describes the tint: paradise.

Good examples: Jesus Christ; Mother Teresa.
Problem: Too exotic; an all-or-nothing attitude; stiff.

Pink – hope; receptive; intimate

- Pink is red with white.
- Pink is romantic.
- Pink is affection.
- Pink is kindness.
- The paler it goes the wider, higher and deeper the love extends.
- Pale pink is highly sensitive. It carries the promise of fulfilment. It says, 'We'll meet again'.
- Pink warmth melts and dissolves.
- Pink could show that it's reassessment time.
- Pink is comforting; it mollifies.
- Pink is the colour of the peace-offering; pour pink on troubled waters.
- It's great in a crisis: if you're being mugged, Think Pink!

- Use pink after a person has been assaulted in any way, or if they have had part of their body removed in an operation.
- Pink gets rid of hang-ups.
- Pink is like a magnet, it draws and attracts.
- A newborn baby is born in the pink and, as it develops into adulthood, it becomes a naughty nude.
- A young person drawn to pink can be showing that they are now ready to develop their full potential.
- Wonderful to use in the mid-life crisis when the dissolution of old patterns and reassessment is imperative.
- An older woman drawn to pale pink can be showing that she has unrealistic expectations – she may be still waiting for her unrealised girlhood dreams to come true. Pink will help her to reassess. Time to let old ideas and issues melt and dissolve away.
- A mature man working well with pink will use it as the gentle stimulant to achieve his aims.
- Too much pink shows a need for protection.
- Pink aids the digestion: affection is nourishment.
- Baby pink says: 'I need nurturing and taking care of.'
- Pink is universal harmony. Unconditional love.
- When we are truly in the pink, we can fall in love again, again, and again.
- It is said 'To love another person is to see the face of God.'

Good examples: Marilyn Monroe; Mum and Dad.

Problem: Too much pink indicates a desire to dominate and control; becoming too soft and silly; too emotional.

Magenta – the great improver

- Magenta is red and violet.
- Magenta wields the invisible energies of infra-red and ultra-violet.

- It has a beneficial effect on the entire endocrine system.
- Magenta is nature's antibiotic colour. It can also help clear fungus conditions and warts.
- Magenta's powers are not fully seen.
- It is spiritually uplifting.
- In the presence of magenta, one feels better.
- The Magenta person seems to know what you are thinking and feeling.
- Magenta creates achievement through love.
- It takes the tender approach to getting what it wants.
- Magenta abolished slavery.
- It helps recovery from sorrow with dignity rather than distraught expressions of emotion.
- Magenta is the arbiter; it stands between antagonists and attempts to bring them to peace and a common understanding.
- Magenta knows that 'I can have my way, but not always. I must let others have their way, also.'
- It accepts that 'things are the way they are' without being a victim.
- However, magenta is often caught in the past-was-better-than-the-present syndrome.
- Magenta is the greatest organiser of them all.

Good examples: The United Nations; Abraham Lincoln.
Problem: Indifference and disinterest; impersonal; slapdash.

A RED STORY
'Guilt is the gift that keeps on giving'
Old Jewish proverb

Helena was a very vivacious woman in her early thirties. She was good-looking and kept her body slim and taut through regular fasting and exercise. Helena was a very together lady who lived abroad mostly.

I met Helena when she was a participant in a course I was giving. We had just finished the Healing Rainbow experience (see page 347) which is a guided visualisation followed by seven questions which you answer according to what you have just seen. One by one each person can share their experience with the rest of the group who then assess what the person's experience showed.

Helena took her place in the hot seat. She was full of the joys as we started to work with her experience. We all looked at the colour clues that had emerged for her, and one of the colours that sprang out from the rest was red. Red flowers had appeared around the section of the process that represented the last few years. I knew that could signify her zest for life which indeed she had, when I was told to stay with the red as there was more. I then knew that her key to red was guilt.

'Helena, what are you feeling guilty about?' I asked. No reply. I continued softly, 'This guilt is ruining your life.'

'Yes, it is,' she replied, the smile fading from her face. I then told her she could not move on until she had dealt with this, and finally her story emerged. Apparently, while living overseas, she had met a beautiful man – an Olympic-standard athlete. He was a great swimmer and diver. They planned to marry. One day at a party held around a swimming pool, several guests had asked him to dive in and show them how he did it. He didn't want to but after a while Helena persuaded him to dive for her. He did and broke his neck. He has been paralysed. Helena had the guilt feeling it was her fault and also felt that she couldn't marry him now that he was confined to a wheelchair, which put her into deep guilt. Guilt is the loss of the magnificence of being human. The belief is that by being human 'I'm terrible'. Time has helped them both to come to an understanding of this tragedy. Helena has had to work through and let go of the guilt of dark red so that both of them have been able to work through their pain and tragedy to personal healing.

AND A PINK BLANCMANGE STORY

After the war when I was about seven or eight we had school dinners. We had had them for years and they were not the cause of much excitement. But this particular day a rumour shot round that we were going to have a very special treat. We were going to have 'blancmange'.

None of us kids knew what 'blancmange' was exactly – we had never had it before – we just knew it was something special. So we sat there after our normal lunch and waited for this amazing 'something' to come in.

The cooks brought in big metal trays and placed them down on the serving tables. Two hundred children looked at what was on them ... and not one of us got up to collect our share. The big grey trays were covered in the brightest, strongest, most vivid pink mass of wobbly stuff. No one had seen anything like it before. It was made with water, gelatine and bright pink powder – no milk available to soften the colour. It *glowed*! We had never seen any such colour in our lives, far less food that colour.

There was a silence in the room in which the drop of the proverbial pin would have sounded like silver thunder. We had been used to very dull-coloured foods. After six years of wartime experience, we kids knew that life was grey. Even foods were grey: dishwater vegetables, grey fish, dingy substitute-milk powder puddings. Now, if it had been nice grey mashed potatoes on the trays we would have galloped to the table. This we knew. Grey blancmange – we would even have understood that. But *pink*! Very suspect. We knew you didn't *eat* anything that colour, not if you wanted to live that is. Pink's vibrations of comfort and unconditional love just had not existed for us up to this point in our short lives.

'While we are talking, envious time is fleeing:
Seize the day, put no trust in the future.'
Quintus Horatius Flaccus (Roman poet)

Orange

'The more things change, the more things stay the same.'
Alphonse Karr, French writer

Orange polarity:
Activity – Laziness
Positive orange keywords:
Strength; flamboyance; warm-hearted; generous;
tolerant; excitement; untiring energy;
fearlessness; sociable; just; freedom.
Negative orange keywords:
Over-proud; pessimistic; overbearing; exhibitionistic;
sponging; self-indulgent; misleading.
Orange is assimilation.
Orange is our gut instincts.
Orange is the colour of the sacral chakra.
The ability to be free; to explore.
Orange is focused on the physical necessities of life.
Orange is taking for oneself what is needed.
Orange draws towards itself.
Orange is self-reliance.
Orange is practical knowledge.
Orange is physical intuition.
Sportsmen relate to the colour orange.

In its role of assimilator, orange is
our intestinal laboratory.
It tests, and accepts
or rejects.
Orange has impetus.
Orange is extremely persistent.
But where red bullies, orange bides its time.
Orange is the great rejuvenator.
Orange is optimistic.
Orange is positive.
Orange is genial.
It is tolerant and warm-hearted.
Orange is friendship.
It is the life and soul of the party.
Orange is the practical joker.
Orange has mental vigour.
It unfolds the mentality.
Orange has the power to illuminate
through creative activity.
Orange loves to cook.
Orange sees the whole . . . and develops the whole.
It is very constructive.
It's the get-it-together-again colour.
Orange is expansion.
It breaks down barriers.
Orange shatters.
It breaks open blocks which causes
a freeing action.
The breakthrough of orange frees the spirit.
Orange broadens life and is very purposeful.
Orange moves on.
It is the colour of divorce!
Whatever red is, orange will be, but without
the aggressive force.

Orange has strength,
but not the physical strength of the red.
Orange strength is more subtle.
It stimulates gently.
Orange believes in the community.
It likes social gatherings.
It loves to use the telephone.
Orange is party time.
Orange likes
to work in groups.
It has pride in the achievement
of the group rather than in
its own success.
Negative orange has an inferiority complex.
Orange is benign.
Orange shows you that things are not so bad after all.
An overload of orange can restrict
and make rigid.
Orange can eradicate.
It brings up the energy of past events that
need to be assimilated so that they can be completed.
Orange will not let sleeping dogs lie.
Orange is the most rejected colour in our time.
An aversion to orange could point to
deep feelings of outrage at having been cruelly treated.
An aversion to orange
could indicate someone holding
themselves back socially – particularly in
business gatherings, office parties, meetings, etc.
Orange gives the courage to face the consequences.
It accepts what is – and then changes it.
Orange also knows that change for change's sake
is not necessarily change for the better.
Change is not always visible.

Orange and parts of the body

Orange is the area of the lower back and lower intestines, the abdomen and the kidneys. It governs the adrenal glands which are attached to the kidneys (although the actual colour of the adrenal glands is yellow).

The use of orange

If the orange is out of harmony, the next chakra above, the solar plexus (yellow), and the root chakra (red) below, will not be functioning fully.

These three are the magnetic colours and are concerned with the action of earthing, making life happen for us in a real way rather than just imagining. If their balance is dislocated, we will not be able to put into practice any course of action we may think or feel able to do. Physically, orange links us to our intuition which enables us to be masters of our own destiny. This feeling is gut instinct.

Orange is *the* colour for dealing with grief, bereavement and loss.

When a person feels that they have been deeply outraged – 'It isn't fair' – orange will bring them up through the shock. Orange can reveal hidden shock and help to expel it.

A person's dislike of, or resistance to, orange can indicate a fear of moving forward in life because they cannot bury the past. Orange can show that there is a hidden grief that cannot be faced. Often this shows up when a person has lost a loved one and feels that it wasn't fair. Orange is the colour to give the strength to face and break such blocks. Orange pulls you through. Orange will always stir up dormant conditions. It provokes change.

Orange removes inhibitions and psychological paralysis. This fear of moving forward is related to the assimilation aspect of orange: the person has not been able to accept the past. The profound meaning of this is that *all* experiences, no matter how painful, have nutrients that we need. Orange helps us to absorb life's nutrients in the same way that our intestines draw off the nutrients of goodness from the food we eat. Refusing to take one's experiences into oneself stops the flow of the life processes. This is often the basis of anorexia. Orange helps to increase the appetite.

Orange is connected to our gut instincts and feelings. When a person is working with the orange aspect within their system, they intuitively know what to do or what is right, regardless of the intellect.

Orange is useful for any intestinal disorders or bowel disturbances, also for kidney complaints. Orange also clears away any mucus or catarrh that may be in the system.

Orange can help in cases of mental breakdown, depression, rape, divorce, and accidents. Autistic children respond to orange. It helps develop abilities that are blocked. Orange can bring in freedom from any emotional paralysis.

Orange can aid with asthma and bronchitis; epilepsy and mental disorders; rheumatism; torn ligaments and broken bones. Orange binds together. It can be applied directly to limbs and muscles in physiotherapy.

Orange is useful during the menopause particularly combined with yellow. It is also an aid for infertility problems. It balances the hormones (for both sexes).

Orange can also reveal hidden phobias. Orange gives support to fight against unknown fears: 'I'm frightened all the time, but I don't know what I'm frightened of.'

To restore equilibrium we need to introduce orange into our system through wearing orange clothes; bathing in orange light; using the Star Breath (pages 158–61), the Rainbow Tonic (pages 157–8) and Water Solarisation (pages 183–4) techniques.

Orange foods

Include oranges, carrots, tangerines, apricots, peaches, swedes and sweet potato. Have a bowl of oranges on the table as a focal point.

Orange is the doctor in the garden – the marigold and its essence, calendula. Orange blossom essence is known as Nerali. It relaxes. This is why orange blossom was a traditional head-dress for brides. It was believed to encourage the bridge to be 'laid back' on her wedding night! Nerali is also good for insomnia. Like the colour orange, it promotes a feeling of well-being which allows you to go to sleep.

Orange is the great reaper, it produces the fruits of the Earth – the harvest of the sun.

THE MANY MOODS OF ORANGE
The shades and tints

Dark orange – opportunist

- A person relating to the dark orange shade always feels thwarted.
- Ambition is the downfall of dark orange; it tries too hard. The person who assures you they can when you know they can't – the 'Do-it-yourself bodger'.
- Dark orange usually has a chip on its shoulder.
- A dark orange person might say, 'I'm going to be a brain surgeon' and have one 'O' level at twenty-five.
- Dark orange can do more harm than good.
- Dark orange is a compulsive hoarder.

Good examples: The addicted gambler; Inspector Clousseau in *The Pink Panther* films.
Problem: Not understanding the reality of one's potential (or lack of potential); the outcast.

Amber – progressive; supportive strength

- Amber removes doubt and suspicion and gives confidence.
- An amber personality is very willing and tries anything.
- Amber helps one trust one's own judgement.
- Give amber to a Doubting Thomas.
- It is the colour of mental vigour. Amber promotes quiet activity.
- Amber sheds light in dark places. It is the colour of realisations and understandings.

Good examples: Live Aid Concert's organiser, Bob Geldof; Martin Luther King.

Problem: Jack of all trades, master of none; restlessness.

Peach – gentle persuasion

- All the qualities of orange without the impetus.
- Peach walks instead of runs.
- Peach encourages communication.
- Peach is a flow of movement: in-breathing/out-breathing in perfect harmony.
- Peach creates a safe environment for confronting difficult or painful memories.
- Good when working with teenagers who have no idea of what they are going to go with their lives.
- Peach assures us that things will be all right. Peach has impeccable manners.
- Orange makes us jump: peach tells us whether or not it is safe to jump.
- Peach is cautious.
- Peach can find that it is giving out love for no return.

Good examples: Mother and elders; the perfect gentleman.

Problem: Evading; putting off until tomorrow; giving out love for no return.

AN ORANGE DAY
The ups and downs

I woke up looking forward to a very busy day – I was to
be a guest lecturer at the Mind, Body and Spirit Exhibition in London. 'I'll need energy today,' I thought, so I
busied myself applying orange herbal oil to the soles of
my feet, the sides of my legs, and around my lower back.
While I was doing this, I noticed feelings of sadness
passing through my body; they were real pangs. There
was no apparent reason for these feelings so I kept
pushing them away.

By 9 am I was dressed. I had chosen peach and orange
as my colour scheme for the day. I was about to leave the
house when the phone rang. An ex-wife of a friend whom
I had not spoken to for some years said, 'I have bad news
for you. Our dear friend, Robert Patterson, has died.'

I was shocked, I had known him for twenty years. I sat
quietly. The car was waiting outside to take me to the
exhibition. Collapse was out of the question, I had to go.
I spent the day using up all the orange I could get. Using
the Star Breath technique, I kept myself bathed in orange.
The loss had destroyed my appetite, but I made myself eat
orange foods.

During the day, several incidents connected to orange
occurred. One was when I was giving a woman a colour
and palm reading. When I asked her how much love she
was giving out for no return – a peach question – she had
a deep and painful realisation that this pattern had been
running through her life as far back as she could
remember. Her constant refrain had been, 'It's not fair'.
Which is a classic orange belief.

A second incident: I had been working with a married
couple. The husband was impotent and believed he was

infertile. They were in great distress. I suggested orange and gold. Some time later, I happened to bump into a highly respected man in the colour world in one of the exhibition halls. I asked him what he would suggest for a man who was impotent. He paused. 'I would think half an hour in bed with Marilyn Monroe should put him right,' he said as he moved away. He said this so seriously that I had thanked him earnestly before realising that he had been, in fact, working on the joker side of orange.

Then, just before I left the exhibition, I saw a group of people standing in the hall. I knew one of them and had a gut feeling that I should join the group. A momentary shyness made me hesitate, but I plucked up courage and went over. Within fifteen minutes, I had been offered a trip to Brazil to lecture the following year.

When I got home, I looked back through the day and saw how subtly dominated by orange it had been. Awakening full of optimism is an orange start. This continued into my preparation with orange for energy. The telephone call – communication comes under the orange ray, as does grief and bereavement. I had also felt – like the woman I was to counsel a few hours later – that it wasn't fair that Robert should die so young. Pulling myself together for the purpose of the day – orange is both motivation and the discipline necessary to achieve purpose. Using orange to encourage appetite. Witnessing the woman releasing her negative orange belief. My genial friend with his joke. The negative orange of my hesitation in a social situation. This countered by orange at its best breaking down the barriers of my shyness – which led to the orange of business through social contacts.

When you review your day in terms of colour, you may find that, like mine, it spans the positive and negative limits of one colour. On the other hand, some days will be clearly multi-coloured. These are the days when you don't know whether you are coming (the red end of the spectrum) or going (the blues).

> 'I make the most of all that comes
> And the least of all that goes.'
> *The Philosopher*, *Sara Teasdale*

Brown

'And you all know security is mortal's chiefest enemy.'
Macbeth, Shakespeare

Brown polarity:
Birth – Decay
Positive brown keywords:
Solidity; reliability; moderation; sober;
self-assurance; caring;
confidentiality; loyalty; informality.
Negative brown keywords:
Self-doubt; withdrawal; depression;
frustration; discontentment; barren;
obsession with decay.
Brown is absorption and solidarity.
Brown is reliable
Brown is down-to-earth.
Brown is capable; it copes.
Brown is as safe as houses.
Brown is the salt of the Earth.
Brown is the colour of conservation.
Brown is calm, and calming.
It is the colour of moderation.
Above all, brown is stable.

Not too much excitement about brown, perhaps,
but much plain common sense.
Brown loves to be safe.
Being safe is brown's passion.
Brown will have a modest manner.
Brown goes about life with a quiet assurance.
There is still a touch of red in brown.
Brown is a slow but sure developer.
Brown holds its own counsel.
Brown has to understand before acting.
It doesn't take chances.
When the euphoria is rising and the castles
are building up high in the sky,
Brown sobers things up.
Brown is the deep thinker.
Brown understands that
there is more to life than one can see.
The person working with the brown vibration
is deeply studious.
Brown is the swot.
Brown is single-minded.
It will often be found deep in thought.
Brown can fathom out where things went wrong.
It has depths of concentration.
Brown contemplates with quiet confidence.
Brown is four-square.
If you are
seeking to employ someone
reliable, loyal and steady, and a candidate
turns up for the interview wearing a
brown suit, they may be your man.
Or woman.
Brown will not let you down.
It will follow your instructions to the letter.

Those under the influence of brown are capable
of being your right-hand man.
Or woman.
Brown will hold the fort while you are away
without plotting to get your position,
and relinquish it gladly when
you come back.
Brown does not desire the spotlight.
It is quite happy for someone else
to be in command.
Brown likes to work behind the scenes.
To be found off stage waiting in the wings.
It believes in the final curtain.
Brown believes everything leaves and ends.
Brown marks time.
Brown is often waiting for the right moment –
which never comes.
If you need a pushy salesman,
brown is not your man.
Brown hates any kind of
bartering or wheeler-dealing.
Working for an established institution
suits brown best.
Brown is the colour of striving hard to do well.
Brown's personal life can be quite hard.
It often experiences life as
a bit of a struggle.
Brown can become so absorbed in work
that it becomes single-minded to an extreme.
This can lead brown to withdraw within.
Brown can doubt itself
and feels unsettled.
There is often suffering from painful conditions and
problems that

brown feels nobody can solve.
This can also make brown retreat inwards.
Depression sets in and Brown becomes
consumed with an obsession with
the decay of life.
Brown doesn't like travel much.
It prefers to stay in its own environment.
Brown feels safer, when it, and the world
around it, is settled
and steady.
Brown dislikes having the order of its life disrupted.
As Goldilocks found when she visited the
Three Brown Bears.
Brown is the colour of the earth.
Most animals are brown.
Brown can hide its light under a bushel.
Brown has hidden potential.
Brown
is the seed in
the husk, afraid to
burst forth and pop up
from below the ground so that
it can develop its full potential.
Brown needs the nurturing of
the pinks and the gold
to develop
trust.
Brown likes to appear solid.
It can even refuse to allow itself to be ill as this
is a sign of weakness.
Brown can have a deep fear of the process of decay.
Thus, it is unable to allow the breakdown phase
of the growth–decay cycle
to take place.

Brown desperately seeks consistency.
Brown has it all – potentially.
But brown also has a fear of life itself – and of
claiming its full due.
This is the costly side of brown's quietness, reliability
and willingness to take a back seat.
Out of its own yearning to be safe, brown
tries to make others safe.
But this safety is often bought at the expense of life.
Brown tries to make life safe by keeping it
still and static.
Dogged by fear, with an irresistible need to be safe
and secure, rather than go out and face
whatever seems to be the problem,
brown tends to
dig in.
Which may be why
brown is the colour of hibernation.

Brown and parts of the body

Brown is not associated with any specific parts or organs in the body but nature makes us aware of its symbolic significance by our elimination process from the bowel.

The use of brown

Being close to the Earth, brown can give a cloak of security and earthy support during times of storm and stress. Brown is soothing; it allowed us to snuggle up to the bosom of Mother Nature. Man is dependent upon life that comes from the soil.

Wearing brown introduces the virtues of the colour into our system as does having it in our environment in any form of interior decoration.

The Star Breath technique can be used with brown (see

pages 158–61). An extremely therapeutic way of working with brown is to do the garden! Particularly turning the earth over and planting.

Brown foods

Nuts, mushrooms, brown rice, many of the herbs and species such as nutmeg and ground ginger, sultanas, dates, cereals – any food, skin or shell that has the brown Mother Earth colour.

People suffering from negative brown need to stand up and show their true colours once in a while. Cinderella is the perfect example of this. She had to leave the cinders and get to the ball to find her Prince! Positive brown has the secret of renewal. Browns know that it will return. Recycling.

THE MANY MOODS OF BROWN
The shades and tints

Dark brown – self-centred; biased

- A dark brown personality sometimes can't see the wood for the trees.
- Dark brown cares nothing for anyone else's opinion. As such, it is associated with selfishness of all kinds.
- It is the person who cuts back on a company's finances; it reduces.
- Dark brown also has a fear of being buried alive.
- However, there is a positive side to dark brown: history. History is 'dead and buried'. This is the black in dark brown. It is all our yesterdays. But it is also a guide – we can consider our current situation in the light of history. History is brown: it is the manure that fertilises and prepares the ground. Dark brown is the Earth's oven.

There is always something cooking. Dark brown also knows it has the secret of rebirthing. Everything reverts back to the soil. Sick soil, diseased people.

Good example: The doctor of the soil – the farmer.

Problem: Stasis; unable to break down. Earthquake.

Rich russet brown – quiet assurance; intuition; concentration

- Things move a little faster with rich russet brown.
- This is the basis colour of most orders of monks and monasteries. Contrary to the modern image of them, monks were hard-working, earthy people. They personify the 'activity with restraint' of russet brown.
- This colour has an intuitive trust in the order of things on Earth.

Good example: St Francis.

Problem: Superstition; secretiveness.

Browny pink – stable affection

- The brown element in browny pink will give single-mindedness, while the pink gives love and affection.
- This is summed up in the traditional Italian Mama who is Mother Earth to her family, but doesn't concern herself with the outside world. She takes care of her own patch of ground.

Good examples: The 'housewife'; marriage bureaux.

Problem: Selfishness; blinkered.

Stone – intuition; clairvoyance

- Stone is a tint of brown.
- It is less heavy than brown, so the aspect of the intuition is clearer.
- Stone shuns glamour and glory.

- It is the medium or clairvoyant working away quietly at home.
- Stone is the people of any country. Without the backbone of the ordinary person, there would be nothing for the politicians to parade in front of.
- Stone is the audience.

Good examples: The dedicated nurse; healers of all kinds.
Problem: Dormouse-ism; no personal identity.

Cream – softness

- Cream softens.
- As every interior decorator knows, cream softens a space – but at the same time enlivens it.
- Cream brings an expansion of the space.
- The spartan quality of the white is warmed by the brown.
- The white provides a safety net that allows you to face the decay side of the recycling process that is an aspect of brown.
- Cream compensates and helps one appreciate what is.
- Cream gives the reassurance that whatever happens, you will be all right.

Good examples: The psychiatrist; the sincere friend.
Problem: Slackness; dribbling; senility.

Coppery bronze – flowingness; balance

- Coppery bronze encourages quick passage with the minimum of disruption. All secret services relate to this colour.
- Copper pans and pots are prized for their ability to allow the heat through with the minimum of resistance, and also to spread the heat evenly. The great warmer-upper.
- It absorbs – as in copper bracelets worn on the wrist against rheumatism.

- It takes away acidity; it is nature's sweetener, it pours oil on troubled waters.
- Coppery bronze represents quiet but effective activity.
- It has several colours in it, which is why it has multiple aspects.
- Coppery bronze activates the understanding that allows personal change to take place without dramatic displays.

Good example: Marriage guidance counsellor.
Problem: Playing the 'fixer'.

A BROWN STORY
Baby knows best

A participant in a course I was giving told us a story about her son. When he was a baby, Brian would never settle to go to sleep at night. His parents tried everything, even resorting to alcohol.

One night when he was shouting and bouncing up and down in his cot as usual, the mother noticed that the top cover of his cot was orange. She wondered if this had anything to do with her son's behaviour. On an impulse, she took it off and, as she couldn't afford to buy a new one, the next day dyed it brown.

The first night she put it on her son's cot he lay down and straight away went to sleep. There was no more trouble in getting Brian to go to sleep at night after that. Social orange had been put to rest, the party was over. Mother, they say, knows best. Not only did this mother know best, she acted upon her intuition and in so doing was being a natural healer.

'A bird in the hand is worth two in the bush.'
Anonymous

Yellow

'All things be ready if our minds be so.'
Henry V, Shakespeare

Yellow Polarity:
Wisdom – Stupidity
Positive yellow keywords:
Quickness; mental agility; joy; originality;
rigour; expansion; perceptive; tolerant;
probing; honesty; justice;
confident.
Negative yellow keywords:
Analytical; acidic; sarcastic; treacherous; absent-minded;
ignorant; intellectually rigid; chatterbox;
critical; impatient; judgemental; contract; vague; folly.
Yellow is the mind.
Yellow is control through the intellect.
Yellow is known as the ray of mental wisdom.
Yellow is the colour of the solar plexus chakra.
The ability to get things in life; self-worth.
Yellow is the colour of the scientist.
Yellow is inquisitive.
It unravels and reveals.
Yellow leaves no stone unturned.

Yellow helps think through difficulties
and will explore all avenues.
Yellow is the brightest colour of the spectrum.
Yellow is flexible and adaptable.
Yellow is penetrating.
Yellow is the concentration
that gets through to the
core of the matter.
Yellow desires to learn.
Yellow is smart.
Yellow is clarity of thought.
Yellow has agility of the mind.
Yellow is precise.
Yellow is very clear about life . . .
and still optimistic.
Yellow is continually striving.
It does not give in.
Yellow is very much the twentieth century.
Yellow is information.
Yellow is civilisation.
Yellow
focuses attention.
It looks for fresh angles.
Yellow loves new ideas.
Yellow is modern; it has the latest.
Yellow has no hesitation.
It decides quickly, and quickly acts.
Yellow does not suffer fools gladly.
Yellow smartens the reflexes.
Yellow is the Great Communicator.
It has no shortage of words.
Yellow is the journalist.
Yellow is the unifier.
It connects.

One of yellow's favourite pastimes is networking.
Whether on a jungle drum or the telephone.
When something is revealed to yellow,
it immediately thinks of editing it
for the public rather than
feeling it for
itself.
Gossip is yellow.
The physical level of yellow communication is
the media – press, radio, TV,
entertainment.
The quiz master and the whizz kid are yellow.
On a higher level the yellow mode is telepathy.
Yellow is mental intuition.
Yellow possesses an agility of mind.
Yellow is the orator.
Yellow goes to battle
in the name of justice and the law.
But with words and intellect, not the red sword.
The negative yellow of this trait appears in
the gangster and criminal.
Yellow is the censor.
Yellow can become a mental dictator.
Negative yellow is the fanatic who believes he has a
mission to do or set right regardless.
Hitler is the twentieth century's
dreadful example
of this
aspect of negative yellow.
Negative yellow can be a coward.
Yellow is the executive level of business.
It is the ability to get things done.
Yellow is diplomatic.
It has self-control, style and sophistication.

Yellow likes to be well known.
Yellow loves admiration as much as red and orange.
It is just more subtle – the pen is
mightier than the sword.
Furthermore, those who use the pen live longer –
and Yellow is *very* interested
in longevity.
Yellow can misuse words cleverly.
Instead of being an instrument of perception,
words then generate a fog of evasion.
Yellow does not like being cornered.
It responds to pressure
with evasiveness.
Yellow can be the first to
see and the last to
understand.
Yellow has the ability to make money,
usually by mental talent.
Keeping it may be more difficult.
Yellow thinks big when it comes to money.
Yellow despises pettiness.
Yellow is broadminded.
Yellow has no personal boundaries – just the same as love.
Yellow is freedom and joy, laughter and fun.
Yellow intends to keep its sunny side up.
Yellow's emphasis on reason can make it seem lacking in
compassion, even callous.
Yellow's reason is that it must add up.
The antidote is to allow intuition to
over-ride the head.
Yellow separates the human from the animal.
Yellow invented the fence.
This penned in the animals so that
they no longer had to be tracked down in the

forest.
So yellow discovered domestication,
which is the cornerstone of
civilisation.
Yellow is not fat – it keeps one in trim.
Yellow is so quick that excess has
no time to gather.
Yellow is sunny and willing –
unless upset, when it can become
acid and sharp-tongued.
Yellow is
connected to the seat of
self-confidence and self-esteem in the body.
Butterflies in the stomach are yellow.
'Am I good enough? Will they like me?'
are yellow questions.
Yellow is not good at pacing itself;
one thing leads to another.
Yellow finds it difficult to rest.
Which makes it prone to nervous strain and breakdown.
Overuse of the intellect can lead
to mental collapse.
Yellow resists recognising physical limitation.
Chronic fatigue and lethargy are common
complaints of yellow.
Yellow's inability to stop can lead either to the stars –
Or to death by sheer exhaustion.
Yellow
needs to get its priorities right.
Sacrificing sense for cleverness is neither.
Yellow does not like pie in the sky thinking. It prefers
reality.
Yellow is: As you think so you become.
It knows that one's own mind

is the master of life.
Yellow always broadcasts a feeling of well-being.
People feel good around those under the
yellow ray . . . which is exactly what
the yellow ray people
would wish.

'Earnest men, never think in vain, though their thoughts
may be errors.'
Bulwer

Yellow and parts of the body

The yellow gland is the pancreas. Yellow is the solar plexus, the pancreas, liver, gall bladder, spleen and middle stomach. The liver is known as the seat of anger where our emotional upsets and hurts are stored. Yellow is also the skin, nervous system and digestive system.

The use of yellow

The solar plexus is the junction that absorbs all the emotions. Emotional upset will register here. Anything that adversely affects the solar plexus, or reveals itself by changes in that area, is likely to benefit from yellow. Yellow is very good for removing cellulite.

Yellow's cleansing means healing. Yellow is the Great Eliminator. It cleans and removes waste from the system. On the physical level, it gets rid of toxins, and promotes the flow of gastric juices. Elimination is the law of life. Faulty elimination is the cause of the beginning of most disease. Yellow tones and cleanses the system. It relieves constipation. Constipation represents holding on to the past.

On the mental level, yellow clears out woolliness and negative thinking. On the emotional level, it clears out low self-esteem. The 'Pardon me for living' syndrome.

Yellow moves things out. Yellow purifies and increases the vital fluid in the body. Yellow is the great weight watcher. It balances the weight.

Yellow stimulates the lymphatic system. It also helps with menopausal flushes, menstrual difficulties and hormone problems. Some people have found that it helps relieve the symptoms associated with diabetes, rheumatism and anorexia and it clears the mind to help correct forgetfulness.

Yellow is also a brilliant colour to use with depressives. It is particularly useful for fears and phobias. Yellow clears congestion/catarrh. It is good for ear problems. Also skin rashes and abrasions.

Yellow is a very good colour in counselling. It tracks down deep-rooted reasons why your disease occurred. If I flood a client with yellow, it usually brings to the surface what the person needs to look at. It gets them talking.

Yellow helps transform 'I can't' into 'I can'. Also shyness and feelings of 'I'm not good enough'. Try using laughter therapy, the best yellow tonic there is. Laughter is internal aerobics; it massages your organs. Give your organs a treat. The best medication is a merry heart.

One of the best and most obvious ways of taking in yellow is to take a sun bath by sitting in the sunlight. If there is no sun, wear yellow clothing, sit in yellow lighting. Introduce yellow flowers, interior decorations and furnishings into your surroundings to get this, the brightest colour of all the spectrum, into your life.

Yellow may also be absorbed through the Star Breath (pages 158–61), the Rainbow Tonic (pages 157–8) and Solarised Water (pages 183–4) techniques.

A special technique for clearing the mind with yellow is given in the Sunshower technique (pages 167–9). This process is also good for a negative trait of yellow which is fear of responsibility which can hinder you – particularly in relationships.

Yellow foods

Fresh ginger, golden syrup, honeydew melon, yellow plums, peppers and cherries, lemons, grapefruit, bananas, pineapple, sweetcorn, avocado, star fruit, squash and buckwheat.

THE MANY MOODS OF YELLOW
The shades and tints

Dark yellow – low self-worth; misplaced confidence

- Dark yellow is a vandal, crafty, treacherous and argumentative.
- This colour exemplifies the truth of: you can fester in the mind just as you can in the body.
- Dark yellow loves to set off rumours.
- Dark yellow is the deceiver.
- It is very cynical, regarding honour as stupidity.
- Those under its influence always expect the worst of others, and themselves.
- When these traits deteriorate even further, we enter the realm of the darker mustard yellow shades.
- Dark yellow is also extremely analytical (the yellow ability to think gone wild).
- Also nagging, complaining and caustic.
- It can be mentally deficient.
- Dark yellow usually feels very unhappy and unloved.
- Eating disorders are connected to this colour.

Good examples: Persecutors; extortionists.
Problem: Life's a problem; joylessness.

Yellow red – rashness; mercy

- The red in this colour creates rashness and impetuosity.
- The justice of yellow may turn into a harsh justice. Then the punishment is likely to far outweigh the crime. Transportation to the colonies for stealing a loaf of bread, for instance, is yellow red.
- The father who cuts off the erring daughter without a penny.
- This colour is the liquidator.
- Organised crime comes under this shade.
- Yellow red has the saving factor of purging, and also the wonderful healing power of unexpected mercy.

Good examples: The hunter; the iron hand.
Problem: Rigidity. Insane authoritarianism.

Lemon yellow – practical

- The lemon yellow statement is: 'No one can pull the wool over my eyes.'
- This can get those under its influence a reputation for having an acid tongue and being critical and suspicious.
- Lemon yellow's comments can sting. On the other hand, its astuteness can be an asset.
- Lemon yellow, because of its make-up of yellow and green, is good for clearing up skin disorders. It acts as an antiseptic for spots and boils.
- Someone drawn to this colour maybe suffering from an acid system. The best antidote is to rectify the diet.
- The good thing about lemon yellows is that they cut through the verbiage and red tape. A great solver of problems is the lemon yellow.
- They have to say what is – which is not always the most popular line. Their disposition can be a bit sour.

Good examples: Margaret Thatcher; the Trade Unionist's motto: 'One out, all out.'

Problem: Can appear uncaring; the misfit.

Citrine yellow – fickleness

- Citrine yellow's emotions will be unstable and often conflicting.
- If under too much pressure, citrine yellows are inclined to run away from responsibilities.
- Those under this hue must watch out for deceitfulness, both in regard to themselves and others. The citrine character can be a bit abrasive.
- Animosity is a trait of Citrine. It will harbour past grudges.
- It can be foolish about money. And probably gave rise to the proverb: 'A fool and his money are soon parted'.
- But citrine yellow can be discriminating, a quality whose positive aspect is fairness.
- This colour can be a tease.

Good example: The coquette.
Problem: Resentment towards others. The malingerer.

Primrose yellow – hyper-spirituality

- Though this colour is associated with great spirituality, it can be an erratic devotion.
- Unreliable is a primrose yellow word.
- It likes others to take over so it can step aside.
- Primrose yellow likes to opt out so that it can spend its time pursuing the unanswerable question: questioning loops that gets you nowhere. When the answer to the question, 'Who made me?' is given as 'God', this colour comes back with, 'Mummy, who made God?'
- A positive aspect: this colour stretches one's mind, inciting it to question a world beyond the obvious. Pale yellow likes to search for an understanding into what is happening.

- Primrose yellow relates to childhood genius.
- Primrose yellow's gift to the intellectual world is the wisdom of the child.

Good examples: The well-intended prophet; St Bernadette of Lourdes; Shirley Temple.
Problem: The false guru; getting nowhere fast; the LSD trip.

A YELLOW STORY
Mr Moneybags

Yellow likes to play games. Those under its influence are very good at them, particularly word games. Someone using this quicksilver yellow talent can defend themselves against taking anything seriously, even their own suffering. It's the Mercury Syndrome: 'I won't be pinned down'.

The client came into my consulting room and slapped his money purse onto the spare chair with á whack. We started working and after about fifteen minutes I could see that we were into the Mercury Syndrome. I stopped him talking and said, 'I'm not playing anymore.'

He blinked.

'You're suffering from the slippery Mercury Syndrome.'

He didn't know what I meant, but he stayed in the yellow: 'Is that serious?' He grinned, ready for the next round.

'You think you can talk your way out of anything.'

'Let's talk about that.' Hard to beat yellow for self-assurance – sometimes better spelt c.o.n.c.e.i.t.

'I'm not going to play ball anymore,' I said. 'I'm putting my racket down.'

He looked at me directly – another of Mercury's laws:

when all else fails, be sincere. 'Why not?'

'Because we can do this until the cows come home, going round and round in circles getting nowhere. It's a waste of my time, and yours. Just when we start to get somewhere, you "slide off".'

He sat there, thinking, looking away into some distance within himself. Five minutes went by. Then he took a deep breath and turned to face me. Tears started to roll down his cheeks as he said quietly, 'Okay, I'm ready. Let's start.'

He had made a brave decision to stop playing games. Because of his fear of being caught he could never take part in life fully. As a child the pain of standing still and experiencing what was happening to him would have been too great to bear. He learned to keep on the move to avoid the suffering of his situation. As a child, being 'nailed down' as he put it represented death, so he had countered by ceaselessly darting about, making himself a slippery customer – particularly verbally.

Now he had decided to stand still and face himself and his feelings.

Instead of using yellow's mental agility to avoid what was happening to him, which was necessary in the past he was going to use yellow's ability to penetrate deeply and to face the truth and life.

'Thinking is the talking of the soul with itself.'
Plato

Gold

'Silence from some is worth more than gold from others.'
Charlton Heston in The Ten Commandments

Gold Polarity
Trust – Deception
Positive gold keywords:
Generosity; experience; maturity; wisdom;
vitality; endless supply; future;
forgiveness; triumphant; access.
Negative gold keywords:
Suspicion; paranoia; crabbedness; limitation;
pessimistic; misfit; under-achiever;
disgrace; conceit.
Gold is purity.
Gold does not seek, it has already found.
Gold is glorious.
Gold expands the power of love.
Gold represents the ultimate victory.
It transforms victimised to victorious.
Gold is the benefactor.
Gold is extremely gracious.
Gold asks that we trust and dare.
Gold's gift is released by trust.

When you trust you can surrender.
And when you surrender,
you can receive.
Gold has no victims nor does it victimise
Gold comes through.
It comes up trumps whatever the odds.
Gold gives access.
It gives entry to the unobtainable.
Gold is well-heeled.
Gold has always been
associated with money and material wealth.
Gold indicates treasure, the chest of golden coins,
the pawnbroker's three gold balls.
But gold's wealth has a higher meaning: gold
is soul experience.
The gold that
we pluck from the Earth
is crystallised
sunlight.
Gold has access to knowledge.
And – most important – to knowledge of the self.
Gold is purely itself.
Parasites are unable to hang on to it.
The saint's golden halo signifies that he has
become spiritually mature.
Gold is wisdom.
Gold can pass on wisdom.
It knows wisdom is given to be handed on to
others, not to be hoarded
for oneself.
Gold is nobody's fool.
Or, as Gordon Gekko puts it in the movie, *Wall Street*:
'A fool and his money are lucky to get together
in the first place.'

Gold absorbs facts quickly.
It is the wise counseller.
Gold is the rain of giving.
Negative gold is the drought of hoarding.
Gold is forgiveness.
The past wrongs we hoard and do not forgive
continue to hurt us.
Forgiveness means letting yourself off the hook.
The martyr's golden halo signifies that he
has moved beyond his trials.
Gold is an old colour, the colour of experience.
Gold is
the colour of autumn.
The young green bud does not fall off the tree
It has to experience the seasons first.
It is letting go the past out of a
deeper understanding.
Gold knows that nature is not always perfect
It experiments continuously.
Gold is the colour of old memory.
Gold means that one has paid one's dues.
Gold radiates vitality and abundance for all.
Gold knows that there is an endless supply.
Whatever seems to have been lost
or taken away
will return.
Gold is the colour of Easter and resurrection.
Gold's beauty wins against all odds.
When lovers glow with the confidence of their love,
the aspect of gold is strong within them.
Gold eventually brings joy and happiness.
It is the sign of completion.
'And they lived happily ever after'
is a golden ending . . .

and beginning.
Gold does not require belief.
When one is working centred in gold,
one just knows.
'I don't have to believe, I just know.'
Carl Jung on being asked about his belief in God.
Gold is the sign of achievement
in the realms of
wisdom and understanding.
Victors can bask in the glory of gold.
The leader
always has a golden streak.
There is a depth of self-knowledge in the
leader that puts him
in front.
The humility of a child
and the wisdom of a true king unite
in the power of gold.
Gold is our following our leader in the trust that
he or she will lead us to liberation.
Gold not only has wisdom,
it knows how to put wisdom into action, as well.
Gold knows what is needed in life.
It has a need to share this
knowledge with
mankind.
Gold believes in the unification of all nations.
It also believes in inherited wealth.
Gold is the solution that yellow is looking for.
Gold in its negativity trusts no one.
This indicates an original mistrust of mother.
Negative gold has a fear of success,
a fear of failure,
a fear of being here at all.

Negative gold has unreal expectations –
fool's gold.
'All that glisters is not gold,'
as Don Quixote (Cervantes' character) has it.
Negative gold will blow its own trumpet.
Yellow's conceit is trivial compared to that of negative gold.
Gold's conceit is that of privilege and belief in one
being inherently more worthy.
Gold is the aristocrat of the conceits.
It is quietly convinced of its own superiority.
True gold is honour among men.
The colours in the rainbow's arch lead
from gold to gold.
Gold means: '*I am.*'
Unearth the gold within that can enrich you.
Gold signifies that which is outside of time.
Gold is immortality.
If you can't take it with you,
it may be because it's
already there!

The use of gold

Gold lifts you up. Thus, it is very beneficial for depressions, both physical and psychological. It is good for suicidal tendencies. Also for underactive thyroids and nervous stomachs. It is good for any kind of digestive irregularity. Also for rheumatics and for irritable bowel syndrome.

As yellow is useful for rashes and skin complaints, so gold, being stronger, is beneficial for scars. The best way of applying gold for this is through lighting techniques – chromatherapy – and bathing the area in solarised water. (See the Solarised Water technique on pages 183–4.)

Gold gives a feeling of well-being. It soothes the nerves.

Gold means 'I am'. For this reason, it is good for depression during the menopause – which is based on a reluctance to let go of the periods and a feeling of being worthless as a female. In certain societies, a woman past the menopause is revered. Freed biologically, she can now enter her most creative time of life.

Gold helps one to come to terms with what is. It also has a useful role during the male menopause.

A golden bandage for the wounded can be applied either materially or as a visualisation. Gold is extremely useful for relief of past hurts, both emotionally and physically.

One interesting aspect of gold is that it helps you shake off any kind of parasite – emotional as well as physical – anything that is not really part of you.

Gold can be introduced into your system through the Star Breath (pages 158–61) and the Rainbow Tonic (pages 157–8) techniques as well as through Water Solarisation (pages 183–4). Also through wearing gold clothing and fabrics, jewellery and gold decor in the home.

Gold foods
Mangoes, some melons and paw paw. Indians eat gold leaf directly in a dessert.

A GOLD STORY
Tom amongst thieves

I was once taken by a burglar to a nightclub that was for burglars only. I knew him, I hasten to add, through friends of friends of friends! It was a most interesting experience. I still don't know where it was exactly – I was led down alleys, through fences, across fields. This was after driving out of London for two hours and changing cars several times.

As we sat in the club talking about his trade, I learned some quite fascinating things about the comradeship and rules among burglars. Things will no doubt have changed today. This was many years ago and these were burglars of the old school, so to speak. Most interesting for me was their respect for gold. There is honour amongst thieves. As my friend's friend put it: 'Whenever we do an house' (he was Cockney) 'we never touch her Tom.'

What, I asked him, was 'Tom'?

'Gold, girl. We take 'er jewellery and everythin' else, but we leave 'er Tom alone. Won't touch that.'

I asked him why not.

'Bring you no luck, girl, if you take that, her Tom, no luck at all. It's the decent thing to do.'

> 'From whom are you to allow liberation?
> None other but from your own mind by correct
> knowledge and perfect understanding.'
> *His Holiness, Param Sant*

Green

'The force that through the green fuse drives the flower
Drives my green age.'
Dylan Thomas

Green polarity:
Balance – Imbalance
Positive green keywords:
Discriminating; tactful; practical; stable; productive;
generous; highly imaginative; progressive; reformer;
commitment; relationships.
Negative green keywords:
Jealous; resentful; forgetful; selfish; greedy;
unimaginative; unsettled; frustration;
hypochondriac; scarcity.
Green is the heart centre.
Green is balance and harmony.
Green stabilises.
Green is the colour of the heart chakra.
The ability to experience wholeness;
love.
Green is agreeable.
Green is the bridge.
It is the gateway in the spectrum –

as the heart is in the body.
The lesson of love needs
to be learned in order to cross green's bridge.
Green reveals the state of your heart.
Green centralises.
The green stem connects the bloom above
with the roots below.
Green always leads you to the root cause.
Green makes progress.
It is dependable.
When we are green we grow.
Green restores.
Green is nature's wheel of unity.
Green is the colour of plants' blood.
Green is diplomatic and tactful.
Green is
midway between
the hot, magnetic colours of
red, orange and yellow
and the cooler, electrical colours
of blue, indigo and
purple.
Green is the bonder of the spectrum –
it bridges the magnetic red side with the
electrical blue side.
Green is a sanctuary – the halfway house of the spectrum.
Green likes partnership; it is always matchmaking.
Green is neither hot nor cold, active nor passive,
acid nor alkaline.
Green can discriminate.
Green compares.
It can see both sides –
which gives it a tendency to moralise.
Green can make right judgement.

It has the ability to weigh things up
and purge that which
must go.
Green can put itself on a moral pedestal.
Particularly when the subject is
the environment.
Green when negative would rather be admired than loved.
Green wants to take its proper place in life.
It wants to be acknowledged
for being who it is.
Negative green believes it can only be loved for what it does
and not for who it is.
Green is clarity and understanding.
It helps one do the
best one can.
Green will encourage.
Green loves harmony and balance.
It achieves this through struggle and conflict.
Green represents the ups and downs of life.
Green is the practical philosopher.
It has great ability in common-sense reasoning.
Green tunes itself into nature.
Green is the great beautician.
Green contemplates.
Green is the reformer.
It makes changes.
Green does not just follow rules,
it creates better ones when the old have failed.
Green can get control of itself because of
its power to stabilise.
Its ability to re-establish balance restores
ease to the system.
Green strives
to keep a balance between

the mental interests of the head
and the emotional concerns of the heart.
Green gets to the core of the matter.
Green is very conscientious.
Green gives encouragement.
Green can indicate difficulty in finding a settled way of life.
There can be a conflict of ideas and emotions
that causes commotion
and upheaval.
But, with green's ability to discriminate and balance,
this conflict can lead to correct
judgement and action.
Green holds the key to memory – it can remember
that which it needs to know.
It unlocks the deep and hidden
that is the cause of our physical
and psychological
illnesses.
Green is an emotional indicator.
If a balance of green is not attained,
it can lead to pains of the heart: envy,
jealousy and heart attacks.
A little green envy can act as a driving
force to achieve the same as others.
A little negative can be
extremely positive –
sometimes.
Green is prosperous, particularly in business.
Green likes the 'good life'.
It wants the best.
Green is productive.
Green knows the value of money.
It is the colour of finance and material wealth,
and of the economist.

Green is interested in property and real estate.
Green loves to collect possessions.
But positive green is the giver.
It is generous and loves to share
what it accumulates.
Green can be very agreeable.
Green is the great host.
Green represents the planet Earth
in its green mantle.
Green must have room to move, to expand.
'Give me space,' it says, 'give me a green field!
Move out of my way, I need to breathe!'
Green opens doors.
Green is an idealist;
It has a social conscience.
But is a practical idealist.
It often helps others, even when this
is at its own expense.
Doctors are on the green ray.
Green loves children, animals, nature.
It represents new beginnings.
Green people love their home –
When you visit, you get a great welcome.
Negative green is the colour of coping,
unquestioning acceptance and hopelessness;
of self-denial and self-suppression;
a refusal to live fully.
The root of cancer lies in this aspect
of negative green.
Green's need for recognition can lead
to ulcers when frustrated.
Green is awareness of the ego and into oneself.
It can show a desire to increase assertiveness.
Green is youth and growth.

Green – the improver for all – brings comfort into the
world.
A new awareness of green may indicate
that you are now prepared to
take your rightful place
in the world.

Green and parts of the body

The green gland is the thymus. Green represents the heart,
shoulders and chest. Also the lower lungs.

The use of green

Green is made up of two colours: yellow and blue. Yellow
is the last colour of the magnetic side of the spectrum, and
blue the first of the electrical side. The yellow clarifies and
the blue brings wisdom. So together as green, they help you
remember that which you need to know. This is important
because most of our physical and psychological illnesses
result from events and conditions in our past. Green is
beneficial in cases of claustrophobia.

Green restores stability to anything malignant. Malig-
nancy is the result of cells that have accelerated out of
control. Green lowers this over-stimulation (get professional
advice for correct dosage). Recent tests in the USA led by Dr
Paul Tacancy have found that eating broccoli fights cancer.
It seems that a very potent compound, sulforaphane, has
been found in broccoli that behaves as if it should be an anti-
carcinogen.

Green is best used as a bridge, a gateway to freedom. It
can reveal the state of your heart emotionally and physically,
and your ability to relate. Green discriminates rightly.
Unfortunately judgement and discrimination have become
dirty words. But the truth is, without applying both, we

could not continue to exist. Only when they become harsh, rigid and condemning do they not serve us. After all, if you have two apples before you and one is good and one is bad, not using the green of judgement and discrimination could mean that you end up with the bad one.

Green is the colour that blends with all. It is a general healer. If anyone is into an overload of any colour, just apply green to neutralise it.

An aversion to green often indicates that we don't feel happy with our emotions: Our conditioning as a child would have been: 'We don't want any of that emotional stuff, thank you.' It would have been stiff upper lip regardless.

Green helps dispel negative emotions. Green applied during stormy periods in a relationship will calm and cool the emotions. Green gives direction – so it can be used when you are trying to make up your mind or heart. It brings back into focus.

Green is a tonic. For this reason, green is a good colour for therapists to use after seeing a lot of clients. If you're feeling scattered and frazzled, relax in a chair, and put a green silk scarf behind your head; it will bring you back to the centre of yourself.

Green helps biliousness, soothes headaches. It is a good detoxifier and good for controlling blood pressure and liver complaints. It is excellent for the treatment of shock, fatigue and for people who don't know what to do next!

Green is soporific. Green's calming qualities can be used with the hyperactive child. Green heals the nerves. It gives reassurance and so is particularly indicated for children coming from neglected and disturbed environments. Green gives you a different view of the garden. If nothing is new then nothing is old. From the coloured bloom of the flower, which is our head, we go down the green stem of our body into the root cause. Green leads you to it – the diagnostic colour.

Green can be worn, used in decor around the house,
eaten. A particularly good, easy and pleasurable way of
absorbing green is through gardening, walking in the
country under trees, or through the grass. House plants and
foliage are a must!

For absorbing green through the Star Breath (pages
158–61), Rainbow Tonic (pages 157–8) and Solarised Water
(pages 183–4) techniques.

Green foods

Salads, green leafy vegetables, green herbs and spices,
alfalfa, avocado, green fruits – kiwi fruit, greengages,
gooseberries, apples, limes, etc.; pistachio nuts, green lentils,
peas and green peppers.

THE MANY MOODS OF GREEN
The shades and tints

Dark green – resentment

- Dark green is always on the defensive.
- Dark green suffers from extreme possessiveness, greed,
  envy and jealousy.
- It can become blind to another's needs, wishes and
  emotions and come to believe that everything revolves
  around its existence.
- The tax system comes under dark green. Originally, tax
  was an imposition by the rich and powerful on the poor
  and weak. Robin Hood (red) had it right! Dark green
  never has enough money, or if it does it is reluctant to
  part with it.
- Dark green needs to break away and create a life of its
  own.
- Someone under the influence of this vibration gives his or

her power to other people.
- The darker the shade of green, the longer the struggle has been going on.
- It can show that the person is full of remorse.
- Dark green can bring on illness.
- Someone under the influence of this colour can be unreliable.

Good examples: The narcissist; 'I'm all right, Jack'; the miser.
Problem: Never learning to say 'No'.

Emerald green – charity; tolerance; adaptability

- The ray of great healers and healing.
- It is connected to great wealth – ideas as well as material – and abundance.
- Emerald green harmonises and desires of the heart are gained.
- Heartfelt choices succeed without struggle.
- Emerald green has the key to unlock your heart.
- Emerald green gives in easily.
- Emerald green's magic makes you feel that it's good to be alive.

Good examples: Your favourite grandparent and teacher.
Problem: Don't give a monkey's; nobody's at home; get lost.

Olive green – treachery

- Olive green is made up of green and grey.
- It deceives, but it deceives no one but itself.
- Animosity is the other pitfall; an envy of anyone more advanced than itself.
- If someone was drawn to this colour, I would look for the areas in their lives where they were not being honest with themselves. Unfortunately, the person will truly

believe that they are totally honest with themselves.

- Olive green has no imagination.
- Olive green refuses to recognise disastrous relationships.

Good example: The underling.

Problem: It is always somebody else's fault.

Green/gold – supply

- Green with gold in it becomes the supplier.
- It produces whatever is needed.
- The 'can get' personality, the one who has the connections, who comes up with the goods.
- This colour is useful for nervous tics and stammering and for anyone suffering from a severe neurosis. It brings the confidence of the gold and the calmness of the green to the person.
- The negative of this is the person who wants but never gets.

Good examples: The black marketeer; the buyer for a big store.

Problem: Not asking for what you want; always the bridesmaid.

Green/blue – confidentiality

- This is the colour of someone who can be trusted with your deepest secrets. They have the ability to keep quiet about another's affairs.
- Green/blue has compassion and understanding for others, yet it is never one of the crowd.
- They do not get attached to their own generation.
- The scoutmaster who gives his life in the service of his troop.
- If drawn to this colour, you may be facing some important decisions in affairs of the heart.
- A good aid for the physical heart, e.g. angina.

- The negative is the blabbermouth.

Good examples: The confidant; the priest in the confessional.

Problem: Two-facedness; loneliness.

Pale green – beginnings; immaturity; the bud
'My salad-days
When I was green in judgement.'
Antony and Cleopatra, *Shakespeare*

- Pale green is tender, the new shoot, the learning time.
- Pale green is a fresh start. Thus its connection with early childhood (birth to seven years).
- It is the development of the will (see the story of 'Adele' on pages 48–9). Thus the person with the 'Should I? Shouldn't I?' syndrome. An inability to make up one's mind.
- An adult drawn to pale green can be indicating childhood deprivation.
- Pale green can show sympathy and compassion. It encourages others to begin again.
- The negative of pale green is drought; nothing grows. It can show someone who starts things up but never finishes them.
- Also mutton done up like lamb – not willing to be one's age.

Good example: Peter Pan.

Problem: Not taking responsibility; immature.

Silver green – misty
- Silver green is the time prior to conception.
- The silver reflects and the green is young – thus it's wonderfully useful in past life regression work.
- Even in past life work, silver green will go to the youthful time of that life rather than the heavy dramas of the

incarnation. I use it when I want the lives that were *not* traumatic to come up. This way, I get to see the essence that keeps recurring life after life – the sailor followed by the swimmer followed by the water engineer, all connected through water.

- Silver green shows me what a person could have been, not only in past lives but also in this lifetime. I look at the 'could-have-beens' in order to see what the person can be.

- This colour has a connection to money: you either have it or you don't.

Good examples: The play *Blithe Spirit*; the spiritual channel.

Problem: Wallowing in the past; the snobbery of class distinction.

Jade green – worldly wisdom; generosity

- Jade green is the true giving of self from the heart. When I give a piece of jade to someone, I am trusting them with a piece of my self. I give with my heart without expecting anything in return.

- Jade green gives space for psychic knowledge.

- Useful for manic-depressives. Give a piece of jade; apply a jade light; or drink solarised water, etc.

- Negative jade looks for the hidden motive; it cannot trust the purity of just giving.

Good example: The unknown soldier.

Problem: Over-giving; imbalanced.

A GREEN STORY
Expectations

Marcus was a lawyer and in his late forties. He had been

suffering for some years with panic attacks. He had been in therapy and attended several clinics – with no permanent success. Now the problem had become acute.

He found it was affecting his work and that it had begun to prevent him from appearing in court. Just as he was about to enter the courtroom, he would be seized with fear, start trembling and have to retire to the gentlemen's room, where he would hang onto a door, unable to leave and go back to appear for his client. Dinner parties were also a hazard. He would be gripped by panic before he started the meal.

The last psychiatrist he had visited had suggested that he carry a small doll in his pocket and, when he found the next attack coming on, grip the doll and see if the symptoms disappeared; they hadn't. I wonder if the psychiatrist knew that she was following on old remedy that witches employed. They would get you to transfer your problem onto another object in the same way.

After observing Marcus, I decided I would flood him with the green light. We needed to find the key to his attacks and green would do that. While he was in the green light, I asked him to go back to the first time he could remember an attack.

It was while he was at a health farm trying to lose weight. He had been doing some press-ups in the gym. He was also on a very low calorie diet and feeling very tired from both that and the exercise.

Marcus remembered the gym instructor saying to him: 'Go on, Marcus, just do one more press-up.' He struggled to obey and collapsed.

'I suddenly felt panic stricken. I just couldn't do another press-up. He expected me to but I couldn't.'

Marcus had given us the clue for which we had been looking. The green light had produced the keyword:

'expected'. After this, we unravelled the whole story.

Marcus had always been expected to do things. He came from a very religious family and there was an older brother who was homosexual and who had been turned out of the family because of it. Marcus was supposed to fulfil all the expectations the family had had of the older brother. He had to be a lawyer like his brother; he had to be a gymnast like his brother; he had to have the girlfriends his brother had never been interested in having.

When he realised this, Marcus could understand that the last press-up the gym instructor had asked him for was the last straw that broke the camel's back. He had taken over his family's expectations of himself. He expected himself to go into the courtroom, to be able to be sociable at a dinner, to be a success. But something in him did not want to live like this. Some part of him was rebelling against being forced to live the life his family had planned for his erring brother.

Having found the root cause of his panic attacks, Marcus also began to realise that he might be a homosexual himself. If he was honest with himself, the girls he was always taking home to mother were only a sham. For years he had been going out late at night when his parents were asleep to lead his secret private life elsewhere. He was going to have to tell his family the truth and end the terrific strain of the pretence.

I suggested that now he had had this realisation about his problem, Marcus get a notebook and keep it by him at all times. He was going to be ready for the next attack. Indeed, he would welcome it and would record every detail from start to finish. He would witness how his body reacted, how he felt emotionally, who said what and when. He was positively looking forward to the experi-

ence. I asked him to do this eight years ago. Marcus has
not had an attack since.

> 'He makes me lie down in green pastures,
> and leads me beside the waters of peace . . .'
> *Psalms xxiii, 2*

Turquoise

'Me, me, me, myself and I.'
Anonymous

Turquoise polarity:
Sociable – Withdrawn
Positive turquoise keywords:
Calmness; self-questioning; self-sufficient;
personal; balance; harmony;
ambitious; success.
Negative turquoise keywords:
Reticent; fence-sitting; unreliable;
boastfulness; deception;
off-handed.
Turquoise looks to itself first.
Turquoise is single-minded.
Turquoise is emotional control.
Through the stillness of turquoise comes a deep peace.
It is nature's great natural tranquilliser.
Turquoise is the colour of balance.
Turquoise calms the nerves of the public speaker.
It feeds the central nervous system.
Turquoise is
the opener of the heart

and the healer of the emotions.
It penetrates into depths of feelings.
However, turquoise can be unaware of
its own heart's desires.
Turquoise's basic motivation in life is
emotional relationship.
It can also be a sexual two-timer because of its
refusal to decide which is the one.
Turquoise loves good friendship.
Turquoise aims to be a success.
It needs to make its own way in the world.
Turquoise has a need to be popular.
It likes to enjoy life.
Turquoise has a longing to know about life.
Turquoise has the gift of being able to see
who is going to win. It is very perceptive.
Not through prophetic powers, but out of an
ability to weigh up the odds.
Turquoise has a discriminating eye –
useful in antique dealings.
Turquoise can be extremely decisive.
it is good in an
emergency.
Turquoise says what it feels rather than
what is appropriate.
The turquoise is often asked to be the arbitrator.
It likes to get things settled.
Turquoise is the only colour that says:
'Stand still! What do I think?
What do I feel? What do I want? What do I need?
Me, me, me!
Not mama, papa, the kids,
the cat and the Universe,
but myself!'

Turquoise is a very human colour.
It loves sharing and togetherness, being together
and having a family.
Negative turquoise can be deceived about itself
It can be over-emotional.
Turquoise can be an emotional manipulator.
Turquoise quite often has problems with affairs of the heart.
Turquoise can be in love with two people at the same time.
and be indecisive about making a choice.
Extreme turquoise will be the narcissist.
The turquoise need to be popular can
lead to some boastfulness
and deception.
Turquoise is afraid of being alone. It hates being single.
In friendship, negative turquoise can
become cold and stand-offish.
Turquoise can be very lonely.
Turquoise can
find itself sitting on the fence
through trying to fix it so that everyone is happy.
But when turquoise gets down off the fence,
looks to its own wants and needs
and makes a stand, it sticks
to its guns, come what may.
Turquoise is the beginning of ambition for the self.
Turquoise has an affinity with animals.

Turquoise and parts of the body
Turquoise is connected to the throat and chest.

The use of turquoise
The healer for the emotions of the heart. Turquoise can talk
from the heart. It is the unity of the green and the blue (with

yellow thrown in). The green of the heart unites with the blue of the throat – then you can say what you feel instead of what is appropriate.

As it calms the nerves, it is a great colour to wear if you have to appear before the public (especially when combined with a pink room which makes the audience more receptive to what you have to say). It subdues. Turquoise is the slow but sure healer. It can sometimes take a while before you feel the benefit. Don't abandon using it as a healer just because you don't get instant relief.

Turquoise feeds the central nervous system. Thus, it is helpful in situations of nervous stress and breakdown. The stillness of turquoise calms the panic that can follow emotional shock. It stops the person running away from their hurt self, and the painful situation. A good colour to use when encountering problems in relationships. It encourages you to be able to speak what's in your heart.

It subdues fevers and cools inflammations of the nerves, particularly good for neuralgia. The inner resistance to turquoise that I sometimes encounter in clients is the fear of facing emotions.

Turquoise will be of benefit to anyone unable to decide between them or me; or between this side and that side of the question. It also encourages self-questioning; coming to know what one wants. Useful in overcoming self-sabotage and in centering oneself. If a person is drawn to this colour, you know they are getting down to the real issue of looking at themselves and how life affects them personally.

In Indian mythology, the blue sky represents the masculine and the green of nature represents the feminine. When we wear turquoise we are uniting the sexes. The negative form of this shows coldness in relationships and unforgivingness.

It is important when using turquoise in any kind of

therapy to remember that it is composed of three colours: blue, green and yellow. The practical effect of this is that the body will always be aware of the hidden yellow in the turquoise. Therefore, if you are going to use turquoise therapeutically, consult the yellow listing in this section. Turquoise is also good for any skin rashes or inflammations. Use also for scar tissue. Use turquoise to subdue fevers.

Turquoise may be introduced through clothing, jewellery, ornaments, fabrics and furnishings, decor and lighting. Also more directly through using the Star Breath, the Rainbow Tonic and Solarised Water techniques (see pages 000–00). There are no purely turquoise foods, but combinations of green, yellow and blue foods (skins included) can be eaten.

A TURQUOISE STORY
The kingfisher

A friend of mine had a picture sent to him by a woman friend of his in Australia. She had done this herself quite recently.

The picture was of a kingfisher and it had not been done with conventional paints. It was made up of thousands of crushed crystals. There were several colours and these had been sprinkled onto the picture instead of paint and held in place by glue. It is a technique that was used in Renaissance times.

What was interesting for me was that the picture and its colours showed exactly where the artist was psychologically. In ancient symbolism, a bird depicted pure power and its beak showed the direction the power was going. If the bird's beak pointed up, the painter was going upwards in life – up signified rebirth and immortality. If it pointed down, one was going down. This kingfisher's beak was dipping into water, which showed that the artist was delving into her emotions and the subconscious.

The bird always represents where we are in ourselves at the time. The fact that the kingfisher was painted only with turquoise crystals indicated that she was looking at herself and her own life and asking herself what she wanted.

In its beak, the kingfisher had a frog of several colours. When it is coloured this way, according to ancient mythology, the frog depicts poison. If it had been transparent, it would have shown that the person had transformed adversity and emotional suffering into balance. The colours in this frog were dark green – which indicated past resentment – two yellows, one dark – which showed a lack of value for the self – and a paler yellow – which indicated her search for an understanding of all that had occurred recently. It also revealed that she was rising above whatever it was that had happened. There was also black – which showed that her life had been on hold for some time – and orange – which showed that there had been a past shock and grief and that this was still buried deep within her.

I told my friend what I saw and felt in the picture. He confirmed that the artist had had a severe shock some months previously. She had lost her home and her family in an accident and her life had ceased since that time. She was, he said, just beginning to pick up the pieces and make a future for herself.

'Please hear what I am not saying.'
Charles C. Finn

Blue

'We are all here on earth to help others.
What I can't figure out is what the others are here for.'
W.H. Auden

Blue polarity:
Knowledge – Ignorance
Positive blue keywords:
Wisdom; patience; truth; mental attainment; spiritual;
philosophical; contemplative; quiet;
healer; integrity; loyal.
Negative blue keywords:
weak; emotionally unstable; spiteful; superstitious;
intellectual conceit; sentimental love;
frigid; deceitful; unforgiving.
Blue is the Spirit of Truth.
Blue is the higher order of intelligence.
Blue is the colour of the throat chakra.
The ability to speak the truth and be heard;
self-expression.
It communicates by the voice.
Blue is the Word.
Blue has a healing voice.
Blue can show that you need to speak up for yourself.

Blue is the connection between
the body and the head.
The head and the heart speak through
the blue throat.
Blue listens closely to what you say –
and plays it back to you.
Blue reasons things out slowly and quietly with integrity.
Blue is the teacher.
Blue is the colour of truth.
Or, as Mark Twain put it: 'You can't pray a lie'.
Blue is peace with a purpose.
Blue has to be careful that it isn't peace at any price.
Blue will not draw attention to itself.
Blue doesn't like to sell, especially not itself.
Compared to the reds and oranges, blue is quiet.
Blue helps you through any problems.
Blue brings rest.
It cools and calms.
It slows down and even retards growth.
Blue is reserved.
Blue is the tranquil spirit.
It is the colour of contemplation.
Blue has higher philosophical thoughts. It is the
philosopher-scientist.
Blue's thinking is quiet, discriminating and deep.
'Still waters run deep' is a blue motto.
Blue can be reticent.
But, like the sky, it is always there.
Blue values intellectual integrity.
The great writers are born
with the energy of the blue ray.
Blue works in a discreet and tactful way.
It prefers to maintain the status quo.
Ambassadors are blue.

Blue does not like upsets – yet often causes them.
Blue is family roots.
It takes one back to rituals that
marked out the family's identity.
Negative blue can show there was a lack of values in the
family.
Blue does things with honour and sincerity.
But its lofty ideals can make it rather aloof and remote.
Blue is highly inventive
in the realms of science and the arts.
Blue has the discrimination of wisdom, and
the wisdom of discrimination.
Blue is the refined mental attainer and recognises that there
is something to be learned in everything.
It penetrates to the soul.
Blue's wisdom is the antidote for an imagination run wild.
Blue is a spiritual sedative.
Particularly apt in counter-balancing fears of
'The end of the world is nigh' variety.
Blue has the ability to sober one up.
Blue brings a wisdom into love.
Blue doesn't always go by the book.
And even when it does, it will do so for only
so long as it suits blue's purposes.
Although honesty is a blue keyword, blue
also has a fear of honesty.
Honesty often requires confrontation and commotion,
both of which blue abhors.
Blue is a master of manipulation.
So good that you may not even know
you have been
manipulated!
Blue can be loyal, if it chooses.
Blue *will* do things its own way.

Blue longs for a change.
Usually a change of its situation.
Blue looks before it leaps – but it *does* leap.
All the religions use blue as one
of their dominant
emblematic
colours.
Blue is as safe as heaven.
Blue can indicate that the person
is not happy in their present
circumstances.
Negative blue can be very separate,
snobbish and cold.
Blue can be frigid and spiteful.
Blue can show a moody and unforgiving
temperament.
Blue's diplomacy can be deceit using nice words.
Blue can be 'smother-love'.
Blue can get stuck in a rut.
Negative blue can have difficulty concentrating.
When blue becomes emotionally upset,
it is liable to let things slide.
It becomes the victim, the doormat.
Negative blue is the martyr syndrome:
'I am going to punish myself in order to
make you suffer.'
Blue is the seeker into all aspects.
Blue has an acceptance of that which
cannot be changed.
It makes the best of what is.
Blue has a great belief that it all turns
out right in the end.
And so blue can go
with the flow.

The Bible says: 'And the truth shall set you free.'
Blue uncovers the Truth.

Blue and parts of the body

Blue's glandular domain is the thyroid and parathyroids.
Blue depicts the throat area, and is linked to the upper lungs
and arms, the base of the skull, and weight.

The use of blue

Blue is the colour of the present time, the Aquarian Age. The
Aquarian is the Seeker of Truth. However, he or she must go
forward in truth. If they do not go forward, they will go
backwards out of fear. Blue combats fear.

Because blue governs the throat, infections in this area are
psychologically related to 'talking inwards', i.e. not speaking
out. Psychologically speaking, coughing is because a person
has swallowed their thoughts and cannot trust themselves to
speak out. Blue will help this by counteracting the fear of
'spitting it out'. People trapped in this negative blue syndrome need to learn the power of the spoken word – not so
much to help others but to help themselves. They need to
understand that what you don't ask for you rarely get.

Stiff necks can benefit from the application of blue. A stiff
neck comes because of rigidity of thought, a fear of going
with the flow, of being flexible. The blue will help dissolve
fear.

Blue hates arguments. Rather than have a row, blue will
refuse to say what it wants, will put up with the situation.
They need *more* blue to get the courage to speak up. Bright
blue is needed in such a case.

Blue is useful for children's ailments, and for teething and
ear infections. Also for childhood throat infections and
speech and vocal problems. Remember that your child may

be unable to speak out from fear of the row that will follow! Also, a child takes the energy of the parents' arguments. If the child is unable to say how upset it is, its throat tightens and becomes sore. The needy child is in the negative blue and needs to be encouraged to stand on its own two feet.

Blue can be used for the bedwetting child, and for adult incontinence. Add pink to blue for greater effectiveness. The bedwetting child feels it is unlovable. Introducing pink with the blue counters this.

Blue in the sickroom cools and calms, particularly useful in reducing fevers, and for the terminally ill. Use a blue light bulb to flood the room with blue light.

Blue can make you aware of the need to rest and relax. Blue is *the* colour for modern-day stress and anxiety. Blue can help to bring down blood pressure. Introduce blue for the relief of pain. Blue cools inflammation, helps nose bleeds, internal bleeding, and varicose veins. It reduces the inflammational pain of sciatica and soothes stomach ulcers. Blue alleviates sunstroke and sunburn.

A psychological use: blue counteracts harshness. If somebody is acting insensitively in a situation, blue may help them become more compassionate. Blue compensates: it can help a person realise the good to be found in the bad event or situation that cannot be reversed. Blue has an acceptance of that which cannot be changed. Blue gives relief from pain, both physical and psychological, and combats cruelty and brutality.

Blue is not a good colour to wear if you want to lose weight. It is too static. I have observed that many people who are overweight feel an attraction to blue. This is because negative blue aids and abets them in remaining just as they are. Losing weight will bring confrontation, conflict and change.

To introduce blue into your system wear blue clothes and

jewellery; bathe in blue light; use the Star Breath (pages 158–61), Rainbow Tonic (pages 157–8) and Water Solarisation (pages 183–4) techniques.

Surround yourself with blue in the home. And bring in blue flowers: bluebells, harebells, hyacinths, Canterbury bells, Michaelmas daisies. And most obvious of all, spend time under the blue sky! I believe because there is the blue sky, there is no need to have a profusion of blue foods.

Blue foods
Blueberries, blue plums, bilberries, the herb flower borage.

THE MANY MOODS OF BLUE
The shades and tints

Sky blue – selfless love
- Sky blue is the universal healer.
- Sky blue remains calm and can overcome all obstacles.
- But, just like the sky, this colour is variable but constant.
- The blue sky will return if you wait long enough.

Good example: Monarchy.
Problem: Fear of not continuing.

Azure blue – ambition; on the path
- Azure blue reaches for the stars, for high spiritual attainment.
- This rich blue colour has finished the waiting period.
- It can release a person from bondage.
- Those under its influence have found what they want and are ready to go all out for it.

Good example: The Oxford–Cambridge boat race.
Problem: Missing the boat.

Pale blue – inspires

- Pale blue uplifts.
- It is the soul searching for its maturity.
- It is a guide for the guides, it cares for the carers.
- It has constant faith and has the purity of innocence about it
- It has a lovely lulling quality; it tones down the harsh and abrupt.
- Pale blue gives great encouragement to break loose from one's chains.
- Pale blue is constantly struggling towards a purpose.
- It can spark off the beginning of ambition.
- Pale blue can show that there is not much depth to the character – tries hard but doesn't succeed easily.
- Pale blue can do a great deal of work without much to show for it.

Good example: The free spirit.
Problem: Ignoring; turning the back on opportunity.

Dark blue – single-mindedness

- The black in this blue indicates a restriction and a hardness.
- Dark blue is inclined to give justice without mercy. This can show up as a single-mindedness, whether for good or not-so-good ends.
- It can be a rather gloomy disposition.
- Dark blue is the worrier.
- Someone dissatisfied with their lot.
- This colour can also indicate locked-up emotions.
- It can give the cold shoulder.
- Dark blue can be the bigot.
- Blue has clairvoyant ability; but in the dark blue it can be the charlatan.

Good examples: The pessimist; the misery.

Problem: Nothing is going to work.

A BLUE STORY
Family roots

Doreen was a client who came to me when she was
working in the negative of blue. As a child, Doreen and
her brother were subjected to a family ritual every evening
after dinner. Before the children were allowed to leave the
table, Father would ask Mother, 'Have these two children
been good today?'

If the answer was yes, each child would be given a
sweetie from the huge jar standing on the sideboard. If it
was no for either one of them, the sweetie would not be
forthcoming.

Doreen said to me: 'Every evening I dreaded this
ceremony. I hated it.' She looked at me, tears streaming
down her face, and said, 'God forgive me, I can't help it.
I'm doing exactly the same with my own children.'

'Truth, Sir, is a cow.'
Samuel Johnson

Indigo

'She would rather light candles than curse the darkness.'
Adlai Stevenson about Eleanor Roosevelt

Indigo polarity
Devotion – Blind faith
Positive indigo keywords:
Perception; structure; regulations; idealism;
fortitude; purging; unflinching;
obedience.
Negative indigo keywords:
Fanatical; fascist; conformity; ritualistic;
self-righteous; liar; addiction.
Indigo has force and power.
It transmutes and purifies.
Indigo is the third eye, the brow chakra.
The ability to plan for the future.
Indigo can see more than is seen.
Indigo has a devotion to truth.
It unravels the unknown.
Indigo strives for the future.
It says, 'I'm going to do it', instead of just thinking about it.
Indigo is purity of thought.
Indigo is the transformer.

Indigo is the priest.
As a duck to water, indigo to reverence.
Indigo raises rules into holy rites.
The Commons raised to the House of Lords.
If blue avoids argument and row,
indigo has raised and refined this tendency to an
absolute belief in the pre-eminence
of the hierarchy.
Terror for indigo is no structure.
'I am structure' is indigo's identity.
Indigo is the third eye opener.
Indigo's third eye sight allows it to see
through the material world, but
leaves it lost
in space.
To anchor itself, it devotes its
energies to maintaining
ancient ways.
Indigo creates structures in which no deviation
or difference is considered either
possible or desirable.
Structure is indigo's safety net.
Indigo pares down to the bone.
There is no in-between for indigo.
It is all or nothing.
Indigo has unshakeable beliefs.
Indigo upholds
the Establishment to the end.
And if it cannot find an Establishment,
it will create one.
Indigo loves law and order.
Indigo is a lover of justice. It is the judge and jury.
It will defend people's rights.
Creating law and order is like an aphrodisiac to indigo.

Indigo
is very conscious
of the rungs of the ladder.
To be out of step for indigo is a
fate worse than
death.
Indigo is extremely conscientious and reliable
in a crisis.
Indigo's
devotional aspect
combined with its reforming fervour
enables it to reconstruct organisations – religious
or otherwise.
Indigo must watch that devotion to work does not become
its sole interest.
Indigo holds the fort.
Indigo must learn to let someone else hold the fort for a
while.
Indigo thinks it's indispensable.
Look to indigo, it always comes up trumps.
It finds that loan or gets that signature.
Indigo always springs to the rescue.
Indigo aspires to be the spiritual master.
Indigo is spiritual antiseptic.
Intuition commences with indigo,
the first step to higher knowledge.
Indigo is a very dramatic colour – the drama queen.
The acting profession comes under the indigo ray.
Like the priest, the actor must give himself up
in order to play out a role.
Indigo can be moody; it's
never middling.
The indigo temperament is up in the clouds one minute,
or down in the dumps the next.

Workwise it can have great enthusiasm for a project one
minute
and then drop it suddenly.
Indigo is the devoted servant.
Intellectual
fervour has partly replaced
indigo's religious fervour in our society.
The addiction to qualifications is the indigo giveaway.
Indigo is hungry for the meaning of life.
Indigo is the inspired preacher and writer.
Indigo can reconcile science and the religion.
Its third eye allows it to see the
true cause behind effect.
You will have to work with your indigo to understand this!
Indigo keeps telling you to pray –
but it doesn't tell you what is going to happen
when you do pray!
Indigo knows when to move energy
and when to hold fast.
Indigo constantly
pushes you into reviewing your
thinking.
Indigo gathers together and makes whole,
so that the journey towards
'somewhere else'
can begin.
Indigo moves us on.
Indigo prepares for the realm of mysteries and
psychic dimensions.
Indigo personalities
can be intoxicating.
On the sexual level, it can be the Don Juan
or the *femme fatale*.
Indigo can make incredibly sweeping statements.

Indigo *knows*.
Furthermore, you know they know...
And they know you know they know that you know...
Negative indigo can be low on trust.
Negative indigo has to beware of self-deception
and a desire to show off which could make it unpopular.
Indigo's love of ritual can translate into addiction.
Rituals are a preparation for our intent;
unfortunately, we tend to forget what
our intention was.
Rituals are not the path.
They are a reminder that there is a path.
Blind devotion is an indigo failing.
Negative indigo can show a disturbing lack of purpose –
a belief in bad luck.
It can be faithless and disloyal.
Just as indigo can see what cannot be seen,
It can also be blind to what is obvious.
Blinkered is the word.
Indigo without both eyes open can
become the fanatic.
Misplaced faith is the great weakness of indigo.
Negative indigo is the bigot.
Deep, dark indigo has a total lack
of understanding.
All addictions relate to negative indigo.
Addiction says:
'There is something wrong with the structure of your life.'
The desire for drugs
shows a desire for access to
indigo's powers of perception.
Unfortunately, the knowledge gained
through drugs will usually be
unable to be brought back.

Indigo's devotion is of the order:
'Even though thou slay me, I will not doubt thee.'
Indigo represents
an ocean of darkness.
But nonetheless it beckons us to cross.
Indigo is the threshold to other spheres.

Indigo and parts of the body

The indigo gland is the pituitary, sometimes known as the conductor of the orchestra – this being the endocrine system. Physically, indigo represents the skeleton, particularly the backbone, lower brain, the eyes and sinuses.

The use of indigo

Indigo is made up of dark blue and dark violet. It is the one colour that shows up hidden fear – so if it appears in any process, look for a fear that you may not know you have. One strange aspect of this is that indigo can show a very deep fear of fire. This is very often related to an experience in a past life. Indigo is the colour that looks beyond the complaint itself and gets to the structural cause of the trouble.

Indigo is the strongest painkiller in the spectrum. It is an astral antiseptic that can clear up any bacteria, the results of air, water and food pollution – and astral toxins.

Because the area of the eyes and nose fall under its dominion, indigo is good for acute sinus problems and cataracts. Sinusitis and allied problems are uncried tears from childhood. It is very good for lung and chest complaints, bronchitis, asthma, etc., and for the treatment of lumbago and sciatica, migraine, eczema, bruising and inflammations. Indigo helps to control diarrhoea. It is useful for bringing down high blood pressure. Indigo is the best antidote for insomnia that I know. I had a client who had not had a good night's sleep in fifteen years. I suggested he use indigo with the Star Breath technique (pages 158–61). Two weeks later he told me he was getting a sound sleep every night.

It is particularly effective for an over-active thyroid. Aids with kidney complaints. Indigo disperses growths, tumours and lumps of any kind. Visualise an army of indigo warriors in your bloodstream moving towards the tumour, passing through it and breaking it up. Follow this with the visualisation of a green wash passing through the blood to the tumour site and sweeping away the debris of the battlefield.

Indigo is said to promote tissue growth – which is why it is good for burns. Use an indigo bandage. Or flood the burn with indigo light. Or drink indigo solarised water.

Because of its particular relationship to the body's bones, indigo is beneficial in any kind of spinal complaints and backaches. Psychologically, backaches may indicate that we are holding ourselves back in life. Lower back problems relate emotionally to insecurity, usually money worries. Mid-back to emotional problems with relationships. High back and shoulder blades, taking too much on – life's a burden. Put on by circumstances. If you are drawn to indigo, it may be an indication that you need to look to the structure, i.e. the bones, of your life. Similarly with addictions of any kind, drugs, cigarettes, alcohol, etc.

Indigo is the great healer of painful memories. It is the great cleanser and purger, cleaning away addictive emotional ties. A dislike of indigo can show a person has problems with their emotions and life set-up. It helps a person to regain direction when they have been emotionally shattered. It helps prepare the way for the next step. Indigo helps you release yourself from imposed or self-acquired conditioning. Indigo will work if there is a real need. It is the power of mind and thought with understanding. It unravels the unknown.

To introduce indigo into your system, wear indigo clothes, jewellery, bathe in indigo light. Also use the Star Breath (pages 158–61), Rainbow Tonic (pages 157–8) and Water Solarisation (pages 183–4) techniques.

Go easy with indigo decor – too much of it can cause melancholy. Combine it with another colour, such as rich cream. And bring in indigo flowers: irises, pansies, primulas for decoration.

Indigo foods
Indigo-skinned grapes and plums, sloes, damsons, bilberries.

AN INDIGO STORY
Business problems

A lawyer came to me seeking answers to a business problem. It turned out to be connected to an emotional problem – it often is.

Martha was about to marry a Swiss man and live abroad. Would she be able to practise law in Switzerland? Should she sell her property in the UK? She already had a house of her own in Switzerland. She went on for some time about the pros and cons of the 'business' situation. Towards the end of the session I said, 'I'm going to put you in a healing light for five minutes.'

She protested saying that light was not necessary, that what she needed to do was to talk about it all. I suggested that she should give herself five minutes, anyway. She agreed reluctantly. I darkened the room, wrapped a sheet of indigo silk round her body and flooded her with rich indigo light. She sat in silence with her eyes shut. Within three minutes, beads of perspiration broke out on her upper lip and then spread all over her face and I could see that her body had begun to tremble.

The session ended and we said our goodbyes. Later that evening Martha rang me. She said, 'I can't believe what has happened. I didn't tell you, but I've had chronic back pain for a year, I haven't even been able to bend. I've been going to specialists and physiotherapists for months. Since the healing this afternoon, I've been able to touch my toes with no problem.'

She also said that she was clearer and knew what to do about the 'business' problems: 'I don't want to live abroad. It's such a relief to realise that I don't have to go.' Martha had been forcing herself towards a new set of life circumstances that her head favoured but her heart did not want. She had been subconsciously stiffening against something she did not really want to do, which had given her backache. It is a classic example of the relationship between indigo and the structure of a person's life.

'Though I disapprove of what you say, I will defend
to the death your right to say it.'
Voltaire

Purple

'Man is a spiritual being who, in order to be
truly spiritual, needs a body.'
St Thomas Aquinas

Purple Polarity
Peace – Conflict
Positive purple keywords:
Rulership; selflessness; dignity; humanitarianism;
inventiveness;
orator; mentally creative; unlimited;
psychic; mystic leader; faith.
Negative purple keywords:
Fraudulent; ruthless; spiritual arrogance; pompous;
corruption; social climber;
delusions of grandeur.
Purple is the Royal Ray.
Purple is the ruler.
Purple is associated with the seventh chakra.
The ability to appreciate time in
all its dimensions.
Purple is the spiritual master.
Purple is the protector.
Purple is the spirit of mercy.

Purple is very dignified.
Purple is visionary.
It works with the highest levels of thought.
Purple is the aristocracy of the spirit.
Purple is the highest note of the scale.
It is seeing and hearing without using
the physical senses.
'My words fly up, my thoughts remain below.' *Hamlet*,
Shakespeare
Purple commands respect.
It strives for spiritual perfection.
Purple is people in high places.
Purple sees a richness with quality.
Purple uses its psychic perception on an everyday basis.
Purple comes to understand that the price it
must pay for its royal attributes
is sacrifice.
Purple has access to power. Has no limitations.
Purple has true greatness.
It can sacrifice itself for the benefit of all
without being a victim or martyr.
Purple came in with the Romans.
Only the Emperor was allowed to wear purple robes.
Purple encourages you to become your own leader and
master.
Purple prefers to be self-employed.
Purple is found in the corridors of power.
Purple is always the leader of the pack.
Purple is always playing a leading role in the community.
Purple is highly inventive.
Purple is full of inspiration and originality.
Purple is the great teacher who realises
that the pupil has to understand.
Facts alone are not enough.

Purple is the humanitarian who has the wisdom of the king
and the humility of the child.
Purple's kindness is never mistaken for weakness.
Purple is poise and humility.
Purple's motto is: 'Be ye wise as serpents and harmless as
doves' *Matthew X, 16*.
The highest level of the purple ray
produces the great mystical leaders.
The colour of the psychic and pure spiritual qualities.
Purple's downfall is wanting
power for power's sake.
Purple desires perfection in all things.
Purple's lower levels can result in an inclination to
the black side and black magic.
Negative purple can show
a love of pomp and self-importance.
It can be insanely ruthless and corrupt.
In an Emperor, this can result in a Nero.
Pride can rear its ugly head in negative purple.
Negative purple can be belligerent and treacherous.
Purple has a universal conscience.
It is the enlightened guru.
Purple is idealism.
The purple ray is that of the gifted poets, writers,
painters and musicians – the masters
in any creative field.
Purple is the peace-maker.
It combines power with gentleness.
Purple is self-assured.
It encourages others' self-esteem.
Purple makes your inner candle burn brighter.
Purple marches to the beat of a different drum.
It will not mix with the crowd.
Purple, being

made of red and blue,
has the body of red and the spiritual nature of blue held in
perfect union.
Purple is the bridge to higher planes of consciousness –
the springboard to the infinite.
Purple is the heart of the Universe in your hands.

Purple and parts of the body

The purple gland is the pineal. Physically, purple represents
the top of the head, the crown, the brain, the scalp.

The use of purple

Purple is to be used sparingly. It is a 'heavy' colour, and too
long an exposure to purple can be depressing, even bring out
suicidal tendencies. Purple can find itself going round and
round in circles to find an answer. When there is no
solution, it can decide to depart – in more ways than one.
Purple can be beneficial to help calm people who are
emotionally erratic. Should anyone have an overload of
purple, the antidote is exposure to gold – gold lighting,
decor, clothes, etc.

Purple is useful for any kind of *internal* inflammation. It
is also useful to help skin eruptions subside.

Purple can bring about its own form of isolation. If you
have ever felt lonely, or apart from life, just acknowledge
your own individuality. Leaders are always apart – and be
assured that it is all right to march to the beat of a different
drum.

Purple is not a colour recommended for use with children.
If it is used with children, exposure times should be very
short.

Purple is good for subduing palpitations of the heart.
Purple is a good colour for head, scalp and concussion
problems, jangled nerves and the immune system.

Note: Purple light should never be directed onto the face. If needed for a head treatment, it should be applied only to the back of the head.

One very positive way of using purple is have it help you bring your leadership qualities to the fore. To introduce purple into your system: wear purple clothes, ornaments, jewellery, coverings, etc. Use purple flowers for decorative purposes including foxglove, stocks, delphiniums. For more direct absorption, use the Star Breath (pages 158–61), Rainbow Tonic (pages 157–8) and Water Solarisation (pages 183–4) techniques.

Purple foods

Aubergines, purple grapes and plums, passion fruit, fresh figs, purple broccoli, purple cabbage, King Edward potatoes (with skin), purple onions and sweet potato.

THE MANY MOODS OF PURPLE
The shades and tints

Deep purple – overbearing

- Because of the greater proportion of black in deep purple, it can use power corruptly.
- This colour can become dedicated to an ideal at the expense of human reality.
- Deep purple marries for position rather than for love.
- Deep purple can be very arrogant. It can be a ruthless seeker of power and have delusions of grandeur.
- It can also show a tendency towards suicide and deep depression.
- Dark purple can be very dogmatic.

Good example: Dark purple can be very dogmatic; the drug barons; tyrants.

Problem: Suppressors of freedom.

Violet – spiritual service; celestial

- Violet adores to revere.
- It is very like purple, but not so intense.
- It is the rebuilder of ideals.
- It will sacrifice old ritual formats for the new, even allow you to change religions.
- Violet likes to busy itself with occult and spiritual matters.
- It has spiritual dedication.
- Violet yearns for emotional security and shies away from responsibility.
- Violet calms emotional turbulence.
- As a friend, violet can be here one minute, gone the next, like a cream cake. Naughty but nice.
- Violet is intuition, not intellect.
- It can see into the future and seems to receive the divine nudge.
- Violet aids psychic ability.
- Those under violet seem to have the knack of bridging time.
- It helps with the pain of neuralgia and acute inflammation of the nerves.
- Can be used for eye complaints. Breathing techniques – the Star Breath on pages 158–61 – are safe enough for this. But the direct application of violet light should only be done under the supervision of a chromatherapist. The deep violet pansy flower is an old-fashioned remedy and was known as eyebright. Applied to the closed eye, it gives considerable relief from eyestrain.
- Violet is good for use in regression to acknowledge your child from other lives.
- It is linked to the unborn child, thus its use in infertility.

- Good for when working with one's own little child.
- Negative violet can flaunt its powers; it can be the misinformed mystic. It can lose its mind in this area. Cults built upon brainwashing techniques are in the negative violet.
- It does not adjust well to a decline in its circumstances.
- Usually outstanding in its life work.
- Violet has a deep inner knowing of its destiny.
- Cinderella was working with the violet.

Good examples: The selfless mystic; visionary.
Problem: Flowery and dramatic.

Amethyst – protector

- Amethyst links one with mystical powers. It is the spiritual ray which protects you while you reach out to the beyond.
- The great preparer for ceremonial magic.
- Enables you to see visions beyond the human eye.
- The monks who were employed in the distilleries knew that amethyst sobers up!
- Helps one pass through boundaries and to acknowledge karmic debts.
- Amethyst has both the crimson and the blue rays within it.
- Idealism is its key.
- It protects those who are unable to protect themselves – small children, the sick and vulnerable, and animals.
- Missionaries relate to this colour: the amethyst vibration sends them out of the unknown to guide and help mankind.
- Amethyst goes beyond the most calculated academic reasoning. It helps one assess who is sincere and who is not.
- Negative amethyst has no method at all and completely

lacks mastership, often getting caught up with imprac-
tical ideals.
Good examples: Democracy, Statue of Liberty.
Problem: Impractical.

Mauve – aristocrat

- Mauve is majestic.
- It can make right choices peacefully and calmly.
- The classic mauve type is the person who has been born
  the right side of the blanket.
- Mauve is the colour of dynasties.
- It is the state that the social climber imagines they will
  find when they reach their goal.
- Negative mauve believes that in some circles it is a
  serious blunder to use the wrong knife and fork.

Good example: Lord Mountbatten.
Problem: Lack of etiquette; common.

Plum – fullblown

- Plum doesn't have to strive to attain anything. It already
  has it.
- It is the privileged who knows it is so and take full
  advantage of it.
- Plum is old fashioned.
- The name-dropper.
- Plum is in love with its own publicity.
- Plum is indulgent.
- In the spiritual field, it has false pride and an holier-than-
  thou attitude.
- Plum never talks to you, it always gives a sermon. The
  personality is so earnest. Plum can be so pompous and
  boring.
- The plum personality is drawn to the land and livestock.
  It has an interest in good breeding.

- Positive plum can be the inspiring school teacher that the child never forgets.
- Plum's aim is to be established.

Good examples: Blue blood; family crests and tradition.
Problem: Impostors; ageing starlet.

Lavender – delicate

- Lavender is sensitive.
- Lavender is the lady in silk.
- Also elusive and fragile. Lavender can be very evasive.
- The colour of convalescence, also the colour to use to clear anaesthetics from the system.
- Because lavender works on the brain's pain centres it helps with drug addiction. Drug addiction is suicide of the soul.
- Lavender is not always as delicate as it seems – the iron butterfly. Lavender is the love of beautiful things.
- Lavender attracts.

Good example: Exquisite porcelain beauty.
Problem: When the chips are down, you can't find it.

Lilac – self-appreciation

- Lilac represents vanity, too much or too little. There is nothing wrong in looking in a mirror so long as it's not at every one you pass.
- It also has great healing powers. Lilac strengthens the immune system.
- Lilac loves glamour, romance and magic!
- It is immaturity, adolescence.
- Lilac's personality is bright and bubbly, the life and soul of the party. Lilac does not like to dig too deep.
- Lilac is springtime.
- It is the colour that says, 'When I am grown up I am

going to be . . .'

Good example: The teenager.

Problem: Lilac can reveal a lost childhood; growing up too soon; lost youth.

A PURPLE STORY
Happy in their misery

There was a power struggle in the relationship. The wife, Sarah, came to me first. She told me of her concern about the marriage. Her husband, she said, was an impossible man and she was unable to cope with this and be herself.

We spent a couple of sessions discussing whether she should leave to go and live with another man she had become involved with. I suggested that she wait before making a decision, and that she should look at herself before jumping either way.

Sarah immediately said that she would ask her husband to come and see me. I got the impression that she had no intention of looking at herself and was using her sessions to remain stuck.

Her husband, Daniel, came to see me. He, too, was pondering whether to stay in the marriage or whether to go and live with *his* lady friend. But his emphasis was on finding out what Sarah wanted. 'I've got to think of Sarah,' he kept saying.

They both commented several times on the position they had in life together – the respect they had as a couple in the community – and how reluctant they were to sink this boat.

Sarah continued her therapy. It was clear to me that neither one would leave the other. Those with the real problem were the two people Sarah and Daniel were involved with outside the marriage. They were waiting in the wings for a cue that was never going to come. Being used, in fact, to keep the marriage together.

Sarah and Daniel shied away from actually looking at themselves individually. They didn't really want change at all, and they were using their therapy, and myself as the therapist, to aid and abet them in remaining stuck in a situation which suited them both very well.

This was a relationship that had sunk into one of the dark aspects of purple. Nothing changed. In fact, Sarah came back a year later and began with the same list of complaints about Daniel's flaws. She never came even close to admitting what was the dynamic of the situation. Both she and Daniel were quite happy with the continuing saga of the power struggle that was their marriage. It was a brilliant example of deep negative purple's refusal to sacrifice position for love.

'New faith means that we are confident of what we hope for, convinced of what we do not see.'
Hebrews II, 1, 2.

Grey

'Parting is such sweet sorrow.'
Romeo and Juliet', Shakespeare

Grey Polarity
Black – White
Positive grey keywords:
Informed; sanity; realism; linking; opposites;
respectable; stoicism.
Negative grey keywords:
Fear of losing; poverty; illness;
criticism; melancholy; sorrow;
depression; austere.
Grey is the bridge between black and white.
Grey is the transitional stage.
Innocence and ignorance meet in grey.
Thus, grey's vulnerability.
These two traits were once considered essential and
most desirable in bringing up young ladies.
Unfortunately all they ever led to was disaster.
Grey feels it doesn't belong anywhere.
Grey is not wanted.
Grey is the colour of the Puritan epoch.
They were respectable people.

Grey is never first.
Children perceive grandparents as the colour grey.
Grey is as firm as a rock.
Grey strives for a harmonious stability.
Grey does not believe in emotional pain.
It likes to control emotional outbursts.
Grey believes emotions should be in their proper place.
This is hardly ever right now!
Grey reveals stark reality and blocks deception.
It can stabilise the disturbed.
Grey can restore sanity.
Dark grey can lead to loss of perspective
and bizarre behaviour.
A dark grey statement is 'I'm solidly behind whichever side
eventually wins.'
The black and white of grey symbolises
the female/male.
Grey always seems to be split in two.
In ancient teachings the male
was thought to light up
the dark womb.
Grey is mainly attached to negativity.
People usually work on the negative of grey.
Negative grey is critical.
It fears its own lack of definition.
Grey is illness – it never feels well.
Negative grey is sadness and melancholy.
There is no future for grey.
It knows it's frail, old and about to die.
Grey is always old; it knows no youth.
Old dry bones are grey.
Grey is a reminder to man of what he will become
'Ashes to ashes, dust to dust'.
Grey puts a dampener on things.

Grey at its weakest
believes it cannot have it today.
It might get it tomorrow – but tomorrow never comes.
'There is never enough,' is the negative grey statement.
The Victorian workhouse that punished
Oliver Twist for not having
poverty consciousness
was under the negative of the grey ray.
Grey at its best is optimistic,
and knows that the best is yet to come.
Grey, like steel, knows that it has to be tempered
before new shape and form can emerge.
Dark grey has usually been knocked about a bit.
Grey must armour itself.
Our modern-day armour is the grey suit.
Grey is always out of date.
Positive grey – nothing is out of date if you love it.
Grey lends strength to someone who feels
inwardly weak and vulnerable.
Too much grey hardens.
Persistence and endurance are the grey aspects
of the life force, and will
eventually lead
to serenity.
The person drawn to grey can be
looking for the ideal emotional relationship.
Positive grey is the release from bondage.
People during the war were living
the negative of grey.
However, their belief
that they would come through
was working with the positive of grey.
Concentration camp survivors,
the hostages who 'knew they would make it',

were all working with the positive of grey.
Because grey is rock bottom, the only
way left to go is up!
Grey represents mouldiness and mildew,
but penicillin was discovered in a mould!
Grey symbolises transitions of all earthly things.
It leads our thoughts beyond destruction of all that's
material to the external.
Grey is divine in its destruction because rebirth can occur
and the flow continue.

The use of grey

The positive of grey is that it is useful for diagnosis. Grey's ability to show up blemishes and shadows in the body is used in X-rays. Grey is not a colour that is used for healing specifically. Rather, it can predict illness – it gives information on the state of the person, mentally, emotionally and physically.

Grey is the light that is dimmed. It shows a fear of circumstances that calls for colours.

When life is grey and bleak it is colourless and flat.

People who wear grey suits are armouring themselves against the negative aspects of grey – illness, criticism, fear and restriction. My father wouldn't have been seen dead without his grey suit. This definitely depicted the restriction of the times.

However, grey can free from the chains that bind. It provides an alternative. A bleak view of the future can be turned around by grey. It gives the inner strength necessary to face up and begin changing a hopeless situation.

Black and white decor in a house often shows that the owner/s may be approaching the grey state that says: 'I want to leave.'

If the whites of the eyes are grey, or if the fingernails, the skin, or the urine has a greyish tint, it shows a thickening of phlegm or catarrh in the nose, chest, stomach or bowels. The antidote is orange.

Grey restores sanity and it stops self-deception. It can also be used profitably with someone who is utterly reckless and irresponsible – it can sober up such a person. Grey is a great colour to subdue the nerves when shattered.

A particularly good, easy and pleasurable way of absorbing grey is to take a walk under a grey sky. Grey can also be worn or used in decor around the house. A soothing silver grey is beneficial in aiding sleep.

Grey foods
Raw fish, caviars, cooked meats. Any food that is going grey is lifeless and off – its life-energy is waning.

THE MANY MOODS OF GREY
The shades and tints

Light grey – salvation; transmutation
- Light grey is a higher vibration of grey because it has more white in it.
- It is the Rescuer. Sister Teresa wore pale grey – this showed she was working on the aspect of salvation.
- It is extremely soothing.
- It brings about great peace of mind and tranquillity.
- Pale grey is the beginning or end of a journey.
- Pale grey can feel it doesn't belong – it's not staying.

Good examples: Ghosts; visions.
Problem: Obscurity; unattached.

Dark grey – stricture; prison

- Dark grey is conventional to the point of narrow-mindedness.
- It can produce unpleasant emotions.
- Dark grey is self-deception.
- It is the shade of suffering and poverty; and so of shame and humiliation.
- Dark grey is austerity. There is a belief that there is never going to be enough.
- It is the tortured mind. Always trying to escape from some unknown anxiety.
- 'Why hast thou forsaken me?' – Christ on the Cross.
- Leprosy is the dark grey disease.
- Wretched, disgusting, sordid, derelict, are dark grey words.
- Dark grey is not wanted.
- The dark grey personality always manages to put a blemish on the proceedings.
- The person feels caged, trapped, that there is no way of escape, at the end of the line. The animals in the zoo.
- Dark grey is bizarre behaviour rather than clinical insanity – the person in the bed-sitting room with forty dogs and thirty cats and old newspapers piled to the ceiling.
- The expression 'their wings are clipped' sums up the dark grey syndrome perfectly.

Good examples: The down-and-out-but-still-living; grandparents.

Problem: As an ex-inmate of Auschwitz put it: 'I think that God has gone on holiday.'

A GREY STORY
Not wanted

A celebrity came to see me. He wore a plaid shirt which was pale grey with dark grey and orange lines. He had no career worries and was planning a world trip for pleasure.

What was bothering Malcolm was that he feared that he was going mad. For one thing, he had begun to feel that he 'didn't belong anywhere'. But what really concerned him was that he kept feeling that somebody was standing near him. There was the presence of another person, but when he looked no one was there.

These feelings had come to a head at a press conference. Many famous people were present. Malcolm had seen that each one of them was trying to be the one who was most well known. Though he was as famous as any of them, he felt that no one wanted to know him.

'I sat by myself and looked at them all and I thought, "Why do they all have such a need to be recognised?"' Intuitively, he knew the reason: 'I thought that perhaps they felt unwanted as people.'

Furthermore, he had had no one at the press conference to give him support. When the time came for his interview with the press, his agent had managed to disappear. This disturbed him deeply.

I suggested that before his next visit, Malcolm asked his mother how she had felt about being pregnant with him, and what happened when he was born. When he came back, I could see a difference in him, a complete change. It was as though something had rocked the foundations of his existence. In fact, Malcolm had found out from his mother that he had been adopted. His real mother had not wanted him because he was a boy. Furthermore, he had been a twin and she had kept the girl.

The dark grey lines in Malcolm's shirt on his first visit had indicated this unwantedness that he had experienced at birth. Unwantedness also explained his pattern of not feeling welcome wherever he went, even though he was famous and apparently so sought after.

The lighter grey background revealed that he was concerned with questions of sanity. But I knew from this hue that Malcolm was not insane. The orange lines in the shirt indicated suppressed grief and shock, and that what had happened to him was 'not fair'.

Malcolm said that he realised that the person he could feel near him but never find was his twin, the sister he had been separated from. He said that a remark he had made for many years was: 'I only feel that half of me is here'.

In a regression, Malcolm was reunited with his sister. He never felt it necessary to find her or his real mother. And he no longer felt unwanted and the presence disappeared. 'Now that I've communicated with my sister, I'm content to go along my own path.'

'All cats are grey in the night.'
Anonymous

Silver

'Every cloud has a silver lining.'
Anonymous

Silver Polarity
Waxing – Waning
Positive silver keywords:
Illuminates; reflects; unbiased;
penetrating; yearning;
fluidity.
Negative silver keywords:
Two-faced; split; elusive; lunatic;
crocodile tears; deceptive.
Silver illuminates.
Silver is the feminine.
Silver has the quality of endurance.
Silver stills the emotions.
It's the great natural tranquilliser.
Silver is flowing.
It is the fluid state of consciousness.
Silver always brings freedom from emotional restriction.
Still waters run deep.
Silver is the penetrator. It pierces.

Silver seeks money. It likes to have its hand crossed with
silver.
Silver yearns for spiritual harmony.
Silver restores equilibrium.
It solves disputes.
Silver is unbiased. It will allow you to have your own
opinion
without having a desire to change it.
The quick-silver mind pours out what is required.
Silver can be a bit slippery. It likes to move on.
The silvered mirror reflects.
It shows you as you are.
Silver is the movies.
Silver's ambition is to become a film star.
Silver lays bare.
It does not cover up mistakes.
Silver illuminates; it lights up the path.
'By the light of the silvery moon . . .'
When the moon is favourable the celestial conditions will
enable man to succeed in his efforts to transcend his mind.
It can show that a person is full of illusion
and living a life that doesn't exist.
Silver loves to fantasise.
Silver has always been connected with the moon,
the seat of astral glamour.
An invisible silver cord is said to attach
us to 'the other side'.
At death, the cord is severed from
our human body and
we move on.
Negative silver is schizophrenia.
Or simply someone who is unable to make decisions.
The full moon is when silver is at its most powerful.
Negative silver shows up in relationships where there is

no substance, just delusion.
Negative silver is mutton done up as lamb.
Negative silver loves to wallow in emotion.
People who fall in love with stars of the
silver screen are under the negative of silver.
Silver is the thread of Cosmic Intelligence.
It governs the waxing and waning of life
through everything on
our planet.
The rise and fall of sap in trees,
the tides, the menstruation
of women.
The
expression,
'I don't know whether
I am coming or going' is
working with this aspect of silver.

The use of silver

Silver reflects back mistakes without distortion, apology or bias. A mistake is not necessarily negative. We have our greatest teachings and learning from our mistakes. A mistake is growth. It's only a mis-take after all. Like filming, you just do it again until you get it right. This ability to mirror is very useful in therapy. A mirror never lies. 'Mirror, mirror on the wall . . .'

Silver is very good for calming the nerves. The spiritual tranquillity and harmony associated with silver brings about a fluid state of consciousness. It calms the hormones. Silver is good for the functioning of the kidneys, beneficial in the use of fluid flows in the body.

To restore equilibrium, you can introduce silver through jewellery, wearing silver clothes – evening gowns and suits, carrying a silver handbag, silver shoes and accessories. A very good way of absorbing silver is to fling your curtains back and bathe in the moonlight.

Star-gazing is a therapeutic silver pastime, also. Making love in the moonlight is said to be a magical and mystical experience! Silver can be absorbed through the Star Breath technique (see pages 158–61).

Silver foods

Any silver-scaled fish, silver-coated sugared almonds, silver-leaf cake and dessert decorations.

A SILVER STORY
Prison doors

A woman rang. She wanted me to see her daughter, Suzanne, who was twenty-eight, and had 'lots of problems and was schizophrenic'. No therapy had had much effect and the woman said she and her husband were desperate.

Two days later, Suzanne and her mother arrived for the first appointment. Suzanne was very beautiful and wearing a rich rose pink dress.

I gave her the basic palm and colour assessment. Throughout the session she just smiled sweetly and said not a word. From this I felt that verbal counselling would be a waste of time. I wondered which way we should go for the second session. Suzanne arrived for this session wearing a light grey dress with silver threads through it. She was also wearing silver earrings and bracelets. I knew there was a clue in the silver. Silver coming from the grey indicates freedom coming from restriction. The word that came to me was 'freedom'. I felt that Suzanne had been imprisoned and decided to have her do a drawing.

I gave Suzanne paper and pencils and asked her to draw five doors any way she liked. When I saw the doors I knew what to do: every one of them was a prison door, and each had a little barred window. To get to the truth behind these doors I knew we needed to see other lifetimes. I put Suzanne in a blue light, which is truth, and wrapped her in red silk for safety. Blue is also the throat chakra, the ability to speak.

In regression, Suzanne went back to only one past life. 'It's dull and dark,' she said, 'and I'm sitting on straw. The walls are dark grey stone ... I'm in a prison cell. There's a window in front of me with bars.' She went silent for a minute, then said, 'I'm looking out through the bars to the sky.'

I got the impression that she was going out through the bars. Her spirit had found release. I knew from this that Suzanne had come into this life schizophrenic. Checking with her mother later, I found that she had been schizophrenic from birth. In that past life she had left her body and gone out through the bars. It was her only way to freedom.

I brought her out of the regression and started to talk with her. She told me about the man she was living with, David, and how he beat her. Her hope was to marry him and have children, but it seemed impossible. Apart from the violence, she was infertile. Tests had confirmed that she could not become pregnant. I asked her whether she could see that, in the pattern of the relationship, the man she was living with was playing the role of her gaoler? She sat silently.

I didn't see Suzanne again. Three years later, I met her mother by chance. She was pleased to see me. 'My daughter has changed after she came to see you. Her life is now completely transformed. She is married to David,

who treats her wonderfully well now that she has become
herself, and they have a beautiful baby.'

'Blue curtains of the sky, scatter thy silver dew
On every flower that shuts its sweet eyes
in timely sleep . . .
And wash the dusk with silver.'
To the Evening Stars, William Blake

Black

'The most beautiful thing we can experience is the mystery.'
Albert Einstein

'Any colour, so long as it's black.'
Henry Ford

Black Polarity
Fullness – Emptiness
Positive black keywords:
Right use of power; creativity; instructor;
visionary ability; contained;
hidden riches.
Negative black keywords:
Destructive; power used out of weakness and selfishness;
dominance; depression; withholding;
empty; restrictions.
Black contains and hides.
Black is visionary ability;
the seeing of that which is hidden.
Black is connected to higher philosophical
thoughts and ideals.
Black can be restricted and restricting.
One of the first questions

I ask myself when I see
someone dressed all in black is:
'What have they got bottled up inside of them?'
Black
indicates that
something is lying dormant or buried.
The black of winter contains the
seeds for the next
spring.
Black is an end.
But out of black come all new beginnings.
Black is connected to mystery – the dark.
It points to magic and esoteric knowledge.
Black is the colour that holds
the power of judgement.
Thus, the black robes of High Court judges.
Black is control.
Not control by the physical dominance (red),
but by the occult.
Black does not want to give up anything in order to keep
control.
Black can show that a person has a need to be in control.
A state that is often caused by fear.
Nothing is as black as it seems.
Pure black is rare.
Black holds on to every colour within itself and
lets no colour escape.
Black makes you stand on your own.
Thus, it is the colour of the person who
keeps control by not giving
information to others.
Black is the absorber that gives nothing out.
The challenge for each of us in black is to bring our
true self out of the night.

Like breathing, this is a two-way process.
Every morning we
pull ourselves out of the dark
and go out into the world to do our day's work.
Every evening we return gratefully
for a night of restoring
sleep.
The black of night
holds the promise of rest
from the daily battle to survive.
We retreat within black to rest and
wake into the light again.
Black, in this aspect of withdrawal and retreat from the
glare of the day, from the publicity of the spotlight,
indicates an urgency to relinquish oneself,
one's identity and ego,
so that one can experience
the realm of purity.
'I want to be alone' as Greta Garbo put it.
But you can only merge yourself with black safely
if you have selfless love.
Thus the danger in black magic that is done for the
self only – in contrast to white magic
done for the good of all.
Nuns are working on the higher order of black when they
undertake to
relinquish their personality as
they embark upon a life of
worldly restriction and
hiddenness.
Black will renounce again and again and again.
There is nothing weak about black.
Which is probably why it is feared.
Black is a promise.

It only becomes negative when depression sets in
because of disappointments in life.
Then we see everything
in a muddy light.
The Devil is the epitome of negative black.
Remember all that walks in the sun casts shadows.
Black is seductive.
The villain twirling his black moustache
has a subtle temptation.
In old black and white Westerns,
the baddie always wore
the black hat.
Black, when used for the wrong reasons, brings in
the worst aspect of the will and power:
harsh behaviour, treachery
and deceit.
Black used in the right way is the dark earth
out of which all new life springs.
But remember: a little black goes a long way.
Overdoing the black causes regression
instead of progression.
Black is the end –
and the beginning.
The day begins with the dark, and ends in the dark.
Our life begins in the unknown and
ends in the unknown.
Black is silent.
Death is silent.
But if we listen to silence we hear that this
silence has a sound.
Black's great challenge is to go beyond our fear of
losing our individual life in order to merge
into Cosmic Unity.
Going into our personal dark to discover

the Universal Light.
Black brings us face-to-face with the
personal death that is the door to liberation.
This is black as the dark night of the soul
where all that is familiar
is swept away.
Depression is a black colour.
Negative black is the fear of what is next.
Because black can be tragic mourning.
Black says, 'Do not seek death – it will find you.'
Death is an eternal opportunity.
The symphony of life swells up and down.
How about making the finale the best?
There is always something coming from the darkness,
whether it's the Christmas rose through
the sunless silence of winter
or a newborn babe from a
mother's dark womb.
Black reminds us that at the end is death, and the pleasure
of the certainty.
Positive Black is going forward to meet
the new with a light heart, regardless.
'"Come to the edge," he said.
They said, "We are afraid."
"Come to the edge," he said.
They came. He pushed them and they flew.' *Guillaume
Apollinaire*

Black parts of the body

Black spots in the body indicate disease. If black is seen in
the aura it means illness or a darkness of the soul.

The use of black

The basis of the positive use of black lies in the paradox that in the heart of black there is light. A simple indication of this is something that we experience every night: we are asleep in a dark room and dreaming. Where does the light in our dream come from? This light in the heart of darkness is the secret of black. One everyday expression of our understanding of this is: the light at the end of the tunnel. This is an ancient teaching about the mystery of light and dark. Or, as the Bible says in the first paragraph of Genesis, the mystery of the Creation: 'God saw that the light was good, and he separated light from darkness. He called the light day, and the darkness night. So evening came, and the morning came, the first day.'

Our problem with black is not going far enough into it to discover the light. No colour is either 'good' or 'bad'. Even the negative aspects of black can be used positively. Sometimes we need to destroy the old and habitual in order for the new to come in. We can overcome the fear that as the sun sets, it sinks not to rise again.

Black, for all its holding, constrictive qualities, can also be wonderfully liberating. Of course, there are positive and negative ways of going about destroying the old. Black more than any other colour shows up one's vices and virtues. Darkness always indicates a loss of energy which only comes when there is weakness or congestion. Just bathe in the white light to clear it, followed by orange.

Someone wearing black continuously may be saying that there is something absent, something lacking, from their life. If someone is held back by circumstances that they are fearful of breaking free from, black may become the colour they feel most comfortable in. Why? Because in black they do not have to move on; they can remain on hold. It is what they cannot face that keeps a person in the black. Black in this case is like the womb; a safe and hidden place in the world.

However, black will keep a person from discovering what is missing. Or it will keep them caught in the circumstance. Better for the person to get out of black and into colour. Knowing what other colour to introduce is where the art of applying colours to your life lies. It is not as difficult as it might seem at first glance. Your own common sense plus the colour information that you have already read in this section will be enough to begin experimenting.

The person taking refuge in black is in a state of depression. Life's disappointments have sent them into the *negative* of black having lost the promise of growth that the *positive* of black gives us. They have decided it is time to retreat. They have lost faith in tomorrow. They want to black out for a while. Black is their personal no-man's land.

The age of the person choosing black must be taken into account when its significance is being interpreted. A teenager wearing black will be making a different statement to someone wearing it in their forties.

To break the hold of black, colours must be introduced. This will begin to allow some movement into the static state the person is caught in. Black combined with another colour can show the outcome. Red and black will make up for all that is deficient. Yellow and black shows a happening will put it right. Blue and black shows that the person is only prepared to enter into life in a calm and tranquil way.

Black also completes the incomplete. Nowhere is this seen more clearly than when we use the black of sleep to complete our life's unfinished business in our dreams. Black gives access to the material of our lives.

Another aspect of the light in the heart of black is discipline and freedom. Black is discipline, it has a restrictive quality. It brings order out of chaos. You can use the restriction and discipline of black to gain true freedom. You do not have to go to sleep to use black in this way.

Meditation and visualisation are a way of dreaming while awake. For instance, a therapist could use black at the right time to help an addicted patient look at the original cause of his addiction by putting him in a dark room and leading him through a visualisation. The dark room will envelop the person and keep him or her on hold long enough to break through and see the light, i.e. the cause of the addiction.

Remember with black, it will always encourage you to work from what you know rather than from what you see.

Black foods
Liquorice, black pepper, black olives, caviar, prunes, black-currants, blackberries and black truffles.

A BLACK STORY
The managing director

I was to give a lecture for a very large company. The organisation had many factories worldwide. Just before I was due to begin, the person who had engaged me said that her Managing Director would be attending. She was a bit difficult and we wouldn't be able to start until she had arrived.

The lady arrived late. In arriving late, she was already demonstrating that she had control of the proceedings. Her clothes confirmed this. She was wearing a black suit with a pale pink blouse. Black and pale pink – a strong combination.

I deduced that, given her age – mid-forties – she was engaged in reassessing her life and probably reconstruct-ing her environment at work, as well. Which might include firing people. Dominance and control. The pink also depicted dominance in this case. It is important to note that these two colours would read differently if we were working from the positive aspects of black and pink.

After the lecture a lot of people were fussing around the Managing Director. The executive who had hired me for that evening looked across at this and said to me, 'Most of them will be fired at the end of the month. She's doing a hatchet job for the company at the moment!'

'I died to the inorganic state and became
endowed with growth, and then I died to vegetable
growth and attained to the animal. I died from animality
and became Adam (Man):
why then should I fear? When have I become less by dying?'
The Persian Poet, Rumi.

Pearl

'Neither cast ye your pearls before swine.'
Matthew VII, 6

Pearl Polarity
Acceptance – Rejection
Positive pearl keywords:
Lustre; soft; glowing; roundness;
perfection; strength; calm; multiple.
Negative pearl keywords:
Irritable; weakness; dull; uneven;
flawed; impenetrable.
Pearl is luxury.
Pearl gives strength and purifies the mind.
Pearl is culmination.
One can find every colour in pearl,
if one looks long enough.
Pearl has a subtle warmth.
It responds to the warmth of the human skin.
Pearl is organic.
Pearl has an open-and-shut quality.
The pearl personality does not like to be intruded upon,
they have a habit of clamming up like their cousins.
The hypersensitive person is under the

negative aspect of pearl.
Also the recluse and hermit.
Pearl is the subtle mixer and merger.
Someone who refuses to answer may be
working with the negative of pearl.
Their mouth is shut
like an oyster.
The pearl personality
may seem remote and impenetrable – even dowdy.
But it is a case of the pearl in the grey shell.
Pearl is the unexpected achiever.
Pearl is balmy.
Pearls have a mysterious relationship with the moon.
An old remedy for keeping pearls
in perfect condition was to
bathe them in
moonlight.
An Indian belief is that pearls represent
solidified semen.

Pearl and parts of the body

Gallstones are made of the same substance as pearls, called aragonite. Gallstones are a gift to us if we understand its meaning, which is that our emotional life has been disturbed. As children we are usually emotionally vulnerable. It takes experience to learn to be quick enough to protect ourselves from invasion. An aversion to pearls could indicate problems with the gall bladder. Spasms and cramps of the body are related to the pearl aspect.

The use of pearl

Pearl aids digestion by promoting a dislike for fatty foods, so it is a good colour for the overweight person. Pearl is also a general healer for the body's subtle energies.

The best way to introduce pearl is to wear it. It can also be absorbed through mother of pearl accessories, decor and furnishings. A pearl food is oysters.

Pearl can be absorbed through the Star Breath visualisation technique (pages 158–61). It can also be drunk if a real or cultured pearl is left overnight in a glass of pure water. One of the best ways of taking in pearl for therapeutic purposes is through bathing in the sea. Seaweed baths are a good substitute. Another way is to have a clear glass full of pearl beads (without water) standing beside the bed or in the room.

A PEARL STORY
An open and shut case

When I was in my teens it was said that if a young man gave his girlfriend pearls it would end in tears.

When I was sixteen, my first date sent a package round to my house. I opened it and found a pearl necklace inside. He was the son of the richest family in the neighbourhood.

'Tears! Tears!' said my father triumphantly, content that the necklace symbolised I wouldn't be running off with this one. As I looked at the necklace I remember thinking to myself, 'Well, I guess that's that then.' But I also had the thought: 'How can it be the end? It hasn't even begun yet.'

But it was.

> 'Full fathom five, thy father lies;
>   Of his bones are coral made.
> Those are pearls that were his eyes;
>   Nothing of him that doth fade, …'
> The Tempest, Shakespeare.

Useful addresses

The *Healing Rainbow* is an original, unique and active process tape in colour created by Lilian Verner Bonds. It takes you through a colour-oriented meditation with specially selected music, which is followed by seven questions relating to your meditation experience. The tape will help you to interpret the discoveries you have made during the process. It also provides a detailed explanation of the psychology of the colours based on Lilian's twenty years of practical experience. The tape is available from:

Penscot
20 Whitehill Park
Liphook Road
Near Bordon
Hampshire GU35 9DS

For copies of the *Healing Rainbow* Tape and information on Lilian's workshops in Australia, contact:

Sirius Connections
PO Box 937
Rozelle NSW 2039
Australia
Tel: (02) 555 1581
Fax: (02) 818 5961

If you would like to obtain Vicky Wall's coloured bottles, please contact:

Aura-Soma
Dev Aura
Little London
Thetford
Lincolnshire LN9 6QL

Index

All Optima books are available at your bookshop or newsagent, or can be ordered from the following address:

   Little, Brown and Company (UK) Limited,
   P.O. Box 11,
   Falmouth,
   Cornwall TR10 9EN.

Alternatively you may fax your order to the above address. Fax No. 0326 376423.

Payments can be made as follows: cheque, postal order (payable to Little, Brown and Company) or by credit cards, Visa/Access. Do not send cash or currency. UK customers and B.F.P.O. please allow £1.00 for postage and packing for the first book, plus 50p for the second book, plus 30p for each additional book up to a maximum charge of £3.00 (7 books plus).

Overseas customers including Ireland, please allow £2.00 for the first book plus £1.00 for the second book, plus 50p for each additional book.

NAME (Block Letters) ....

....

ADDRESS ....

....

....

☐ I enclose my remittance for _____

☐ I wish to pay by Access/Visa Card

Number ☐☐☐☐☐☐☐☐☐☐☐☐☐☐☐☐

Card Expiry Date ☐☐☐